Microprocessors

Book 1

Including Programming Experiments

HEATH COMPANY
BENTON HARBOR, MICHIGAN 49022

Model EB-6401A
595-3429-05

Copyright © 1978, 1985

Heath Company
Not affiliated with D.C. Heath, Inc.
Printed in the United States of America

Library of Congress Cataloging in Publication Data
Main entry under title:

Microprocessors : including programming experiments.

    Includes index.
    1. Microprocessors.   2. Motorola 6800
(Microprocessor)   3. Microprocessors—Programming.
I. Heathkit/Zenith Educational Systems (Group)
QA76.5.M52245   1985   001.64   85-784
ISBN 0-87119-105-9

CONTENTS

Introduction VI
Course Objectives IX

UNIT ONE — NUMBER SYSTEMS AND CODES

Introduction 1-2
Unit Objectives 1-3
Decimal Number System 1-4
Binary Number System 1-9
Octal Number System 1-18
Hexadecimal Number System 1-27
Binary Codes 1-40
Unit 1 Summary 1-57
Positive Powers of 2 1-62
Negative Powers of 2 1-63
Positive Powers of 8 1-64
Positive Powers of 16 1-64
Negative Powers of 16 1-64

UNIT TWO — MICROCOMPUTER BASICS

Introduction 2-2
Unit Objectives 2-3
Terms and Conventions 2-4
An Elementary Microcomputer 2-12
Executing a Program 2-26
Addressing Modes 2-41
Unit 2 Summary 2-69

UNIT THREE — COMPUTER ARITHMETIC

Introduction 3-2
Unit Objectives 3-3
Binary Arithmetic 3-4

Two's Complement Arithmetic 3-24
Boolean Operations 3-33
Unit 3 Summary 3-43

UNIT FOUR — INTRODUCTION TO PROGRAMMING

Introduction 4-2
Unit Objectives 4-3
Branching 4-4
Conditional Branching 4-18
Microcomputer Programming 4-27
Algorithms 4-37
Additional Instructions 4-54
Unit 4 Summary 4-67

UNIT FIVE — THE 6800 MICROPROCESSOR — PART 1

Introduction 5-2
Unit Objectives 5-3
Architecture of the 6800 MPU 5-4
Instruction Set of the 6800 MPU 5-13
New Addressing Modes 5-34
Unit 5 Summary 5-51

UNIT SIX — THE 6800 MICROPROCESSOR — PART 2

Introduction 6-2
Unit Objectives 6-3
Stack Operations 6-4
Subroutines 6-15
Input — Output (I/O) Operations 6-25
Interrupts 6-35
Unit 6 Summary 6-49

MICROPROCESSORS

PROGRAMMING EXPERIMENTS

Experiment 1 — Binary/Decimal Training Program 3
Experiment 2 — Hexadecimal/Decimal Training Program 13
Experiment 3 — Straight Line Programs 23
Experiment 4 — Arithmetic and Logic Instructions 41
Experiment 5 — Program Branches 53
Experiment 6 — Additional Instructions 89
Experiment 7 — New Addressing Modes 111
Experiment 8 — Arithmetic Operations 121
Experiment 9 — Stack Operations 133
Experiment 10 — Subroutines 141

EXAMINATIONS

Unit 1 Examination — Number Systems and Codes 165
Unit 2 Examination — Microcomputer Basics 169
Unit 3 Examination — Computer Arithmetic 173
Unit 4 Examination — Introduction to Programming 175
Unit 5 Examination — The 6800 Microprocessor — Part 1 ... 177
Unit 6 Examination — The 6800 Microprocessor — Part 2 ... 185

APPENDIX A — DEFINITION OF THE EXECUTABLE INSTRUCTIONS

INDEX

PROGRAMMING CARD — 6800/6808 INSTRUCTION SET
    (BOOK 1 TEAR-OUT)

INTRODUCTION

The Microprocessors course is designed to teach you the fundamentals of the microprocessor unit (MPU), or as it is also known, the central processor unit (CPU). This is the decision maker, or brain, of the computer. Like the brain in your body, the MPU needs support from many peripheral devices to maintain the system. Because of that interrelationship, a course on microprocessors is not complete without a through discussion of how the MPU interfaces to its support devices and the outside world. To that end, we will show you how the MPU is structured, how you communicate with the MPU (its language), and how the MPU communicates with you and the system under its control.

The course is arranged into two broad topics or sections: microprocessor theory and programming, and microprocessor interfacing. The first topic is covered in the textbook set "Book 1" and "Book 2." In addition to the text material, these books contain related "programming experiments" and an appendix with a description of the complete 6800/6808 microprocessor instruction set. The second topic is covered in the "Student Workbook." In addition to interfacing theory, this textbook contains related "interfacing experiments" and an appendix with data sheets for all of the more complex IC's such as the 6800/6808 MPU.

Microprocessors communicate with numbers. They use the simplest number system, binary, to process data. Then, depending on the computer, they use the octal, decimal, or hexadecimal number systems, and several of codes to communicate with man. The first unit in this course will describe the most common number systems and codes used by computers. Once you have built a foundation in number systems (microprocessor/computer communication), we will introduce you to the basic elements of a microprocessor in Unit 2. This is followed by a unit on computer arithmetic, to show you how a microprocessor manipulates a number system. The fourth unit introduces you to programming the computer. The last two units in the first section of the course expand on the theory of microprocessors and relate it specifically to the 6800 family of microprocessors.

The second section of the course contains two units on interfacing. The first describes interfacing fundamentals; including 3-state logic, all of the interface pins on the 6800 and 6808 microprocessor, and instruction timing. It also describes memory and display interfacing.

The second unit deals with interfacing with switches and the Peripheral Interface Adapter. Keep in mind that after you interface either the 6800 or 6808 MPU you, still have to program its operation. Therefore, you must complete the first section of the course on theory and programming before you attempt to interface the MPU.

There are two trainers that can be used with this course. One has the model number ET-3400, while the other has the model number ET-3400A. You can think of them as first and second generation trainers. The older ET-3400 trainer uses the 6800 MPU and has up to 512 bytes of memory. The ET-3400A uses the 6808 MPU and has 1024 bytes of memory. Both trainers operate in essentially the same manner. Any differences are fully explained in the experiments.

One final point about the 6800 MPU and the 6808 MPU. Both devices are essentially the same. The 6800 MPU uses an external clock while the 6808 MPU has an internal clock. Both microprocessors respond to the same instruction set, and operate in essentially the same manner. Any differences are hardware related and they are fully explained in the interfacing section. If any of the terms used in this introduction are unfamiliar, don't worry, each will be described in detail in the course.

A special programming card is included at the end of "Book 1." It has a perforated edge so that you can easily remove it from the textbook. The card contains all of the data needed to program a 6800 or 6808 MPU. You will find the card very helpful when you begin writing programs.

How to Use this Course

You will find two types of objectives in this course. Broad "Course Objectives" are listed after this Introduction. They give a general overview of the goals of the course. More specific "Unit Objectives" are listed near the front of each unit. They tell you exactly what you will be able to do as a result of studying that unit. This lets you maintain a constant check of your progress through the course.

Each unit is divided into sections. A "Self-Test Review" is included at the end of each section. This gives you an opportunity to evaluate your progress and pinpoint any areas that need review.

At the end of each unit, you will be directed to an experiment. The "Programming Experiments" are located after Unit 6, in "Book 2," while the "Interfacing Experiments" are located after Unit 8, in the "Student Workbook."

The "Unit Examinations" for Units 1 through 6 are located after the "Programming Experiments," while those for Units 7 and 8 are located after the "Interfacing Experiments." Your instructor has the answers.

COURSE OBJECTIVES

When you have completed this course, you will be able to:

1. Program a representative microprocessor.

2. Interface a representative microprocessor with the "outside world."

3. Describe the internal register structure of the 6800 and 6808 microprocessors.

4. Develop a program flowchart to define a problem.

5. Input and output data through a Peripheral Interface Adapter (PIA).

Unit 1

NUMBER SYSTEMS AND CODES

INTRODUCTION

The purpose of this first unit on microprocessors is to give you a firm foundation in number systems and codes. Binary numbers and codes are the basic language of all microprocessors. Octal and hexadecimal numbers allow easy manipulation of binary numbers and data. Thus, a good foundation in numbers and codes is essential to understanding microprocessors.

This unit will reacquaint you with the decimal number system, then expand the basic concept of numbers to the binary, octal, and hexadecimal systems. Understanding these systems fully will help you understand the many digital codes used with microprocessors. Although this unit can only give you a working knowledge of numbers and codes, you will become more proficient with them as you proceed through the units that follow.

A listing of number system tables has been provided at the end of this unit.

Examine the Unit Objectives listed in the next section to see what you will learn in this unit.

UNIT OBJECTIVES

When you complete this unit you will have the following knowledge and capabilities:

1. Given any decimal number, you will be able to convert it into its binary, octal, hexadecimal, and BCD equivalent.

2. Given any binary number, you will be able to convert it into its decimal, octal, hexadecimal, and BCD equivalent.

3. Given any octal number, you will be able to convert it into its decimal and binary equivalent.

4. Given any hexadecimal number, you will be able to convert it into its decimal and binary equivalent.

5. Given any BCD code, you will be able to convert it into its decimal and binary equivalent.

6. Given a list of popular digital codes, you will be able to read and identify them including pure binary, natural 8421 BCD, Gray, ASCII, and BAUDOT.

7. You will be able to convert a letter or number into its ASCII binary code, and convert an ASCII binary code into its letter or number equivalent.

8. You will be able to define the following terms:

Radix	BCD
Integer	Gray Code
Decimal	ASCII
Binary	BAUDOT
Octal	Most Significant Bit (MSB)
Hexadecimal	Least Significant Bit (LSB)
Bit	Most Significant Digit (MSD)
Parity	Least Significant Digit (LSD)

DECIMAL NUMBER SYSTEM

The number system we are all familiar with is the decimal number system. This system was originally devised by Hindu mathematicians in India about 400 A.D. The Arabs began to use the system about 800 A.D., where it became known as the Arabic Number System. After it was introduced to the European community about 1200 A.D., the system soon acquired the title "decimal number system."

A basic distinguishing feature of a number system is its **base** or **radix**. The base indicates the number of characters or digits used to represent quantities in that number system. The decimal number system has a base or radix of 10 because we use the ten digits 0 through 9 to represent quantities. When a number system is used where the base is not known, a subscript is used to show the base. For example, the number 4603_{10} is derived from a number system with a base of 10.

Positional Notation The decimal number system is positional or weighted. This means each digit position in a number carries a particular weight which determines the magnitude of that number. Each position has a weight determined by some power of the number system base, in this case 10. The positional weights are 10^0 (units)*, 10^1 (tens), 10^2 (hundreds), etc. Refer to Figure 1-1 for a condensed listing of powers of 10.

$$10^0 = 1$$
$$10^1 = 10$$
$$10^2 = 100$$
$$10^3 = 1,000$$
$$10^4 = 10,000$$
$$10^5 = 100,000$$
$$10^6 = 1,000,000$$
$$10^7 = 10,000,000$$
$$10^8 = 100,000,000$$
$$10^9 = 1,000,000,000$$

Figure 1-1
Condensed listing of powers of 10.

*Any number with an exponent of zero is equal to one.

We evaluate the total quantity of a number by considering the specific digits and the weights of their positions. For example, the decimal number 4603 is written in the shorthand notation with which we are all familiar. This number can also be expressed with positional notation.

$$(4 \times 10^3) + (6 \times 10^2) + (0 \times 10^1) + (3 \times 10^0) =$$
$$(4 \times 1000) + (6 \times 100) + (0 \times 10) + (3 \times 1) =$$
$$4000 + 600 + 0 + 3 = 4603_{10}$$

To determine the value of a number, multiply each digit by the weight of its position and add the results.

Fractional Numbers So far, only **integer** or whole numbers have been discussed. An integer is any of the natural numbers, the negatives of these numbers, or zero (that is, 0, 1, 4, 7, etc.). Thus, an integer represents a whole or complete number. But, it is often necessary to express quantities in terms of fractional parts of a whole number.

Decimal fractions are numbers whose positions have weights that are **negative powers of ten** such as $10^{-1} = \frac{1}{10} = 0.1$, $10^{-2} = \frac{1}{100} = 0.01$, etc.

Figure 1-2 provides a condensed listing of negative powers of 10 (decimal fractions).

$$10^{-1} = \frac{1}{10} = 0.1$$

$$10^{-2} = \frac{1}{100} = 0.01$$

$$10^{-3} = \frac{1}{1000} = 0.001$$

$$10^{-4} = \frac{1}{10,000} = 0.0001$$

$$10^{-5} = \frac{1}{100,000} = 0.00001$$

$$10^{-6} = \frac{1}{1,000,000} = 0.000001$$

Figure 1-2
Condensed listing of negative powers of 10.

A radix point (decimal point for base 10 numbers) **separates** the **integer** and **fractional** parts of a number. The integer or whole portion is to the left of the decimal point and has positional weights of units, tens, hundreds, etc. The fractional part of the number is to the right of the decimal point and has positional weights of tenths, hundredths, thousandths, etc. To illustrate this, the decimal number 278.94 can be written with positional notation as shown below.

$$(2 \times 10^2) + (7 \times 10^1) + (8 \times 10^0) + (9 \times 10^{-1}) + (4 \times 10^{-2}) =$$
$$(2 \times 100) + (7 \times 10) + (8 \times 1) + (9 \times 1/10) + (4 \times 1/100) =$$
$$200 + 70 + 8 + 0.9 + 0.04 = 278.94_{10}$$

In this example, the left-most digit (2×10^2) is the **most significant digit** or MSD because it carries the greatest weight in determining the value of the number. The right-most digit, called the **least significant digit** or LSD, has the lowest weight in determining the value of the number. Therefore, as the term implies, the MSD is the digit that will affect the greatest change when its value is altered. The LSD has the smallest effect on the complete number value.

Self-Test Review

1. The ___BASE___ indicates the number of characters or digits in a number system.

2. In the decimal number system, the base or radix is ___10___.

3. Write the following numbers using positional notation.

   A. 4563_{10} $4 \times 10^3 + 5 \times 10^2 + 6 \times 10^1 + 3 \times 10^0$
   B. 26.32_{10} $2 \times 10^1 + 6 \times 10^0 + 3 \times 10^{-1} + 2 \times 10^{-2}$
   C. 536.9_{10} $5 \times 10^2 + 3 \times 10^1 + 6 \times 10^0 + 9 \times 10^{-1}$

4. In the decimal number system, the radix point is called the ___DECIMAL POINT___.

5. Convert the following positional notations into their shorthand decimal form.

   A. $(5 \times 10^1) + (2 \times 10^0) + (3 \times 10^{-1}) + (8 \times 10^{-2})$ 52.38_{10}
   B. $(4 \times 10^{-1}) + (6 \times 10^{-2}) + (2 \times 10^{-3})$ 0.462_{10}
   C. $(3 \times 10^3) + (7 \times 10^2) + (1 \times 10^1) + (0 \times 10^0)$ 3710_{10}

6. The radix point separates the ___INTEGER___ and ___FRACTION___ parts of a number.

Answers

1. base or radix.

2. 10.

3. A. $4563_{10} = 4000 + 500 + 60 + 3.$
   $= (4 \times 10^3) + (5 \times 10^2) + (6 \times 10^1) + (3 \times 10^0)$
   B. $(2 \times 10^1) + (6 \times 10^0) + (3 \times 10^{-1}) + (2 \times 10^{-2})$
   C. $(5 \times 10^2) + (3 \times 10^1) + (6 \times 10^0) + (9 \times 10^{-1})$

4. decimal point.

5. A. $(5 \times 10^1) + (2 \times 10^0) + (3 \times 10^{-1}) + (8 \times 10^{-2}) =$
   $(5 \times 10) + (2 \times 1) + (3 \times 1/10) + (8 \times 1/100) =$
   $50 + 2 + 0.3 + 0.08 = 52.38_{10}$
   B. 0.462_{10}
   C. 3710_{10}

6. integer or whole, fractional.

BINARY NUMBER SYSTEM

The simplest number system that uses positional notation is the binary number system. As the name implies, a **binary** system contains only two elements or states. In a number system this is expressed as a base of 2, using the digits 0 and 1. These two digits have the same basic value as 0 and 1 in the decimal number system.

Because of its simplicity, microprocessors use the binary number system to manipulate data. Binary data is represented by binary digits called **bits**. The term bit is derived from the contraction of **bi**nary dig**it**. Microprocessors operate on groups of bits which are referred to as words. The binary number 11101101 contains eight bits.

Positional Notation

As with the decimal number system, each bit (digit) position of a binary number carries a particular weight which determines the magnitude of that number. The weight of each position is determined by some power of the number system base (in this example 2). To evaluate the total quantity of a number, consider the specific bits and the weights of their positions. (Refer to Figure 1-3 for a condensed listing of powers of 2.) For example, the binary number 110101 can be written with positional notation as follows:

$$(1 \times 2^5) + (1 \times 2^4) + (0 \times 2^3) + (1 \times 2^2) + (0 \times 2^1) + (1 \times 2^0)$$

To determine the decimal value of the binary number 110101, multiply each bit by its positional weight and add the results.

$$(1 \times 32) + (1 \times 16) + (0 \times 8) + (1 \times 4) + (0 \times 2) + (1 \times 1) =$$
$$32 + 16 + 0 + 4 + 0 + 1 = 53_{10}$$

$$2^0 = 1_{10} \qquad 2^6 = 64_{10}$$
$$2^1 = 2_{10} \qquad 2^7 = 128_{10}$$
$$2^2 = 4_{10} \qquad 2^8 = 256_{10}$$
$$2^3 = 8_{10} \qquad 2^9 = 512_{10}$$
$$2^4 = 16_{10} \qquad 2^{10} = 1024_{10}$$
$$2^5 = 32_{10} \qquad 2^{11} = 2048_{10}$$

Figure 1-3
Condensed listing of powers of 2.

Fractional binary numbers are expressed as negative powers of 2. Figure 1-4 provides a condensed listing of negative powers of 2. In positional notation, the binary number 0.1101 can be expressed as follows:

$$(1 \times 2^{-1}) + (1 \times 2^{-2}) + (0 \times 2^{-3}) + (1 \times 2^{-4})$$

To determine the decimal value of the binary number 0.1101, multiply each bit by its positional weight and add the results.

$$(1 \times 1/2) + (1 \times 1/4) + (0 \times 1/8) + (1 \times 1/16) =$$
$$0.5 + 0.25 + 0 + 0.0625 = 0.8125_{10}$$

In the binary number system, the radix point is called the binary point.

$$2^{-1} = \frac{1}{2} = 0.5_{10}$$

$$2^{-2} = \frac{1}{4} = 0.25_{10}$$

$$2^{-3} = \frac{1}{8} = 0.125_{10}$$

$$2^{-4} = \frac{1}{16} = 0.0625_{10}$$

$$2^{-5} = \frac{1}{32} = 0.03125_{10}$$

$$2^{-6} = \frac{1}{64} = 0.015625_{10}$$

$$2^{-7} = \frac{1}{128} = 0.0078125_{10}$$

$$2^{-8} = \frac{1}{256} = 0.00390625_{10}$$

Figure 1-4
Condensed listing of negative powers of 2.

Converting Between the Binary and Decimal Number Systems

In working with microprocessors, you will often need to determine the decimal value of binary numbers. In addition, you will find it necessary to convert a specific decimal number into its binary equivalent. The following information shows how such conversions are accomplished.

Binary to Decimal To convert a binary number into its decimal equivalent, add together the weights of the positions in the number where binary 1's occur. The weights of the integer and fractional positions are indicated below.

	INTEGER								FRACTIONAL		
2^7	2^6	2^5	2^4	2^3	2^2	2^1	2^0		2^{-1}	2^{-2}	2^{-3}
128	64	32	16	8	4	2	1		.5	.25	.125

Binary Point

As an example, convert the binary number 1010 into its decimal equivalent. Since no binary point is shown, the number is assumed to be an integer number, where the binary point is to the right of the number. The right-most bit, called the **least significant bit** or LSB, has the lowest integer weight of $2^0 = 1$. The left-most bit is the **most significant bit** (MSB) because it carries the greatest weight in determining the value of the number. In this example, it has a weight of $2^3 = 8$. To evaluate the number, add together the weights of the positions where binary 1's appear. In this example, 1's occur in the 2^3 and 2^1 positions. The decimal equivalent is ten.

```
Binary Number        1     0     1     0
Position Weights    2³    2²    2¹    2⁰
Decimal Equivalent
                     8  +  0  +  2  +  0   = 10₁₀
```

To further illustrate this process, convert the binary number 101101.11 into its decimal equivalent.

```
Binary Number        1    0    1    1    0    1   .1    1
Position Weights    2⁵   2⁴   2³   2²   2¹   2⁰  2⁻¹  2⁻²
Decimal Equivalent
                    32 + 0 +  8 +  4 +  0 +  1 + .5 + .25 = 45.75₁₀
```

Decimal to Binary A decimal integer number can be converted to a different base or radix through successive divisions by the desired base. To convert a decimal integer number to its binary equivalent, successively divide the number by 2 and note the remainders. When you divide by 2, the remainder will always be 1 or 0.

The remainders form the equivalent binary number.

As an example, the decimal number 25 is converted into its binary equivalent.

$$25 \div 2 = 12 \text{ with remainder } 1 \leftarrow \text{LSB}$$
$$12 \div 2 = 6 \qquad\qquad\qquad\quad 0$$
$$6 \div 2 = 3 \qquad\qquad\qquad\quad 0$$
$$3 \div 2 = 1 \qquad\qquad\qquad\quad 1$$
$$1 \div 2 = 0 \qquad\qquad\qquad\quad 1 \leftarrow \text{MSB}$$

Divide the decimal number by 2 and note the remainder. Then divide the quotient by 2 and again note the remainder. Then divide the quotient by 2 and again note the remainder. Continue this division process until 0 results. Then collect remainders beginning with the last or most significant bit (MSB) and proceed to the first or least significant bit (LSB). The number $11001_2 = 25_{10}$. Notice that the remainders are collected in the reverse order. That is, the first remainder becomes the least significant bit, while the last remainder becomes the most significant bit.

NOTE: Do not attempt to use a calculator to perform this conversion. It would only supply you with confusing results.

To further illustrate this, the decimal number 175 is converted into its binary equivalent.

$$175 \div 2 = 87 \text{ with remainder } 1 \leftarrow \text{LSB}$$
$$87 \div 2 = 43 \qquad\qquad\qquad\quad 1$$
$$43 \div 2 = 21 \qquad\qquad\qquad\quad 1$$
$$21 \div 2 = 10 \qquad\qquad\qquad\quad 1$$
$$10 \div 2 = 5 \qquad\qquad\qquad\quad 0$$
$$5 \div 2 = 2 \qquad\qquad\qquad\quad 1$$
$$2 \div 2 = 1 \qquad\qquad\qquad\quad 0$$
$$1 \div 2 = 0 \qquad\qquad\qquad\quad 1 \leftarrow \text{MSB}$$

The division process continues until 0 results. The remainders are collected to produce the number $10101111_2 = 175_{10}$.

Number Systems and Codes | 1-13

To convert a decimal fraction to a different base or radix, multiply the fraction successively by the desired base and record any integers produced by the multiplication as an overflow. For example, to convert the decimal fraction 0.3125 into its binary equivalent, multiply repeatedly by 2.

$$0.3125 \times 2 = 0.625 = 0.625 \quad \text{with overflow} \quad 0 \leftarrow \text{MSB}$$
$$0.6250 \times 2 = 1.250 = 0.250 \quad \quad \quad \quad \quad \quad \quad \quad 1$$
$$0.2500 \times 2 = 0.500 = 0.500 \quad \quad \quad \quad \quad \quad \quad \quad 0$$
$$0.5000 \times 2 = 1.000 = 0 \quad \quad \quad \quad \quad \quad \quad \quad \quad 1 \leftarrow \text{LSB}$$

These multiplications will result in numbers with a 1 or 0 in the units position (the position to the left of the decimal point). By recording the value of the units position, you can construct the equivalent binary fraction. This units position value is called the "overflow." Therefore, when 0.3125 is multiplied by 2, the overflow is 0. This becomes the most significant bit (MSB) of the binary equivalent fraction. Then 0.625 is multiplied by 2. Since the product is 1.25, the overflow is 1. When there is an overflow of 1, it is effectively subtracted from the product when the value is recorded. Therefore, only 0.25 is multiplied by 2 in the next multiplication process. This method continues until an overflow with no fraction results. It is important to note that you can not always obtain 0 when you multiply by 2. Therefore, you should only continue the conversion process to the accuracy or precision you desire. Collect the conversion overflows beginning at the radix (binary) point with the MSB and proceed to the LSB. This is the same order in which the overflows were produced. The number $0.0101_2 = 0.3125_{10}$.

To further illustrate this process, the decimal fraction 0.90625 is converted into its binary equivalent.

$$0.90625 \times 2 = 1.8125 = 0.8125 \quad \text{with overflow} \quad 1 \leftarrow \text{MSB}$$
$$0.81250 \times 2 = 1.6250 = 0.6250 \quad \quad \quad \quad \quad \quad \quad \quad 1$$
$$0.62500 \times 2 = 1.2500 = 0.2500 \quad \quad \quad \quad \quad \quad \quad \quad 1$$
$$0.25000 \times 2 = 0.5000 = 0.5000 \quad \quad \quad \quad \quad \quad \quad \quad 0$$
$$0.50000 \times 2 = 1.0000 = 0 \quad \quad \quad \quad \quad \quad \quad \quad \quad \quad 1 \leftarrow \text{LSB}$$

The multiplication process continues until either 0 or the desired precision is obtained. The overflows are then collected beginning with the MSB at the binary (radix) point and proceeding to the LSB. The number $0.11101_2 = 0.90625_{10}$.

If the decimal number contains both an integer and fraction, you must separate the integer and fraction using the decimal point as the break point. Then perform the appropriate conversion process on each number portion. After you convert the binary integer and binary fraction, recombine them. For example, the decimal number 14.375 is converted into its binary equivalent.

$$14.375_{10} = 14_{10} + 0.375_{10}$$

$14 \div 2 = 7$	with remainder	0 ← LSB
$7 \div 2 = 3$		1
$3 \div 2 = 1$		1
$1 \div 2 = 0$		1 ← MSB

$$\boxed{14_{10} = 1110_2}$$

$0.375 \times 2 = 0.75 = 0.75$	with overflow	0 ← MSB
$0.750 \times 2 = 1.50 = 0.50$		1
$0.500 \times 2 = 1.00 = 0$		1 ← LSB

$$\boxed{0.375_{10} = 0.011_2}$$

$$14.375_{10} = 14_{10} + 0.375_{10} = 1110_2 + 0.011_2 = 1110.011_2$$

MICROPROCESSORS — Number Systems and Codes | 1-15

Self-Test Review

7. The base or radix of the binary number system is ___2___.

8. A binary digit is called a ___bit___.

9. Convert the following binary integers to decimal.

    A. 101101   45
    B. 1001   9
    C. 1101100   108

10. Convert the following binary fractions to decimal.

    A. 0.011   0.375
    B. 0.01101   0.40625
    C. 0.1001   0.5625

11. Convert the following decimal integers to binary.

    A. 63
    B. 12
    C. 132

12. Convert the following decimal fractions to binary.

    A. 0.4375
    B. 0.96875
    C. 0.625

13. Convert 13.125_{10} to binary.

Answers

7. 2

8. bit

9. A. $101101_2 =$
   $(1 \times 2^5) + (0 \times 2^4) + (1 \times 2^3) + (1 \times 2^2) + (0 \times 2^1) + (1 \times 2^0) =$
   $32 + 0 + 8 + 4 + 0 + 1 = 45_{10}$
   B. $1001_2 = 9_{10}$
   C. $1101100_2 = 108_{10}$

10. A. $0.011_2 = (0 \times 2^{-1}) + (1 \times 2^{-2}) + (1 \times 2^{-3}) =$
    $0 + \dfrac{1}{4} + \dfrac{1}{8} = 0 + 0.25 + 0.125 = 0.375_{10}$
    B. $0.01101_2 = 0.40625_{10}$
    C. $0.1001_2 = 0.5625_{10}$

11. A.
$63 \div 2 = 31$	with remainder	1 ← LSB
$31 \div 2 = 15$		1
$15 \div 2 = 7$		1
$7 \div 2 = 3$		1
$3 \div 2 = 1$		1
$1 \div 2 = 0$		1 ← MSB

    $\boxed{63_{10} = 111111_2}$

    B. $12_{10} = 1100_2$
    C. $132_{10} = 10000100_2$

12. A. $0.4375 \times 2 = 0.875 = 0.875$ with overflow   0 ← MSB
        $0.8750 \times 2 = 1.750 = 0.750$ 1
        $0.7500 \times 2 = 1.500 = 0.500$ 1
        $0.5000 \times 2 = 1.000 = 0$ 1 ← LSB

        $\boxed{0.4375_{10} = 0.0111_2}$

   B. $0.96875_{10} = 0.11111_2$
   C. $0.625_{10} = 0.101_2$

13. $13.125_{10} = 13_{10} + 0.125_{10}$

        $13 \div 2 = 6$ with remainder   1 ← LSB
        $6 \div 2 = 3$ 0
        $3 \div 2 = 1$ 1
        $1 \div 2 = 0$ 1 ← MSB

        $\boxed{13_{10} = 1101_2}$

        $0.125 \times 2 = 0.25 = 0.25$ with overflow   0 ← MSB
        $0.250 \times 2 = 0.50 = 0.50$ 0
        $0.500 \times 2 = 1.00 = 0$ 1 ← LSB

        $\boxed{0.125_{10} = 0.001_2}$

   $13.125_{10} = 13_{10} + 0.125_{10} = 1101_2 + 0.001_2 = 1101.001_2$

OCTAL NUMBER SYSTEM

Octal is another number system that is often used with microprocessors. It has a base (radix) of 8, and uses the digits 0 through 7. These eight digits have the same basic value as the digits 0—7 in the decimal number system.

As with the binary number system, each digit position of an octal number carries a positional weight which determines the magnitude of that number. The weight of each position is determined by some power of the number system base (in this example, 8). To evaluate the total quantity of a number, consider the specific digits and the weights of their positions. Refer to Figure 1-5 for a condensed listing of powers of 8. For example, the octal number 372.01 can be written with positional notation as follows:

$$(3 \times 8^2) + (7 \times 8^1) + (2 \times 8^0) + (0 \times 8^{-1}) + (1 \times 8^{-2})$$

The decimal value of the octal number 372.01 is determined by multiplying each digit by its positional weight and adding the results. As with decimal and binary numbers, the radix (octal) point separates the integer from the fractional part of the number.

$$(3 \times 64) + (7 \times 8) + (2 \times 1) + (0 \times 0.125) + (1 \times 0.015625) =$$
$$192 + 56 + 2 + 0 + 0.015625 = 250.015625_{10}$$

$$8^{-4} = \frac{1}{4096} = 0.000244140625_{10}$$

$$8^{-3} = \frac{1}{512} = 0.001953125_{10}$$

$$8^{-2} = \frac{1}{64} = 0.015625_{10}$$

$$8^{-1} = \frac{1}{8} = 0.125_{10}$$

$$1_{10} = 8^0$$
$$8_{10} = 8^1$$
$$64_{10} = 8^2$$
$$512_{10} = 8^3$$
$$4096_{10} = 8^4$$
$$32768_{10} = 8^5$$
$$262144_{10} = 8^6$$

Figure 1-5
Condensed listing of powers of 8.

Conversion From Decimal to Octal

Decimal to octal conversion is accomplished in the same manner as decimal to binary, with one exception; the base number is now 8 rather than 2. As an example, the decimal number 194 is converted into its octal equivalent.

$$194 \div 8 = 24 \text{ with remainder } 2 \leftarrow \text{LSD}$$
$$24 \div 8 = 3 \qquad\qquad\qquad 0$$
$$3 \div 8 = 0 \qquad\qquad\qquad 3 \leftarrow \text{MSD}$$

Divide the decimal number by 8 and note the remainder. (The remainder can be any number from 0 to 7.)

Then divide the quotient by 8 and again note the remainder. Continue dividing until 0 results. Finally, collect the remainders beginning with the last or most significant digit (MSD) and proceed to the first or least significant digit (LSD). The number $302_8 = 194_{10}$. Figure 1-6 illustrates the relationship between the first several decimal, octal, and binary integers.

DECIMAL	OCTAL	BINARY
0	0	0
1	1	1
2	2	10
3	3	11
4	4	100
5	5	101
6	6	110
7	7	111
8	10	1000
9	11	1001
10	12	1010
11	13	1011
12	14	1100
13	15	1101
14	16	1110
15	17	1111
16	20	10000
17	21	10001
18	22	10010
19	23	10011
20	24	10100

Figure 1-6
Sample comparison of decimal, octal, and binary integers.

To further illustrate this process, the decimal number 175 is converted into its octal equivalent.

$$175 \div 8 = 21 \text{ with remainder } 7 \leftarrow \text{LSD}$$
$$21 \div 8 = 2 \qquad\qquad\qquad\quad 5$$
$$2 \div 8 = 0 \qquad\qquad\qquad\quad 2 \leftarrow \text{MSD}$$

The division process continues until a quotient of 0 results. The remainders are collected, producing the number $257_8 = 175_{10}$.

To convert a decimal fraction to an octal fraction, multiply the fraction successively by 8 (octal base). As an example, the decimal fraction 0.46875 is converted into its octal equivalent.

$$0.46875 \times 8 = 3.75 = 0.75 \text{ with overflow } 3 \leftarrow \text{MSD}$$
$$0.75000 \times 8 = 6.00 = 0 \qquad\qquad\qquad\qquad 6 \leftarrow \text{LSD}$$

Multiply the decimal number by 8. If the product exceeds one, subtract the integer (overflow) from the product. Then multiply the product fraction by 8 and again note any "overflow." Continue multiplying until an overflow, with 0 for a fraction, results. Remember, you can not always obtain 0 when you multiply by 8. Therefore, you should only continue this conversion process to the accuracy or precision you desire. Collect the conversion overflows beginning at the radix (octal point) with the MSD and proceed to the LSD. The number $0.36_8 = 0.46875_{10}$. Figure 1-7 illustrates the relationship between decimal, octal, and binary fractions.

Now, the decimal fraction 0.136 will be converted into its octal equivalent with four-place precision.

$$0.136 \times 8 = 1.088 = 0.088 \text{ with overflow } \quad 1 \leftarrow \text{MSD}$$
$$0.088 \times 8 = 0.704 = 0.704 \qquad\qquad\qquad\quad 0$$
$$0.704 \times 8 = 5.632 = 0.632 \qquad\qquad\qquad\quad 5$$
$$0.632 \times 8 = 5.056 = 0.056 \qquad\qquad\qquad\quad 5 \leftarrow \text{LSD}$$
$$0.136_{10} \cong 0.1055_8$$

The number 0.1055_8 approximately equals 0.136_{10}. If you convert 0.1055_8 back to decimal (using positional notation), you will find $0.1055_8 = 0.135986328125_{10}$. This example shows that extending the precision of your conversion is of little value unless extreme accuracy is required.

DECIMAL	OCTAL	BINARY
0.015625	0.01	0.000001
0.03125	0.02	0.00001
0.046875	0.03	0.000011
0.0625	0.04	0.0001
0.078125	0.05	0.000101
0.09375	0.06	0.00011
0.109375	0.07	0.000111
0.125	0.1	0.001
0.140625	0.11	0.001001
0.15625	0.12	0.00101
0.171875	0.13	0.001011
0.1875	0.14	0.0011
0.203125	0.15	0.001101
0.21875	0.16	0.00111
0.234375	0.17	0.001111
0.25	0.2	0.01
0.265625	0.21	0.010001
0.28125	0.22	0.01001
0.296875	0.23	0.010011
0.3125	0.24	0.0101

Figure 1-7
Sample comparison of decimal, octal, and binary fractions.

As with decimal to binary conversion of a number that contains both an integer and fraction, decimal to octal conversion requires two operations. You must separate the integer from the fraction, then perform the appropriate conversion on each number. After you convert them, you must recombine the octal integer and octal fraction. For example, convert the decimal number 124.78125 into its octal equivalent.

$124.78125_{10} = 124_{10} + 0.78125_{10}$

$124 \div 8 = 15$ with remainder $\quad 4 \leftarrow$ LSD
$15 \div 8 = 1 \quad\quad\quad\quad\quad\quad\quad\quad 7$
$1 \div 8 = 0 \quad\quad\quad\quad\quad\quad\quad\quad 1 \leftarrow$ MSD

$\boxed{124_{10} = 174_8}$

$0.78125 \times 8 = 6.25 = 0.25$ with overflow $\quad 6 \leftarrow$ MSD
$0.25000 \times 8 = 2.00 = 0 \quad\quad\quad\quad\quad\quad\quad 2 \leftarrow$ LSD

$\boxed{0.78125_{10} = 0.62_8}$

$124.78125_{10} = 124_{10} + 0.78125_{10} = 174_8 + 0.62_8 = 174.62_8$

Converting Between the Octal and Binary Number Systems

Microprocessors manipulate data using the binary number system. However, when larger quantities are involved, the binary number system can become cumbersome. Therefore, other number systems are frequently used as a form of binary shorthand to speed-up and simplify data entry and display. The octal number system is one of the systems that is used in this manner. It is similar to the decimal number system, which makes it easier to understand numerical values. In addition, conversion between binary and octal is readily accomplished because of the value structure of octal. Figures 1-6 and 1-7 illustrate the relationship between octal and binary integers and fractions.

As you know, three bits of a binary number exactly equal eight value combinations. Therefore, you can represent a 3-bit binary number with a 1-digit octal number.

$$101_2 = (1 \times 2^2) + (0 \times 2^1) + (1 \times 2^0) = 4 + 0 + 1 = 5_8$$

Because of this relationship, converting binary to octal is simple and straight forward. For example, binary number 101001 is converted into its octal equivalent.

$$101001_2$$
REWRITE AS

MSB　　　　　LSB
101　　001

YIELDS

$$51_8$$

To convert a binary number to octal, first separate the number into groups containing three bits, beginning with the least significant bit. Then convert each 3-bit group into its octal equivalent. This gives you an octal number equal in value to the binary number.

Binary fractions can also be converted to their octal equivalents using the same process, with one exception. The binary bits must be separated into groups of three beginning with the most significant bit. For example, the binary fraction 0.011101 is converted into its octal equivalent.

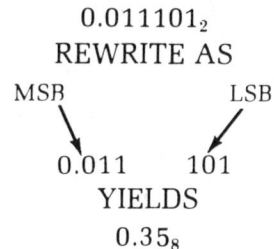

$$0.011101_2$$
REWRITE AS
0.011 101
YIELDS
$$0.35_8$$

Again, you must first separate the binary number into groups of three beginning at the radix (binary) point. Then convert each 3-bit group into its octal equivalent.

To separate binary numbers into 3-bit groups when the number does not contain the necessary bits, add zeros to the number until the number can be separated into 3-bit groups. For example, binary number 10010101.1011 is converted into its octal equivalent.

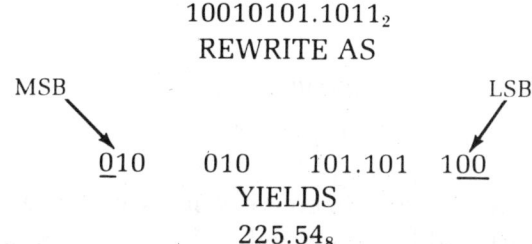

$$10010101.1011_2$$
REWRITE AS
010 010 101.101 100
YIELDS
$$225.54_8$$

As before, the integer part of the number is separated into 3-bit groups, beginning at the radix (binary) point. Note that the third group contains only two bits. However, a zero can be added to the group without changing the value of the binary number. Next, the fractional part of the number is separated into 3-bit groups, beginning at the radix (binary) point. Note that the second group contains only one bit. By adding two zeros to the group, the group is complete with no change in the value of the binary number.

NOTE: Whenever you add zeros to a **binary integer**, always place them to the **left** of the most significant bit. When you add zeros to a **binary fraction**, always place them to the **right** of the least significant bit.

After you have formed the 3-bit groups, convert each group into its octal equivalent. This gives you an octal number equal in value to the binary number. Now convert binary number 1101110.01 into its octal equivalent.

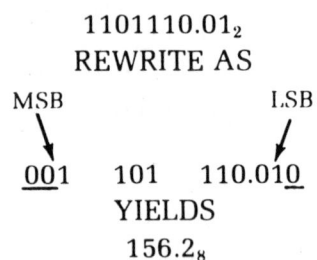

Separate the integer and fraction into 3-bit groups, adding zeros as necessary. Then convert each 3-bit group to octal. **Never** shift the radix (binary) point in order to form 3-bit groups.

Converting octal to binary is just the opposite of the previous process. You simply convert each octal number into its 3-bit binary equivalent. For example, convert the octal number 75.3 into its binary equivalent.

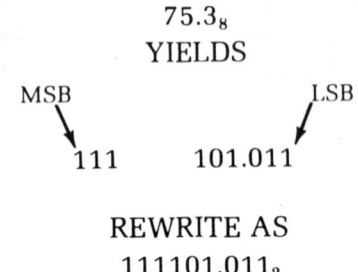

The above example is a simple conversion. Now a more complex octal number (1752.714) will be converted to a binary number.

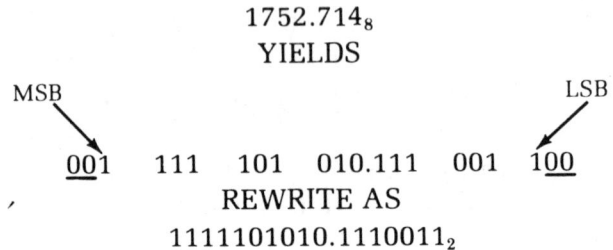

Again, each octal digit is converted into its 3-bit binary equivalent. However, in this example, there are two insignificant zeros in front of the MSB and after the LSB. Since these zeros have no value, they should be removed from the final result.

Self-Test Review

14. The base or radix of the octal number system is _____.

15. Convert the following decimal integers to octal.

    A. 156
    B. 32
    C. 1785

16. Convert the following decimal fractions to octal. Do not use greater than 4-place precision.

    A. 0.1432
    B. 0.8125
    C. 0.6832

17. Convert 735.984375_{10} to octal.

18. Convert the following binary numbers to octal.

    A. 10000111.01101
    B. 11101.0101
    C. 1001101.000001

19. Convert the following octal numbers to binary.

    A. 372.61
    B. 11.001
    C. 3251.034

Answers

14. 8

15. A. $156 \div 8 = 19$ with remainder   4 ← LSD
       $19 \div 8 = 2$ 3
       $2 \div 8 = 0$ 2 ← MSD

$$\boxed{156_{10} = 234_8}$$

     B. $32_{10} = 40_8$
     C. $1785_{10} = 3371_8$

16. A. $0.1432 \times 8 = 1.1456 = 0.1456$ overflow   1 ← MSD
         $0.1456 \times 8 = 1.1648 = 0.1648$ 1
         $0.1648 \times 8 = 1.3184 = 0.3184$ 1
         $0.3184 \times 8 = 2.5472 = 0.5472$ 2 ← LSD

$$\boxed{0.1432_{10} = 0.1112_8}$$

     B. $0.8125_{10} = 0.64_8$
     C. $0.6832_{10} = 0.5356_8$

17. $735.984375_{10} = 735_{10} + 0.984375_{10}$
                   $= 735 \div 8 = 91$ with remainder   7 ← LSD
                       $91 \div 8 = 11$ 3
                       $11 \div 8 = 1$ 3
                       $1 \div 8 = 0$ 1 ← MSD

$$\boxed{735_{10} = 1337_8}$$

               $0.984375 \times 8 = 7.875 = 0.875$ overflow
                                                           7 ← MSD
               $0.875000 \times 8 = 7.00 = 0$ 7 ← LSD

$$\boxed{0.984375_{10} = 0.77_8}$$

     $735.984375_{10} = 735_{10} + 0.984375_{10} = 1337_8 + 0.77_8 = 1337.77_8$

18. A. $10000111.01101_2 = 010\ 000\ 111.011\ 010_2$
                                    $= 207.32_8$
     B. $11101.0101_2 = 35.24_8$
     C. $1001101.000001_2 = 115.01_8$

19. A. $372.61_8 = 011\ 111\ 010.110\ 001_2 = 11111010.110001_2$
     B. $11.001_8 = 1001.000000001_2$
     C. $3251.034_8 = 11010101001.0000111_2$

HEXADECIMAL NUMBER SYSTEM

Hexadecimal is another number system that is often used with microprocessors. It is similar in value structure to the octal number system, and thus allows easy conversion with the binary number system. Because of this feature and the fact that hexadecimal simplifies data entry and display to a greater degree than octal, you will use hexadecimal more often than any other number system in this course. As the name implies, hexadecimal has a base (radix) of 16_{10}. It uses the digits 0 through 9 and the letters A through F.

The letters are used because it is necessary to represent 16_{10} different values with a single digit for each value. Therefore, the letters A through F are used to represent the number values 10_{10} through 15_{10}. The following discussion will compare the decimal number system with the hexadecimal number system.

All of the numbers are of equal value between systems ($0_{10} = 0_{16}$, $3_{10} = 3_{16}$, $9_{10} = 9_{16}$, etc.). For numbers greater than 9, this relationship exists: $10_{10} = A_{16}$, $11_{10} = B_{16}$, $12_{10} = C_{16}$, $13_{10} = D_{16}$, $14_{10} = E_{16}$, and $15_{10} = F_{16}$. Using letters in counting may appear awkward until you become familiar with the system. Figure 1-8 illustrates the relationship between decimal and hexadecimal integers, while Figure 1-9 illustrates the relationship between decimal and hexadecimal fractions.

DECIMAL	HEXADECIMAL	BINARY
0	0	0
1	1	1
2	2	10
3	3	11
4	4	100
5	5	101
6	6	110
7	7	111
8	8	1000
9	9	1001
10	A	1010
11	B	1011
12	C	1100
13	D	1101
14	E	1110
15	F	1111
16	10	10000
17	11	10001
18	12	10010
19	13	10011
20	14	10100
21	15	10101
22	16	10110
23	17	10111
24	18	11000
25	19	11001
26	1A	11010
27	1B	11011
28	1C	11100
29	1D	11101
30	1E	11110
31	1F	11111
32	20	100000
33	21	100001
34	22	100010
35	23	100011

Figure 1-8
Sample comparison of decimal,
hexadecimal, and binary integers.

MICROPROCESSORS

DECIMAL	HEXADECIMAL	BINARY
0.00390625	0.01	0.00000001
0.0078125	0.02	0.0000001
0.01171875	0.03	0.00000011
0.015625	0.04	0.000001
0.01953125	0.05	0.00000101
0.0234375	0.06	0.0000011
0.02734375	0.07	0.00000111
0.03125	0.08	0.00001
0.03515625	0.09	0.00001001
0.0390625	0.0A	0.0000101
0.04296875	0.0B	0.00001011
0.046875	0.0C	0.00011
0.05078125	0.0D	0.00001101
0.0546875	0.0E	0.0000111
0.05859375	0.0F	0.00001111
0.0625	0.1	0.0001
0.06640625	0.11	0.00010001
0.0703125	0.12	0.0001001
0.07421875	0.13	0.00010011
0.078125	0.14	0.000101
0.08203125	0.15	0.00010101
0.0859375	0.16	0.0001011
0.08984375	0.17	0.00010111
0.09375	0.18	0.00011
0.09765625	0.19	0.00011001
0.1015625	0.1A	0.0001101
0.10546875	0.1B	0.00011011
0.109375	0.1C	0.000111
0.11328125	0.1D	0.00011101
0.1171875	0.1E	0.0001111
0.12109375	0.1F	0.00011111
0.125	0.2	0.001

Figure 1-9
Sample comparison of decimal,
hexadecimal, and binary fractions.

As with the previous number systems, each digit position of a hexadecimal number carries a positional weight which determines the magnitude of that number. The weight of each position is determined by some power of the number system base (in this example, 16_{10}). The total quantity of a number can be evaluated by considering the specific digits and the weights of their positions. (Refer to Figure 1-10 for a condensed listing of powers of 16_{10}.) For example, the hexadecimal number E5D7.A3 can be written with positional notation as follows:

$$(E \times 16^3) + (5 \times 16^2) + (D \times 16^1) + (7 \times 16^0) + (A \times 16^{-1}) + (3 \times 16^{-2})$$

The decimal value of the hexadecimal number E5D7.A3 is determined by multiplying each digit by its positional weight and adding the results. As with the previous number systems, the radix (hexadecimal) point separates the integer from the fractional part of the number.

$(14 \times 4096) + (5 \times 256) + (13 \times 16) + (7 \times 1) + (10 \times 1/16) + (3 \times 1/256) =$
$57344 + 1280 + 208 + 7 + 0.625 + 0.01171875 =$
58839.63671875_{10}

$16^{-4} = \dfrac{1}{65536} = 0.0000152587890625_{10}$

$16^{-3} = \dfrac{1}{4096} = 0.000244140625_{10}$

$16^{-2} = \dfrac{1}{256} = 0.00390625_{10}$

$16^{-1} = \dfrac{1}{16} = 0.0625_{10}$

$1_{10} = 16^0$
$16_{10} = 16^1$
$256_{10} = 16^2$
$4096_{10} = 16^3$
$65536_{10} = 16^4$
$1048576_{10} = 16^5$
$16777216_{10} = 16^6$

Figure 1-10
Condensed listing of powers of 16.

Conversion From Decimal to Hexadecimal

Decimal to hexadecimal conversion is accomplished in the same manner as decimal to binary or octal, but with a base number of 16_{10}. As an example, the decimal number 156 is converted into its hexadecimal equivalent.

$$156 \div 16 = 9 \quad \text{with remainder} \quad 12 = C \leftarrow \text{LSD}$$
$$9 \div 16 = 0 \qquad\qquad\qquad\qquad\quad 9 = 9 \leftarrow \text{MSD}$$

Divide the decimal number by 16_{10} and note the remainder. If the remainder exceeds 9, convert the 2-digit number to its hexadecimal equivalent (12_{10} = C in this example). Then divide the quotient by 16 and again note the remainder. Continue dividing until a quotient of 0 results. Then collect the remainders beginning with the last or most significant digit (MSD) and proceed to the first or least significant digit (LSD). The number $9C_{16} = 156_{10}$. NOTE: The letter H after a number is sometimes used to indicate hexadecimal. However, this course will always use the subscript 16.

To further illustrate this, the decimal number 47632 is converted into its hexadecimal equivalent.

$$47632 \div 16 = 2977 \quad \text{with remainder} \quad 0 = 0 \leftarrow \text{LSD}$$
$$2977 \div 16 = 186 \qquad\qquad\qquad\qquad\quad 1 = 1$$
$$186 \div 16 = 11 \qquad\qquad\qquad\qquad\quad 10 = A$$
$$11 \div 16 = 0 \qquad\qquad\qquad\qquad\quad 11 = B \leftarrow \text{MSD}$$

The division process continues until a quotient of 0 results. The remainders are collected, producing the number $BA10_{16} = 47632_{10}$. Remember, any remainder that exceeds the digit 9 must be converted to its letter equivalent. (In this example, 10 = A, and 11 = B.)

To convert a decimal fraction to a hexadecimal fraction, multiply the fraction successively by 16_{10} (hexadecimal base). As an example the decimal fraction 0.78125 is converted into its hexadecimal equivalent.

$$0.78125 \times 16 = 12.5 = 0.5 \quad \text{with overflow} \quad 12 = C \leftarrow \text{MSD}$$
$$0.50000 \times 16 = 8.0 = 0 \qquad\qquad\qquad\qquad 8 = 8 \leftarrow \text{LSD}$$

Multiply the decimal by 16_{10}. If the product exceeds one, subtract the integer (overflow) from the product. If the "overflow" exceeds 9, convert the 2-digit number to its hexadecimal equivalent. Then multiply the product fraction by 16_{10} and again note any overflow. Continue multiplying until an overflow, with 0 for a fraction, results. Remember, you can not always obtain 0 when you multiply by 16. Therefore, you should only continue the conversion to the accuracy or precision you desire. Collect the conversion overflows beginning at the radix point with the MSD and proceed to the LSD. The number $0.C8_{16} = 0.78125_{10}$.

Now the decimal fraction 0.136 will be converted into its hexadecimal equivalent with five-place precision.

$0.136 \times 16 =$	$2.176 = 0.176$	overflow	$2 = 2 \rightarrow$ MSD
$0.176 \times 16 =$	$2.816 = 0.816$		$2 = 2$
$0.816 \times 16 =$	$13.056 = 0.056$		$13 = D$
$0.056 \times 16 =$	$0.896 = 0.896$		$0 = 0$
$0.896 \times 16 =$	$14.336 = 0.336$		$14 = E \rightarrow$ LSD

The number $0.22D0E_{16}$ approximately equals 0.136_{10}. If you convert $0.22D0E_{16}$ back to decimal (using positional notation), you will find $0.22D0E_{16} = 0.1359996795654296875_{16}$. This example shows that extending the precision of your conversion is of little value unless extreme accuracy is required.

Number Systems and Codes

As shown in this section, conversion of an integer from decimal to hexadecimal requires a different technique than for conversion of a fraction. Therefore, when you convert a hexadecimal number composed of an integer and a fraction, you must separate the integer and fraction, then perform the appropriate operation on each. After you convert them, you must recombine the integer and fraction. For example, the decimal number 124.78125 is converted into its hexadecimal equivalent.

$124.78125_{10} = 124_{10} + 0.78125_{10}$
$124 \div 16 = 7$ with remainder $12 = C \leftarrow$ LSD
$7 \div 16 = 0$ $7 = 7 \leftarrow$ MSD

$\boxed{124_{10} = 7C_{16}}$

$0.78125 \times 16 = 12.5 = 0.5$ overflow $12 = C \leftarrow$ MSD
$0.50000 \times 16 = 8.0 = 0$ $8 = 8 \leftarrow$ LSD

$\boxed{0.78125_{10} = 0.C8_{16}}$

$124.78125_{10} = 124_{10} + 0.78125_{10} = 7C_{16} + 0.C8_{16} = 7C.C8_{16}$

First separate the decimal integer and fraction. Then convert the integer and fraction to hexadecimal.

Finally, recombine the integer and fraction.

Converting Between the Hexadecimal and Binary Number Systems

Previously, the octal number system was described as an excellent shorthand form to express large binary quantities. This method is very useful with many microprocessors. The trainer used with this course uses the hexadecimal number system to represent binary quantities. As a result, frequent conversions from binary-to-hexadecimal are necessary. Figures 1-8 and 1-9 illustrate the relationship between hexadecimal and binary integers and fractions.

As you know, four bits of a binary number exactly equal 16_{10} value combinations. Therefore, you can represent a 4-bit binary number with a 1-digit hexadecimal number:

$$1101_2 = (1 \times 2^3) + (1 \times 2^2) + (0 \times 2^1) + (1 \times 2^0) = 8 + 4 + 0 + 1 = 13_{10} = D_{16}$$

Because of this relationship, converting binary to hexadecimal is simple and straightforward. For example, binary number 10110110 is converted into its hexadecimal equivalent.

$$10110110_2$$
REWRITE AS

MSB → 1011 0110 ← LSB

YIELDS

$$B6_{16}$$

To convert a binary number to hexadecimal, first separate the number into groups containing four bits, beginning with the least significant bit. Then convert each 4-bit group into its hexadecimal equivalent. Don't forget to use letter digits as required. This gives you a hexadecimal number equal in value to the binary number.

Now convert a larger binary number (10101101101) into its hexadecimal equivalent.

$$10101101101_2$$
REWRITE AS

MSB → 0101 0110 1101 ← LSB

YIELDS

$$56D_{16}$$

Again, the binary number is separated into 4-bit groups beginning with the LSB. However, the third group contains only three bits. Since each group must contain four bits, a zero must be added after the MSB. The third group will then have four bits with no change in the value of the binary number. Now each 4-bit group can be converted into its hexadecimal equivalent. **Whenever you add zeros to a binary integer, always place them to the left of the most significant bit.**

Binary fractions can also be converted to their hexadecimal equivalents using the same process, with one exception; the binary bits are separated into groups of four, beginning with the most significant bit (at the radix point). For example, the binary fraction 0.01011011 is converted into its hexadecimal equivalent.

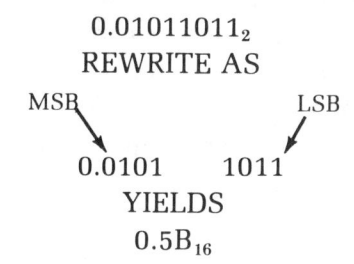

$$0.01011011_2$$
REWRITE AS

MSB → 0.0101   1011 ← LSB

YIELDS

$$0.5B_{16}$$

Again, you must separate the binary number into groups of four, beginning with the radix point. Then convert each 4-bit group into its hexadecimal equivalent. This gives you a hexadecimal number equal in value to the binary number.

Now convert a larger binary fraction (0.1101001101) into its hexadecimal equivalent.

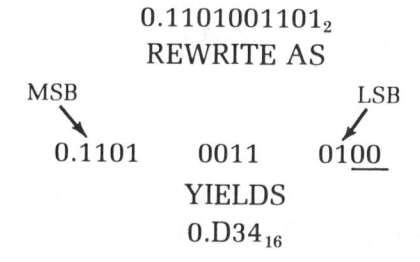

$$0.1101001101_2$$
REWRITE AS

MSB → 0.1101   0011   01<u>00</u> ← LSB

YIELDS

$$0.D34_{16}$$

Separate the binary number into 4-bit groups, beginning at the radix (binary) point (MSB). Note that the third group contains only two bits. Since each group must contain four bits, two zeros must be added after the LSB. The third group will then have four bits with no change in the value of the binary number. Now, each 4-bit group can be converted into its hexadecimal equivalent. **Whenever you add zeros to a binary fraction, always place them to the right of the least significant bit.**

Now, a binary number containing both an integer and a fraction (110110101.01110111) will be converted into its hexadecimal equivalent.

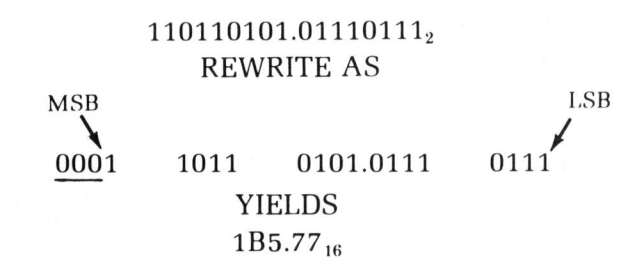

$$110110101.01110111_2$$
REWRITE AS

MSB $\searrow$ LSB $\swarrow$

<u>0001</u>   1011   0101.0111   0111

YIELDS

$$1B5.77_{16}$$

The integer part of the number is separated into groups of four, **beginning** at the radix point. Note that three zeros were added to the third group to complete the group. The fractional part of the number is separated into groups of four, **beginning** at the radix point. (No zeros were needed to complete the fractional groups.) The integer and fractional 4-bit groups are then converted to hexadecimal. The number 110110101.01110111_2 = $1B5.77_{16}$. **Never** shift the radix point in order to form 4-bit groups.

Converting hexadecimal to binary is just the opposite of the previous process; simply convert each hexadecimal number into its 4-bit binary equivalent. For example, convert the hexadecimal number 8F.41 into its binary equivalent.

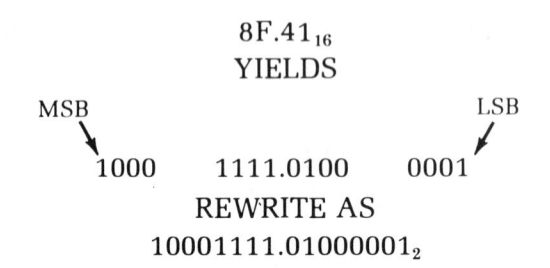

$$8F.41_{16}$$
YIELDS

MSB $\searrow$ LSB $\swarrow$

1000   1111.0100   0001

REWRITE AS

$$10001111.01000001_2$$

Convert each hexadecimal digit into a 4-bit binary number. Then condense the 4-bit groups to form the binary value equal to the hexadecimal value. The number $8F.41_{16}$ = 10001111.01000001_2.

Now, the hexadecimal number 175.4E will be converted into its binary equivalent.

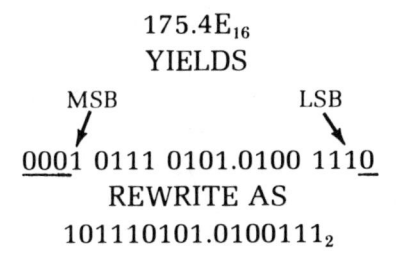

$$175.4E_{16}$$
YIELDS

MSB   LSB

<u>000</u>1 0111 0101.0100 111<u>0</u>

REWRITE AS

$$101110101.0100111_2$$

Again, each hexadecimal digit is converted into its 4-bit binary equivalent. However, in this example there are three insignificant zeros in front of the MSB and one after the LSB. Since these zeros have no value, they should be removed from the final result.

Self-Test Review

20. The base or radix of the hexadecimal number system is _____.

21. Convert the following decimal integers to hexadecimal.

    A. 783
    B. 5372
    C. 957

22. Convert the following decimal fractions to hexadecimal. Do not use greater than four-place precision.

    A. 0.653
    B. 0.109375
    C. 0.4567

23. Convert 1573.125_{10} to its hexadecimal equivalent.

24. Convert the following binary numbers to hexadecimal.

    A. 100001101.01011
    B. 11111011001.01
    C. 110001101.00010010101

25. Convert the following hexadecimal numbers to binary.

    A. AE7.D2
    B. 2C5.21F8
    C. 1B6.64E

MICROPROCESSORS

Number Systems and Codes | 1-39

Answers

20. 16_{10}.

21. A. $783 \div 16 = 48$ with remainder $15 = F$ ← LSD
       $48 \div 16 = 3$ $0 = 0$
        $3 \div 16 = 0$ $3 = 3$ ← MSD

          $\boxed{783_{10} = 30F_{16}}$

    B. $5372_{10} = 14FC_{16}$
    C. $957_{10} = 3BD_{16}$

22. A. $0.653 \times 16 = 10.448 = 0.448$ with overflow $10 = A$ ← MSD
        $0.448 \times 16 = 7.168 = 0.168$ $7 = 7$
        $0.168 \times 16 = 2.688 = 0.688$ $2 = 2$
        $0.688 \times 16 = 11.008 = 0.008$ $11 = B$ ← LSD

          $\boxed{0.653_{10} = 0.A72B_{16}}$

    B. $0.109375_{10} = 0.1C_{16}$
    C. $0.4567_{10} = 0.74EA_{16}$

23. A. $1573.125_{10} = 1573_{10} + 0.125_{10}$
          $1573 \div 16 = 98$ with remainder $5 = 5$ ← LSD
            $98 \div 16 = 6$ $2 = 2$
             $6 \div 16 = 0$ $6 = 6$ ← MSD

          $\boxed{1573_{10} = 625_{16}}$

        $0.125 \times 16 = 2.00 = 0$ with overflow $2 = 2$ ← MSD, LSD

          $\boxed{0.125_{10} = 0.2_{16}}$

        $1573.125_{10} = 1573_{10} + 0.125_{10} = 625_{16} + 0.2_{16} = 625.2_{16}$

24. A. $100001101.01011_2 = 0001\ 0000\ 1101.0101\ 1000_2$
                             $= 10D.58_{16}$

    B. $11111011001.01_2 = 7D9.4_{16}$
    C. $110001101.00010010101_2 = 18D.12A_{16}$

25. A. $AE7.D2_{16} = 1010\ 1110\ 0111.1101\ 0010_2$
                   $= 101011100111.1101001_2$
    B. $2C5.21F8_{16} = 1011000101.0010000111111_2$
    C. $1B6.64E_{16} = 110110110.01100100111_2$

BINARY CODES

Converting a decimal number into its binary equivalent is called "coding." A decimal number is expressed as a binary code or binary number. The **binary number system**, as discussed, is known as the pure binary code. This name distinguishes it from other types of binary codes. This section will discuss some of the other types of binary codes used in computers.

Binary Coded Decimal

The decimal number system is easy to use because it is so familiar. The binary number system is less convenient to use because it is less familiar. It is difficult to quickly glance at a binary number and recognize its decimal equivalent. For example, the binary number 1010011 represents the decimal number 83. It is difficult to tell immediately by looking at the number what its decimal value is. However, within a few minutes, using the procedures described earlier, you could readily calculate its decimal value. The amount of time it takes to convert or recognize a binary number quantity is a distinct disadvantage in working with this code despite the numerous hardware advantages. Engineers recognized this problem early and developed a special form of binary code that was more compatible with the decimal system. Because so many digital devices, instruments and equipment use decimal input and output, this special code has become very widely used and accepted. This special compromise code is known as binary coded decimal (BCD). The BCD code combines some of the characteristics of both the binary and decimal number systems.

8421 BCD Code The BCD code is a system of representing the decimal digits 0 through 9 with a four-bit binary code. This BCD code uses the standard 8421 position **weighting system** of the pure binary code. The standard 8421 BCD code and the decimal equivalents are shown in Figure 1-11, along with a special Gray code that will be described later. As with the pure binary code, you can convert the BCD numbers into their decimal equivalents by simply adding together the weights of the bit positions whereby the binary 1's occur. Note, however, that there are only ten possible valid 4-bit code arrangements. The 4-bit binary numbers representing the decimal numbers 10 through 15 are invalid in the BCD system.

DECIMAL	8421 BCD	GRAY	BINARY
0	0000	0000	0000
1	0001	0001	0001
2	0010	0011	0010
3	0011	0010	0011
4	0100	0110	0100
5	0101	0111	0101
6	0110	0101	0110
7	0111	0100	0111
8	1000	1100	1000
9	1001	1101	1001
10	0001 0000	1111	1010
11	0001 0001	1110	1011
12	0001 0010	1010	1100
13	0001 0011	1011	1101
14	0001 0100	1001	1110
15	0001 0101	1000	1111

Figure 1-11
Codes.

To represent a decimal number in BCD notation, substitute the appropriate 4-bit code for each decimal digit. For example, the decimal integer 834 in BCD would be 1000 0011 0100. Each decimal digit is represented by its equivalent 8421 4-bit code. A space is left between each 4-bit group to avoid confusing the BCD format with the pure binary code. This method of representation also applies to decimal fractions. For example, the decimal fraction 0.764 would be 0.0111 0110 0100 in BCD. Again, each decimal digit is represented by its equivalent 8421 4-bit code, with a space between each group.

An advantage of the BCD code is that the ten BCD code combinations are easy to remember. Once you begin to work with binary numbers regularly, the BCD numbers may come to you as quickly and automatically as decimal numbers. For that reason, by simply glancing at the BCD representation of a decimal number you can make the conversion almost as quickly as if it were already in decimal form. As an example, convert a BCD number into its decimal equivalent.

$$0110\ 0010\ 1000.1001\ 0101\ 0100 = 628.954_{10}$$

The BCD code simplifies the man-machine interface but it is less efficient than the pure binary code. It takes more bits to represent a given decimal number in BCD than it does with pure binary notation. For example, the decimal number 83 in pure binary form is 1010011. In BCD code the decimal number 83 is written as 1000 0011. In the pure binary code, it takes only seven bits to represent the number 83. In BCD form, it takes eight bits. It is inefficient because, for each bit in a data word, there is usually some digital circuitry associated with it. The extra circuitry associated with the BCD code costs more, increases equipment complexity, and consumes more power. Arithmetic operations with BCD numbers are also more time consuming and complex than those with pure binary numbers. With four bits of binary information, you can represent a total of $2^4 = 16$ different states or the decimal number equivalents 0 through 15. In the BCD system, six of these states (10-15), are wasted. When the BCD number system is used, some efficiency is traded for the improved communications between the digital equipment and the human operator.

Decimal-to-BCD conversion is simple and straightforward. However, binary-to-BCD conversion is not direct. An intermediate conversion to decimal must be performed first. For example, the binary number 1011.01 is converted into its BCD equivalent.

First the binary number is converted to decimal.

$$1011.01_2 = (1 \times 2^3) + (0 \times 2^2) + (1 \times 2^1) + (1 \times 2^0) + (0 \times 2^{-1}) + (1 \times 2^{-2})$$
$$= 8 + 0 + 2 + 1 + 0 + 0.25$$
$$= 11.25_{10}$$

Then the decimal result is converted to BCD.

$11.25_{10} = 0001\ 0001.0010\ 0101$

To convert from BCD to binary, the previous operation is reversed. For example, the BCD number 1001 0110.0110 0010 0101 is converted into its binary equivalent.

First, the BCD number is converted to decimal.
1001 0110.0110 0010 0101 = 96.625_{10}
Then the decimal result is converted to binary.
$96.625_{10} = 96_{10} + 0.625_{10}$

$96 \div 2 = 48$ with remainder 0 ← LSB
$48 \div 2 = 24$ 0
$24 \div 2 = 12$ 0
$12 \div 2 = 6$ 0
$6 \div 2 = 3$ 0
$3 \div 2 = 1$ 1
$1 \div 2 = 0$ 1 ← MSB

$$\boxed{96_{10} = 1100000_2}$$

$0.625 \times 2 = 1.25 = 0.25$ with overflow   1 ← MSB
$0.250 \times 2 = 0.50 = 0.50$ 0
$0.500 \times 2 = 1.00 = 0$ 1 ← LSB

$$\boxed{0.625_{10} = 0.101_2}$$

$96.625_{10} = 96_{10} + 0.625_{10} = 1100000_2 + 0.101_2 = 1100000.101_2$

Therefore:

1001 0110.0110 0010 0101 = 96.625_{10} = 1100000.101_2

Because the intermediate decimal number contains both an integer and fraction, each number portion is converted as described under "Binary Number System." The binary sum (integer plus fraction) 1100000.101 is equivalent to the BCD number 1001 0110.0110 0010 0101.

DECIMAL	8421 BCD	GRAY	BINARY
0	0000	0000	0000
1	0001	0001	0001
2	0010	0011	0010
3	0011	0010	0011
4	0100	0110	0100
5	0101	0111	0101
6	0110	0101	0110
7	0111	0100	0111
8	1000	1100	1000
9	1001	1101	1001
10	0001 0000	1111	1010
11	0001 0001	1110	1011
12	0001 0010	1010	1100
13	0001 0011	1011	1101
14	0001 0100	1001	1110
15	0001 0101	1000	1111

Figure 1-11
Codes.

Special Binary Codes

Besides the standard pure binary coded form, the BCD numbering system is by far the most widely-used digital code. You will find one or the other in most of the applications that you encounter. However, there are several other codes that are used for special applications, such as the "Gray Code."

The Gray Code is a widely-used, non-weighted code system. Also known as the cyclic, unit distance or reflective code, the Gray code can exist in either the pure binary or BCD formats. The Gray code is shown in Figure 1-11. As with the pure binary code, the first ten codes are used in BCD operations. Notice that there is a change in only one bit from one code number to the next in sequence. You can get a better idea about the Gray code sequence by comparing it to the standard 4-bit 8421 BCD code and the pure binary code also shown in Figure 1-11. For example, consider the change from 7 (0111) to 8 (1000) in the pure binary code. When this change takes place, all bits change. Bits that were 1's are changed to 0's and 0's are changed to 1's. Now notice the code change from 7 to 8 in the Gray code. Here 7 (0100) changes to 8 (1100). Only the first bit changes.

The Gray code is generally known as an error minimizing code because it greatly reduces confusion in the electronic circuitry when changing from one state to the next. When binary codes are implemented with electronic circuitry, it takes a finite period of time for bits to change from 0 to 1 or 1 to 0. These state changes can create timing and speed problems. This is particularly true in the standard 8421 codes where many bits change from one combination to the next. When the Gray code is used, however, the timing and speed errors are greatly minimized because only one bit changes at a time. This permits code circuitry to operate at higher speeds with fewer errors.

The biggest disadvantage of the Gray code is that it is difficult to use in arithmetic computations. Where numbers must be added, subtracted or used in other computations, the Gray code is not applicable. In order to perform arithmetic operations, the Gray code number must generally be converted into pure binary form.

Alphanumeric Codes

Several binary codes are called alphanumeric codes because they are used to represent characters as well as numbers. The two most common codes that will be discussed are ASCII and BAUDOT.

ASCII Code The American Standard Code for Information Interchange commonly referred to as ASCII, is a special form of binary code that is widely used in microprocessors and data communications equipment. A new name for this code that is becoming more popular is the American National Standard Code for Information Interchange (ANSCII). However, this course will use the most recognized term, ASCII. ASCII is a 6-bit binary code that is used in transferring data between microprocessors and their peripheral devices, and in communicating data by radio and telephone. With six bits, a total of $2^6 = 64$ different characters can be represented. These characters comprise decimal numbers 0 through 9, upper-case letters of the alphabet, plus other special characters used for punctuation and data control. A 7-bit code called full ASCII, extended ASCII, or USASCII can be represented by $2^7 = 128$ different characters. In addition to the characters and numbers generated by 6-bit ASCII, 7-bit ASCII contains lower-case letters of the alphabet, and additional characters for punctuation and control. The 7-bit ASCII code is shown in Figure 1-12.

COLUMN	0 (3)	1 (3)	2 (3)	3	4	5	6	7 (3)
ROW \ BITS 4321 \ 765	000	001	010	011	100	101	110	111
0 0000	NUL	DLE	SP	0	@	P	\	p
1 0001	SOH	DC1	!	1	A	Q	a	q
2 0010	STX	DC2	"	2	B	R	b	r
3 0011	ETX	DC3	#	3	C	S	c	s
4 0100	EOT	DC4	$	4	D	T	d	t
5 0101	ENQ	NAK	%	5	E	U	e	u
6 0110	ACK	SYN	&	6	F	V	f	v
7 0111	BEL	ETB	'	7	G	W	g	w
8 1000	BS	CAN	(	8	H	X	h	x
9 1001	HT	EM	)	9	I	Y	i	y
10 1010	LF	SUB	*	:	J	Z	j	z
11 1011	VT	ESC	+	;	K	[	k	{
12 1100	FF	FS	,	<	L	\	l		
13 1101	CR	GS	–	=	M	]	m	}
14 1110	SO	RS	.	>	N	⌃(1)	n	~
15 1111	SI	US	/	?	O	—(2)	o	DEL

Figure 1-12

Table of 7-bit American Standard Code for Information Interchange.

NOTES:

(1) Depending on the machine using this code, the symbol may be a circumflex, an up-arrow, or a horizontal parenthetical mark.

(2) Depending on the machine using this code, the symbol may be an underline, a back-arrow, or a heart.

(3) Explanation of special control functions in columns 0, 1, 2, and 7.

NUL	Null	DLE	Data Link Escape
SOH	Start of Heading	DC1	Device Control 1
STX	Start of Text	DC2	Device Control 2
ETX	End of Text	DC3	Device Control 3
EOT	End of Transmission	DC4	Device Control 4
ENQ	Enquiry	NAK	Negative Acknowledge
ACK	Acknowledge	SYN	Synchronous Idle
BEL	Bell (audible signal)	ETB	End of Transmission Block
BS	Backspace	CAN	Cancel
HT	Horizontal Tabulation (punched card skip)	EM	End of Medium
		SUB	Substitute
LF	Line Feed	ESC	Escape
VT	Vertical Tabulation	FS	File Separator
FF	Form Feed	GS	Group Separator
CR	Carriage Return	RS	Record Separator
SO	Shift Out	US	Unit Separator
SI	Shift In	DEL	Delete
SP	Space (blank)		

Figure 1-12
(Continued.)

The 7-bit ASCII code for each number, letter or control function is made up of a 4-bit group and a 3-bit group. Figure 1-13 shows the arrangement of these two groups and the numbering sequence. The 4-bit group is on the right and bit 1 is the LSB. Note how these groups are arranged in rows and columns in Figure 1-12.

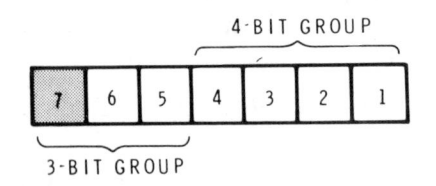

Figure 1-13
ASCII code word format.

To determine the ASCII code for a given number letter or control operation, locate that item in the table. Then use the 3- and 4-bit codes associated with the row and column in which the item is located. For example, the ASCII code for the letter L is 1001100. It is located in column 4, row 12. The most significant 3-bit group is 100, while the least significant 4-bit group is 1100. When 6-bit ASCII is used, the 3-bit group is reduced to a 2-bit group as shown in Figure 1-14.

In 7-bit ASCII code, an eighth bit is often used as a **parity** or check bit to determine if the data (character) has been transmitted correctly. The value of this bit is determined by the type of parity desired. **Even parity** means the sum of all the 1 bits, including the parity bit, is an even number. For example, if G is the character transmitted, the ASCII code is 1000111. Since four 1's are in the code, the parity bit is 0. The 8-bit code would be written 01000111.

Odd Parity means the sum of all the 1 bits, including the parity bit, is an odd number. If the ASCII code for G was transmitted with odd parity, the binary representation would be 11000111.

MICROPROCESSORS — Number Systems and Codes — 1-49

ROW	BITS 4321	65 → 10	11	00	01
		COLUMN 0	1	2	3
0	0000	SP(3)	(	@	P
1	0001	!	1	A	Q
2	0010	"	2	B	R
3	0011	#	3	C	S
4	0100	$	4	D	T
5	0101	%	5	E	U
6	0110	&	6	F	V
7	0111	'	7	G	W
8	1000	(	8	H	X
9	1001	)	9	I	Y
10	1010	*	:	J	Z
11	1011	+	;	K	[
12	1100	,	<	L	\
13	1101	–	=	M	]
14	1110	.	>	N	⌢ (1)
15	1111	/	?	O	— (2)

Figure 1-14
Table of 6-bit American Standard Code for Information Interchange.

NOTES:

(1) Depending on the machine using this code, the symbol may be a circumflex, an up-arrow, or a horizontal parenthetical mark.

(2) Depending on the machine using this code, the symbol may be an underline, a back-arrow, or a heart.

(3) SP — Space (blank) for machine control.

BAUDOT Code While the ASCII code is used almost exclusively with microprocessor peripheral devices (CRT display, keyboard terminal, paper punch/reader, etc.), there are many older printer peripherals that use the 5-bit BAUDOT code. With five data bits, this code can represent only $2^5 = 32$ different characters. To obtain a greater character capability, 26 of the 5-bit codes are used to represent two separate characters. As shown in Figure 1-15, one set of 5-bit codes represents the 26 upper-case alphabet letters. The same 5-bit codes also represent various figures and the decimal number series 0 through 9.

The remaining six 5-bit codes are used for machine control and do not have a secondary function. Two of these 5-bit codes determine which of the 26 double (letter/figure) characters can be transmitted/received. Bit number 11111 forces the printer to recognize all following 5-bit codes as **letters**. Bit number 11011 forces **figure** recognition of all the following 5-bit codes. For example, to type 56 NORTH 10 STREET, the following method is used.

Type — Figures 5 6 Space

Then — Letters N O R T H Space

Then — Figures 1 0 Space

Finally — Letters S T R E E T

Bit Numbers 5 4 3 2 1	Letters Case	Figures Case
0 0 0 0 0	Blank	Blank
0 0 0 0 1	E	3
0 0 0 1 0	Line Feed	Line Feed
0 0 0 1 1	A	—
0 0 1 0 0	Space	Space
0 0 1 0 1	S	Bell
0 0 1 1 0	I	8
0 0 1 1 1	U	7
0 1 0 0 0	Car. Ret.	Car. Ret.
0 1 0 0 1	D	$
0 1 0 1 0	R	4
0 1 0 1 1	J	(Apos)'
0 1 1 0 0	N	(Comma),
0 1 1 0 1	F	!
0 1 1 1 0	C	:
0 1 1 1 1	K	(
1 0 0 0 0	T	5
1 0 0 0 1	Z	"
1 0 0 1 0	L	)
1 0 0 1 1	W	2
1 0 1 0 0	H	Stop
1 0 1 0 1	Y	6
1 0 1 1 0	P	0
1 0 1 1 1	Q	1
1 1 0 0 0	O	9
1 1 0 0 1	B	?
1 1 0 1 0	G	&
1 1 0 1 1	Figures	Figures
1 1 1 0 0	M	.
1 1 1 0 1	X	/
1 1 1 1 0	V	;
1 1 1 1 1	Letters	Letters

Figure 1-15
5-bit BAUDOT code table.

Self-Test Review

26. The BCD code is more convenient to use than the binary code because:

    A. it uses less bits.
    B. it is more compatible with the decimal number system.
    C. it is more adaptable to arithmetic computations.
    D. there are more different coding schemes available.

27. Convert the following decimal numbers to 8421 BCD code.

    A. 1049
    B. 267
    C. 835

28. Convert the following 8421 BCD code numbers to decimal.

    A. 1001 0110 0010
    B. 0111 0001 0100 0011
    C. 1010 1001 1000
    D. 1000 0000 0101

29. Convert the following binary numbers to 8421 BCD code.

    A. 101110.01
    B. 1001.0101
    C. 11011011.0001

MICROPROCESSORS
Number Systems and Codes 1-53

30. Convert the following 8421 BCD codes to binary.

    A. 0001 1000 0010.0101
    B. 0010 1001 0000.0010 0101
    C. 1101 0110 0011.0101
    D. 0110 1000.0001 0010 0101

31. Which code is best for error minimizing?

    A. 8421 BCD
    B. pure binary
    C. Gray

32. The ASCII and BAUDOT codes are a form of _____ _____ codes.

33. To determine if the correct ASCII character has been transmitted, a _____ bit is often added to the code.

34. Which type of parity is used when the 8-bit ASCII character 01000111 is transmitted?

    A. odd
    B. even

35. Refer to Figure 1-12 and convert the following characters into their ASCII 7-bit binary code.

    A. B
    B. X
    C. 3
    D. S

36. Refer to Figure 1-12 and convert the following ASCII 7-bit binary codes to their character equivalents.

    A. 0110010
    B. 1010110
    C. 1011010
    D. 1001110

Answers

26. B. More compatible with the decimal system.

27. A. 0001 0000 0100 1001
    B. 0010 0110 0111
    C. 1000 0011 0101

28. A. 962
    B. 7143
    C. Invalid (1010 represents a decimal digit greater than 9)
    D. 805

29. A. $101110.01_2 = (1 \times 2^5) + (0 \times 2^4) + (1 \times 2^3) + (1 \times 2^2) + (1 \times 2^1)$
        $+ (0 \times 2^0) + (0 \times 2^{-1}) + (1 \times 2^{-2})$
        $= 32 + 0 + 8 + 4 + 2 + 0 + 0 + 0.25$
        $= 46.25_{10}$
    $46.25_{10} = 0100\ 0110.0010\ 0101$
    $101110.01_2 = 0100\ 0110.0010\ 0101$
    B. $1001.0101_2 = 1001.0011\ 0001\ 0010\ 0101$
    C. $11011011.0001_2 = 0010\ 0001\ 1001.0000\ 0110\ 0010\ 0101$

MICROPROCESSORS — Number Systems and Codes — 1-55

30. A.   0001 1000 0010.0101 = 182.5_{10}

$$182.5_{10} = 182_{10} + 0.5_{10}$$

182 ÷ 2 = 91	with remainder	0 ← LSB
91 ÷ 2 = 45		1
45 ÷ 2 = 22		1
22 ÷ 2 = 11		0
11 ÷ 2 = 5		1
5 ÷ 2 = 2		1
2 ÷ 2 = 1		0
1 ÷ 2 = 0		1 ← MSB

$$\boxed{182_{10} = 10110110_2}$$

0.5 × 2 = 1.00 = 0   overflow   1 ← MSB, LSB

$$\boxed{0.5_{10} = 0.1_2}$$

$182.5_{10} = 182_{10} + 0.5_{10} = 10110110_2 + 0.1_2 = 10110110.1_2$

0001 1000 0010.0101 = 10110110.1_2

B. 0010 1001 0000.0010 0101 = 100100010.01_2
C. invalid (1101 represents a decimal digit greater than 9)
D. 0110 1000.0001 0010 0101 = 1000100.001_2

31.   Gray

32.   Alpha numeric

33.   Parity

34.   Even

35. A.   1000010
     B.   1011000
     C.   0110011
     D.   1010011

36. A.   2
     B.   V
     C.   Z
     D.   N

UNIT 1 SUMMARY

1. A basic distinguishing feature of a number system is its base or radix. The binary number system has a radix of 2, octal 8, decimal 10, and hexadecimal 16.

2. A number system is positional or weighted. That is, each digit position carries a particular weight which determines the magnitude of that number. Each position has a weight determined by the power of the number system. In the decimal number system the positional weights are 10^0 (units), 10^1 (tens), 10^2 (hundreds), 10^{-1} (tenths), 10^{-2} (hundredths), etc.

3. In a number, such as decimal 247429, the left-most digit (2) is called the most significant digit or MSD, while the right-most digit (9) is called the least significant digit or LSD. These terms apply to all number systems.

4. The simplest number system is the binary number system. It is called binary because it has a base or radix of 2. The numbers used in the binary number system are 0 and 1.

5. Binary data is represented by binary digits called bits. The left-most bit is generally called the most significant bit (MSB) rather than MSD. By the same token, the right-most bit is called the least significant bit (LSB) rather than LSD.

6. Microprocessors operate on groups of bits which are called words.

7. Positional weight in the binary number system is a positive or negative power of two.

8. To convert a binary number into its decimal equivalent, add together the weights of the positions in the number where the binary ones occur.

9. To convert a decimal whole number into its binary equivalent, successively divide the number by two and note the remainders. When you divide by two, the remainder will always be one or zero. The first remainder is always the LSB, while the last remainder is always the MSB.

10. To convert a decimal fraction into its binary equivalent, successively multiply the fraction by the number two and record the integers produced by the multiplication. The integer produced by the multiplication will always be one or zero. The first integer is the MSB. The MSB is located at the radix (binary) point of the fraction.

11. The octal number system uses the digits 0 through 7.

12. The positional weight in the octal number system is a positive or negative power of eight.

13. To convert an octal number into its decimal equivalent, add together the weights of the number positions.

14. To convert a decimal whole number into its octal equivalent, successively divide the number by eight and note the remainders. These will be some value between zero and seven. The first remainder will always be the ~~MSD~~ LSD.

15. To convert a decimal fraction into its octal equivalent, successively multiply the fraction by the number eight and record the integers produced by the multiplication. The integer produced by the multiplication will always be some number between zero and seven. The first integer is the MSD. The MSD is located at the radix (octal) point of the fraction.

16. Three bits of a binary number exactly equal eight value combinations. Therefore, you can represent a 3-bit binary number with a 1-digit octal number.

17. To convert a binary number into octal, first separate the number into groups containing three bits, beginning with the LSB. Then convert each 3-bit group into its octal equivalent. This applies to both integers and fractions.

18. To convert an octal number into binary, simply convert each octal digit into its 3-bit binary equivalent.

19. The hexadecimal number system uses the digits 0 through 9 and the letters A through F.

20. The positional weight in the hexadecimal number system is a positive or negative power of sixteen.

21. To convert a hexadecimal number into its decimal equivalent, add together the weights of the number positions.

22. To convert a decimal whole number into its hexadecimal equivalent, successively divide the number by sixteen and note the remainders. These will be some value between zero and fifteen. The first remainder will always be the MSD. Any remainder greater than nine must be converted into its hexadecimal letter equivalent.

23. To convert a decimal fraction into its hexadecimal equivalent, successively multiply the fraction by the number sixteen and record the integers produced by the multiplication. The integer produced by the multiplication will always be some number between zero and fifteen. The first integer is the MSD. The MSD is located at the radix (octal) point of the fraction. Any remainder greater than nine must be converted into its hexadecimal letter equivalent.

24. Four bits of a binary number exactly equal sixteen value combinations. Therefore, you can represent a 4-bit binary number with a 1-digit hexadecimal number.

25. To convert a binary number into hexadecimal, first separate the number into groups containing four bits, beginning with the LSB. Then convert each 4-bit group into its hexadecimal equivalent. This applies to both integers and fractions.

26. To convert a hexadecimal number into binary, simply convert each hex digit into its 4-bit binary equivalent.

27. Converting a decimal number into its binary equivalent is called coding.

28. Binary coded decimal (BCD) code combines some of the characteristics of both the binary and decimal number systems. The BCD code is a system of representing the decimal digits zero through nine with a 4-bit binary code. The code uses the 8421 position weighting system of pure binary code. However, there are only ten valid 4-bit code arrangements.

29. The BCD code simplifies the man-machine interface but it is less efficient than the pure binary code. It takes more bits to represent a given decimal number in BCD than it does to represent a given decimal number in pure binary.

30. You cannot make direct conversion between BCD and binary. You must first convert the BCD code to decimal digits, then convert the decimal digits to binary.

31. Gray code is a widely-used, non-weighted code system. It is also known as the cyclic, unit distance, error minimizing, or reflective code.

32. When Gray code is incremented, only one bit changes state. While this permits code circuitry to operate at higher speeds with fewer errors, it is difficult to use in arithmetic computations.

33. American Standard Code for Information Interchange (ASCII) code is a special form of binary code that is widely used in microprocessors and data communications equipment.

34. While ASCII can be used as a 6-bit code, it is generally used in its 7- bit form. The seven code bits are used through a translation table to identify 128 different printable and non-printable characters. The printable characters are the upper-and lower-case alphabet, the numbers zero through nine, and punctuation symbols. The non-printable characters are used to control various "machine" operations such as carriage return, line feed, etc.

35. In 7-bit ASCII code, an eighth bit is often used as a parity or check bit. You use the value of the parity bit to control the parity of the 8-bit word.

36. Older printer peripherals use BAUDOT code for data transmission. It is a 5-bit code that can represent 32 different characters. These characters include the upper-case alphabet, the numbers zero through nine, punctuation symbols, and a number of machine control characters.

Perform Experiments 1 and 2 at the end of Book 2.

POSITIVE POWERS OF 2

n	2^n
0	1
1	2
2	4
3	8
4	16
5	32
6	64
7	128
8	256
9	512
10	1024
11	2048
12	4096
13	8192
14	16384
15	32768
16	65536
17	13107 2
18	26214 4
19	52428 8
20	10485 76
21	20971 52
22	41943 04
23	83886 08
24	16777 216
25	33554 432
26	67108 864
27	13421 7728
28	26843 5456
29	53687 0912
30	10737 41824
31	21474 83648
32	42949 67296

MICROPROCESSORS

NEGATIVE POWERS OF 2

n	2^{-n}
0	1.0
1	0.5
2	0.25
3	0.125
4	0.0625
5	0.03125
6	0.01562 5
7	0.00781 25
8	0.00390 625
9	0.00195 3125
10	0.00097 65625
11	0.00048 82812 5
12	0.00024 41406 25
13	0.00012 20703 125
14	0.00006 10351 5625
15	0.00003 05175 78125
16	0.00001 52587 89062 5
17	0.00000 76293 94531 25
18	0.00000 38146 97265 625
19	0.00000 19073 48632 8125
20	0.00000 09536 74316 40625
21	0.00000 04768 37158 20312 5
22	0.00000 02384 18579 10156 25
23	0.00000 01192 09289 55078 125
24	0.00000 00596 04644 77539 0625
25	0.00000 00298 02322 38769 53125
26	0.00000 00149 01161 19384 76562 5
27	0.00000 00074 50580 59692 38281 25
28	0.00000 00037 25290 29846 19140 625
29	0.00000 00018 62645 14923 09570 3125
30	0.00000 00009 31322 57461 54785 15625
31	0.00000 00004 65661 28730 77392 57812 5
32	0.00000 00002 32830 64365 38696 28906 25

POSITIVE POWERS OF 8

n	8^n
0	1
1	8
2	64
3	512
4	409 6
5	327 68
6	262 144
7	209 715 2
8	167 772 16

POSITIVE POWERS OF 16

n	16^n
0	1
1	16
2	256
3	409 6
4	655 36
5	104 857 6
6	167 772 16
7	268 435 456
8	429 496 729 6

NEGATIVE POWERS OF 16

n	16^{-n}
0	1.0
1	0.062 5
2	0.003 906 25
3	0.000 244 140 625
4	0.000 015 258 789 062 5

Unit 2

MICROCOMPUTER BASICS

INTRODUCTION

A microprocessor is a very complex electronic circuit. It consists of thousands of microscopic transistors squeezed onto a tiny chip of silicon that is often no more than one-eighth inch square. The chip is placed in a package containing anywhere from 40 to 64 leads.

The thousands of transistors that make up the microprocessor are arranged to form many different circuits within the chip. From the standpoint of learning how the microprocessor operates, the most important circuits on the chip are registers, counters, and decoders. In this unit, you will learn how these circuits can work together to perform simple but useful tasks.

UNIT OBJECTIVES

When you have completed this unit you will be able to:

1. Define the terms: microprocessor, microcomputer, input, output, I/O, I/O device, I/O port, instruction, program, stored program concept, word, byte, MPU, ALU, operand, memory, address, read, write, RAM, fetch, execute, MPU cycle, mnemonic, opcode, and bus.

2. Explain the purpose of the following circuits in a typical microprocessor: accumulator, program counter, instruction decoder, controller sequencer, data register, and address register.

3. Using a simplified block diagram of a hypothetical microprocessor, trace the data flow that takes place between the various circuits during the execution of a simple program.

4. Describe the difference between inherent, immediate, and direct addressing.

5. Write simple, straight-line programs that can be executed by the ET-3400 Microprocessor Trainer.

TERMS AND CONVENTIONS

A **microprocessor** is a logic device that is used in digital electronic systems. It is also being used by hobbyists, experimenters and low-budget research groups as a low-cost, general-purpose computer. But a distinction should be made between the microprocessor and the microcomputer.

The microprocessor unit, or MPU, is a complex logic element that performs arithmetic, logic, and control operations. The trend is to package it as a single integrated circuit.

A **microcomputer** contains a microprocessor, but it also contains other circuits such as memory devices to store information, interface adapters to connect it with the outside world, and a clock to act as a master timer for the system. Figure 2-1 shows a typical microcomputer in which these additional circuits are added. The arrows represent conductors over which binary information flows. The wide arrows represent several conductors connected in parallel. A group of parallel conductors which carry information is called a **bus**.

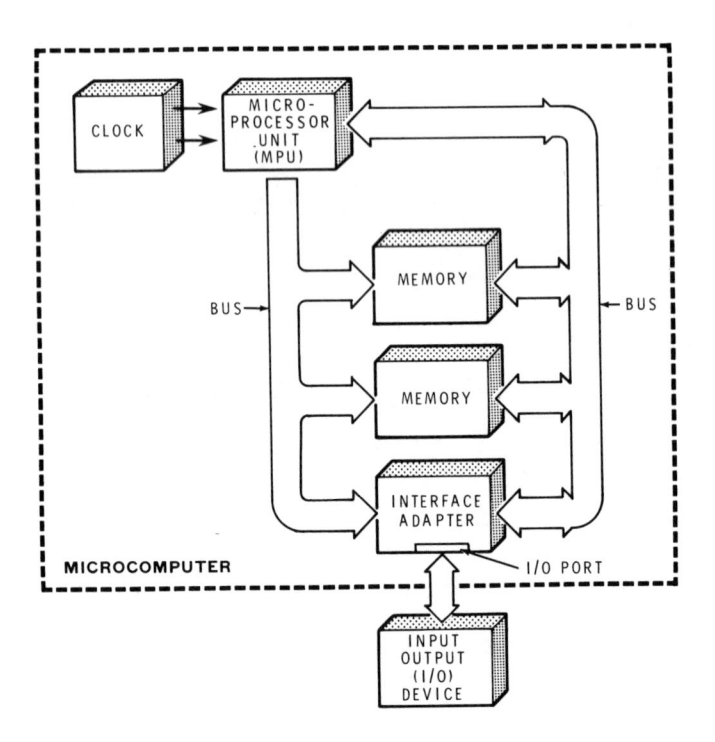

Figure 2-1
A Basic Microcomputer.

The microcomputer is composed of everything inside the dotted line. Everything outside the dotted line is referred to as the **outside world**, and all microcomputers must have some means of communicating with it. Information received by the microcomputer from the outside world is referred to as **input** data. Information transmitted to the outside world from the microcomputer is referred to as **output** data.

Input information may come from devices like paper tape readers, typewriters, mechanical switches, keyboards, or even other computers. Output information may be sent to video displays, output typewriters, paper tape punches, or line printers. Some devices such as the teletypewriter can serve as both an input and an output device. These devices are referred to as **input/output** or **I/O** devices. The point at which the I/O device connects to the microcomputer is called an **I/O port**.

Stored Program Concept

A microcomputer is capable of performing many different operations. It can add and subtract numbers and it can perform logical operations. It can read information from an input device and transmit information to an output device. In fact, depending on the microprocessor used, there may be 100 or more different operations that the microcomputer can perform. Moreover, two or more individual operations can be combined to perform much more complex operations.

In spite of all its capabilities, the computer will do nothing on its own accord. It will do only what it is told to do, nothing more and nothing less. You must tell the computer exactly what operations to perform and the order in which it should perform them. The operations that the computer can be told to perform are called **instructions**. A few typical instructions are ADD, SUBTRACT, LOAD INDEX REGISTER, STORE ACCUMULATOR, and HALT.

A group of instructions that allows the computer to perform a specific job is called a **program**. One who writes these instructions is called a **programmer**. To design with microprocessors, the engineer must become a programmer. To repair microprocessor-based equipment, the technician must understand programming. Generally, the length of the program is proportional to the complexity of the task that the computer is to perform. A program for adding a list of numbers may require only a dozen instructions. On the other hand, a program for controlling all the traffic lights in a small city may require thousands of instructions.

A computer is often compared to a calculator, which is told what to do by the operator via the keyboard. Even inexpensive calculators can perform several operations that can be compared to instructions in the computer. By depressing the right keys, you can instruct the calculator to add, subtract, multiply, divide, and clear the display. Of course, you must also enter the numbers that are to be added, subtracted, etc. With the calculator, you can add a list of numbers as quickly as you can enter the numbers and the instructions. That is, the operation is limited by the speed and accuracy of the operator.

From the start, computer designers recognized that it was the human operator that slowed the computation process. To overcome this, the **stored program concept** was developed. Using this approach, the program is stored in the computer's memory. Suppose, for example, that you have 20 numbers that are to be manipulated by a program that is composed of 100 instructions. Let's further suppose that 10 answers will be produced in the process.

Before any computation begins, the 100-instruction program plus the 20 numbers are loaded into the computer's memory. Furthermore, 10 memory locations are reserved for the 10 answers. Only then is the computer allowed to execute the program. The actual computation time might be less than one millisecond. Compare this to the time that it would take to manually enter the instructions and numbers, one at a time, while the computer is running. This automatic operation is one of the features that distinguishes the computer from the calculator.

Computer Words

In computer terminology, a **word** is a group of binary digits that can occupy a storage location. Although the word may be made up of several binary digits, the computer handles each word as if it were a single unit. Thus, the **word** is the fundamental unit of information used in the computer.

A word may be a binary number that is to be handled as data. Or, the word may be an instruction that tells the computer which operation it is to perform. It may be an ASCII character representing a letter of the alphabet. Finally, a word can be an "address" that tells the computer where a piece of data is located.

Word Length

In the past few years, a wide variety of microprocessors have been developed. Their cost and capabilities vary widely. One of the most important characteristics of any microprocessor is the word length it can handle. This refers to the length in bits of the most fundamental unit of information.

The most common word length for microprocessors is 8 bits. In these units; numbers, addresses, instructions, and data are represented by 8-bit binary numbers. The lowest 8-bit binary number is $0000\ 0000_2$ or 00_{16}. The highest is $1111\ 1111_2$ or FF_{16}. In decimal, this range is from 0 to 255_{10}. Thus, an 8-bit binary number can have any one of 256_{10} unique values.

An 8-bit word can specify positive numbers between 0 and 255_{10}. Or, if the 8-bit word is an instruction, it can specify any of 256_{10} possible operations. It is also entirely possible that the 8-bit word is an ASCII character. In this case, it can represent letters of the alphabet, punctuation marks, or numerals. As you can see, the 8-bit word can represent many different things, depending on how it is interpreted. The programmer must insure that an ASCII character or binary number is not interpreted as an instruction. Later, you will see the consequences of making this mistake.

While the 8-bit word length is the most popular, other word lengths are sometimes used. The earliest microprocessor used a 4-bit word length, and four-bit microprocessors are still used in many cases because of their low cost. A few 12-bit and 16-bit microprocessors have also been developed.

Longer word lengths allow us to work with larger numbers. For example, a 16-bit word can represent numbers up to $65,535_{10}$. However, this capability adds to the complexity and cost of the microprocessor. Because most microprocessors use 8-bit word lengths, we will restrict our discussion to units of this type.

It should be pointed out that just because the word length is 8-bits, it does not mean that we are restricted to numbers below 256_{10}. It simply means that you must use two or more words to represent larger numbers.

The 8-bit word length defines the size of many different components in the microprocessor system. For example, many of the important registers will have 8-bit capacity. Memory will be capable of holding a large number of 8-bit words. And, the bus which is used to transfer data words will consist of eight parallel conductors.

Even 16-bit microprocessors use 8-bit segments of data in many applications. For example, inputs from teletypewriters often consist of 8-bit ASCII characters. To distinguish these 8-bit segments of information from the 16-bit (or longer) word lengths, another term has come into general use: the term **byte**. A byte is a group of bits that are handled as a single unit. Generally, a byte is understood to consist of 8-bits. In the 8-bit microprocessor, each word consists of one byte. But in the 16-bit machines, each word contains two bytes. Figure 2-2 illustrates these points.

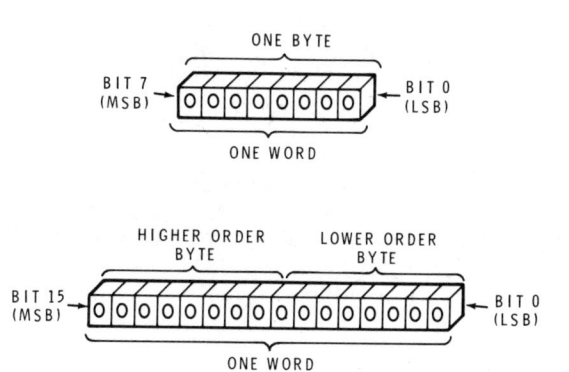

Figure 2-2
Words and Bytes.

Figure 2-2 also shows how the bits that make up the computer word are numbered. The least significant bit (LSB) is on the right while the most significant bit (MSB) is on the left. In the 8-bit word, the bits are numbered 0 through 7 from right to left. In the 16-bit word, the bits are numbered 0 through 15 as shown. The lower 8-bits are called the lower order byte while the upper 8-bits are called the higher order byte.

Self-Test Review

1. Explain the difference between a microprocessor and a microcomputer.

2. What is a bus?

3. Explain the difference between input and output data.

4. Define I/O.

5. The point at which data enters or leaves the computer is called an I/O _____.

6. The operations that the computer can be told to perform are called _____.

7. What is a program?

8. Explain what is meant by "stored program concept."

9. A byte generally consists of _____ bits.

10. A computer word may consist of one or more _____.

11. What is the largest number that can be represented by an 8-bit computer word? By a 16-bit word?

Answers

1. A microprocessor is a logic element that can perform a variety of arithmetic, control, and logic operations. A microcomputer is a system that consists of a microprocessor, memory, interface adapters, clock, etc.

2. A bus is a group of conductors over which information can be transmitted. The conductors may be wires in a cable, foil patterns on a printed circuit board, or microscopic metal deposits in a silicon chip.

3. Input data is information that is entered into the computer from the outside world. Output data is information that is transmitted from the computer to the outside world. The outside world is defined as anything outside the computer.

4. I/O is the abbreviation for input-output. Thus, a device that can send data to and accept data from the computer is called an I/O device.

5. Port.

6. Instructions.

7. A program is a group of instructions that tell the computer the operations to be performed and the sequence in which they are to be performed.

8. The stored program concept refers to the technique of storing the instruction to be performed in the memory section along with the data that is to be operated upon.

9. 8.

10. Bytes.

11. $1111\ 1111_2$ or 255_{10}. $1111\ 1111\ 1111\ 1111_2$ or $65,535_{10}$.

AN ELEMENTARY MICROCOMPUTER

One of the difficulties you may encounter in learning about a microcomputer for the first time is the complexity of its main component — the microprocessor. The microprocessor may have a dozen or more registers varying in size from 1 bit to 16 bits. It will have scores of instructions, most of which can be implemented several different ways. It will have data, address, and control buses. In short, it can be very intimidating to start out by considering a full-blown microprocessor.

A better approach is to start with a "stripped down" version. By initially omitting some of the processor's advanced features, we arrive at a device that can be readily understood and yet maintains the characteristics of an actual microprocessor. Strictly speaking, the microprocessor developed in this unit is hypothetical in nature. However, it is so close to the real thing that the programs we develop for it will actually run on the ET-3400 Microprocessor Trainer. Also, as you will see later, one of the most popular microprocessors in use today is a vastly advanced version of our elementary model.

A block diagram of a basic microcomputer is shown in Figure 2-3, which shows the microprocessor, the memory, and the I/O circuitry. For simplicity, we will ignore the I/O circuitry in this unit. We can do this by assuming that the program and data are already in memory and that the results of any computations will be held in a register or stored in memory. Ultimately of course, the program and data must come from the outside world and the results must be sent to the outside world. But we will save these procedures until a later unit. This will allow us to concentrate on the microprocessor unit and the memory.

Figure 2-3
The Basic Microcomputer.

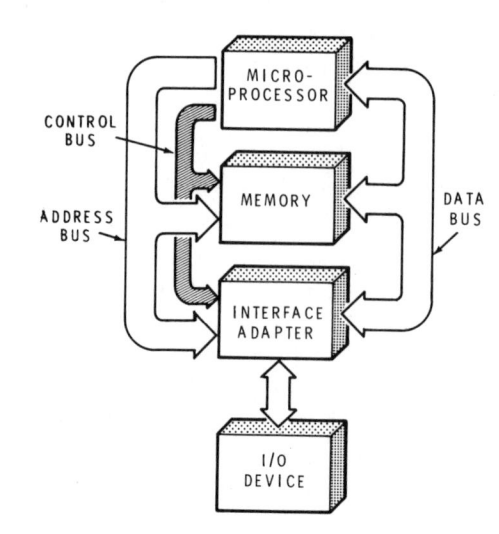

MICROPROCESSORS

The Microprocessor Unit (MPU)

The microprocessor unit is shown in greater detail in Figure 2-4. For simplicity, only the major registers and circuits are shown. In our elementary unit most of the counters, registers, and buses are 8-bits wide. That is, they can accomodate 8-bit words.

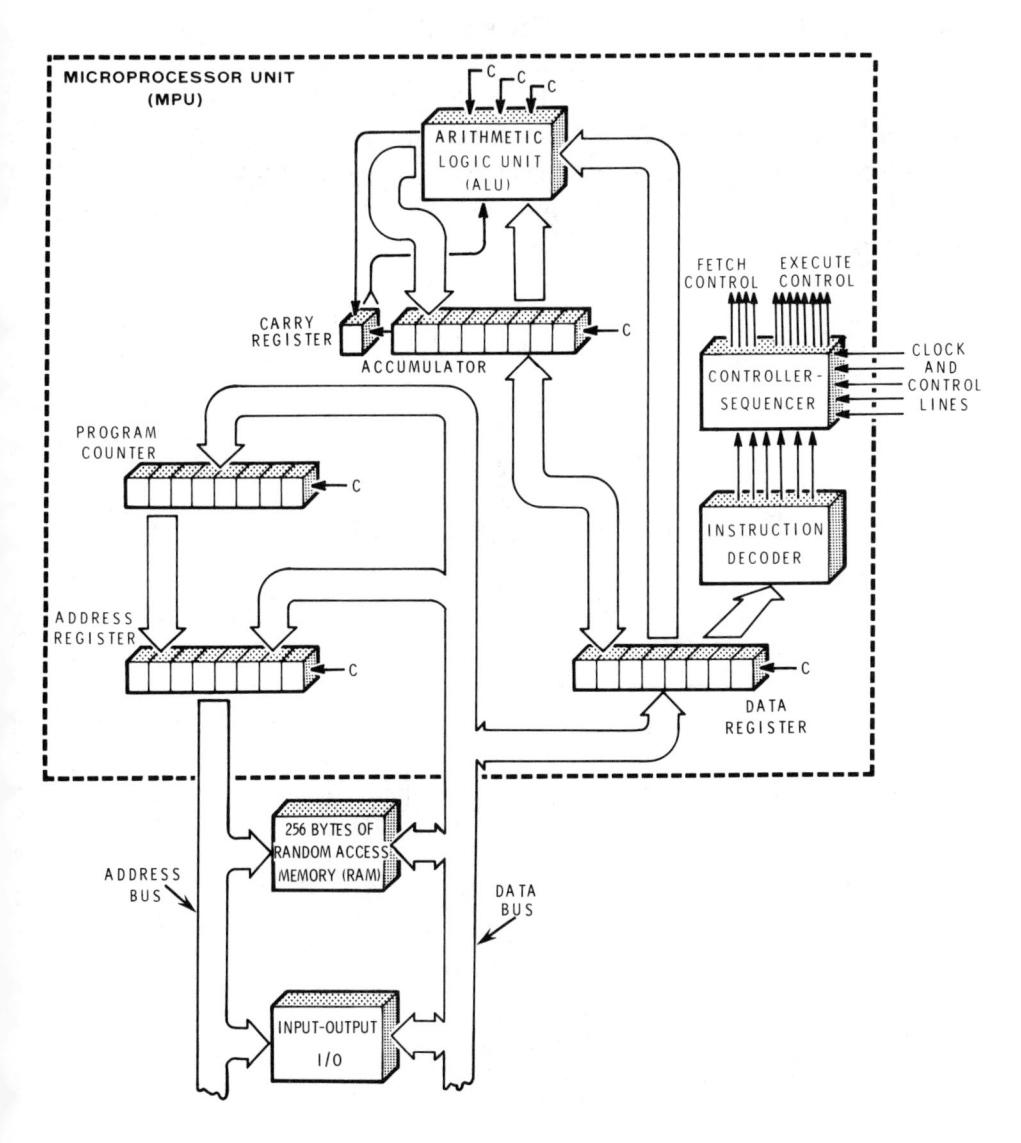

Figure 2-4
An Elementary Microprocessor.

One of the most important circuits in the microprocessor is the **arithmetic logic unit** (ALU). Its purpose is to perform arithmetic or logic operations on the data words that are delivered to it. The ALU has two main inputs. One comes from a register called the accumulator, and the other comes from the data register. The ALU can add the two input data words together, or it can subtract one from the other. It can also perform some logic operations which will be discussed in later units. The operation that the ALU performs is determined by signals on the various control lines (marked C on the block diagram).

Generally, the ALU receives two 8-bit binary numbers from the accumulator and the data register as shown in Figure 2-5A. Because some operation is performed on these data words, the two inputs are called **operands**.

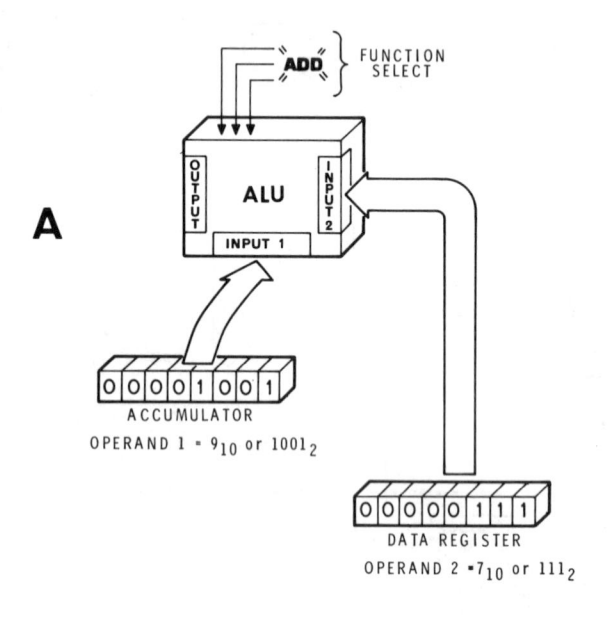

Figure 2-5
The Arithmetic Logic Unit.

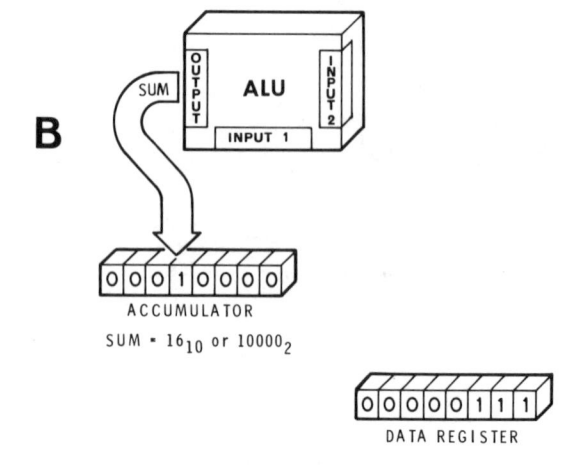

The two operands may be added, subtracted, or compared in some way, and the result of the operation is stored back in the accumulator. For example, assume that two numbers (7 and 9) are to be added. Before the numbers can be added, one operand (9) is placed in the accumulator; the other (7) is placed in the data register. The proper control line is then activated to implement the add operation. The ALU adds the two numbers together, producing their sum (16_{10}) at the output. As shown in Figure 2-5B, the sum is stored in the accumulator, replacing the operand that was originally stored there. Notice that all the numbers involved are in binary form.

The **accumulator** is the most useful register in the microprocessor. During arithmetic and logic operations it performs a dual function. Before the operation, it holds one of the operands. After the operation, it holds the resulting sum, difference, or logical answer. The accumulator receives several instructions in every microprocessor. For example, the "load accumulator" instruction causes the contents of some specified memory location to be transferred to the accumulator. The "store accumulator" instruction causes the contents of the accumulator to be stored at some specified location in memory.

The **data register** is a temporary storage location for data going to or coming from the data bus. For example, it holds an instruction while the instruction is being decoded. Also, it holds a data byte while the word is being stored in memory.

The MPU also contains several other important registers and circuits: the address register, the program counter, the instruction decoder, and the controller-sequencer. These are shown in Figure 2-4.

The **address register** is another temporary storage location. It holds the address of the memory location or I/O device that is used in the operation presently being performed.

The **program counter** controls the sequence in which the instructions in a program are performed. Normally, it does this by counting in the sequence, 0, 1, 2, 3, 4, etc. At any given instant, the count indicates the location in memory from which the next byte of information is to be taken.

The **instruction decoder** does just what its name implies. After an instruction is pulled from memory and placed in the data register, the instruction is decoded by this circuit. The decoder examines the 8-bit code and decides which operation is to be performed.

The **controller-sequencer** produces a variety of control signals to carry out the instruction. Since each instruction is different, a different combination of control signals is produced for each instruction. This circuit determines the sequence of events necessary to complete the operation described by the instruction.

Later you will see how these various circuits work together to execute simple programs. But first, take a closer look at the memory for our microcomputer.

Memory

A simplified diagram of the 256-word, 8-bit read/write memory that is used in our hypothetical microcomputer is shown in Figure 2-6. The memory consists of 256_{10} locations, each of which can store an 8-bit word. This size memory is often referred to as 256 × 8. A read/write memory is one in which data can be written in and read out with equal ease.

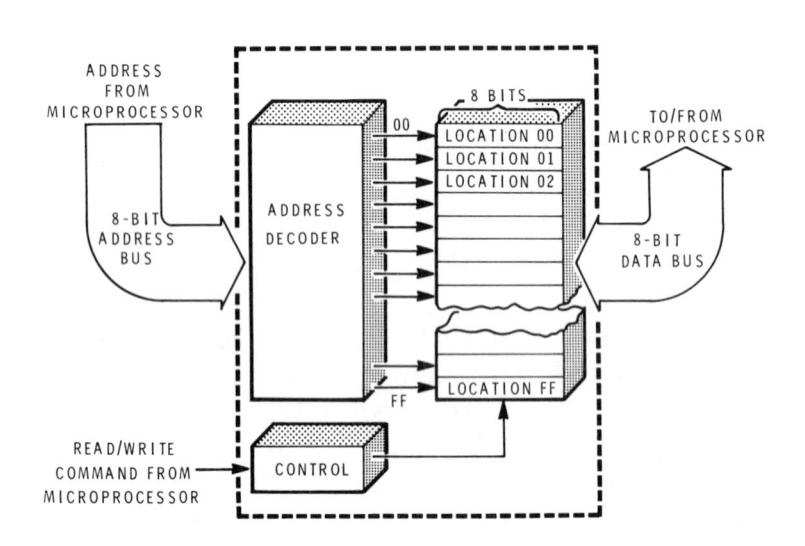

Figure 2-6
The Random Access Memory.

Two buses and a number of control lines connect the memory with the microprocessing unit. The address bus will carry an 8-bit binary number, which can specify 256_{10} locations, from the MPU to the memory address decoder. Each location is assigned a unique number called its address. The first location is given the address 0. The last location is given the address 255_{10}, which is 1111 1111 in binary and FF in hexadecimal. A specific location is selected by placing its 8-bit address on the address bus. The address decoder decodes the 8-bit number and selects the proper memory location.

The memory also receives a control signal from the MPU. This signal tells the memory the operation that is to be performed. A READ signal indicates that the selected location is to be read out. This means that the 8-bit number contained in the selected location is to be placed on the data bus where it can be transferred to the MPU.

The procedure is illustrated in Figure 2-7. Assume that the MPU is to read out the contents of memory location 04_{16}. Let's further assume that the number stored there is 97_{16}. First, the MPU places the address 04_{16} on the address bus. The decoder recognizes the address and selects the proper memory location. Second, the MPU sends a READ signal to the memory, indicating that the contents of the selected location is to be placed on the data bus. Third, the memory responds by placing the number 97_{16} on the data bus. The MPU can then pick up the number and use it as needed.

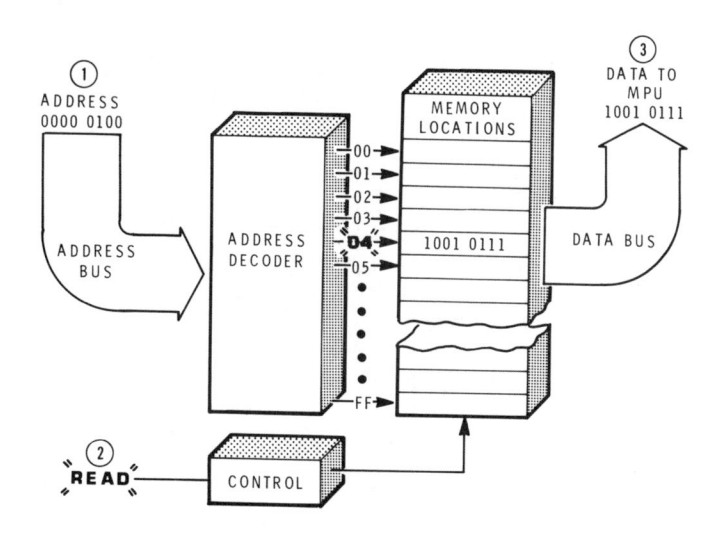

Figure 2-7
Reading from Memory.

It should be pointed out that the process of reading out a memory location does not disturb the contents of that location. That is, the number 97_{16} will still be present at memory location 04 after the read operation is finished. This characteristic is referred to as nondestructive readout (NDRO). It is an important feature because it allows us to read out the same data as many times as needed.

The MPU can also initiate a WRITE operation. This procedure is illustrated in Figure 2-8. During a WRITE operation, a data word is taken from the data bus and placed in the selected memory location. For example, let's see how the MPU can store the number 52_{16} at memory location 03. First, the MPU places the address 03 on the address bus. The decoder responds by selecting memory location 03. Second, the MPU places the number 52_{16} on the data bus. Third, the MPU sends the WRITE signal. The memory responds by storing the number contained on the data bus in the selected location. That is, 52_{16} is stored in location 03. The previous contents of the selected location are lost as the new number is written in that location.

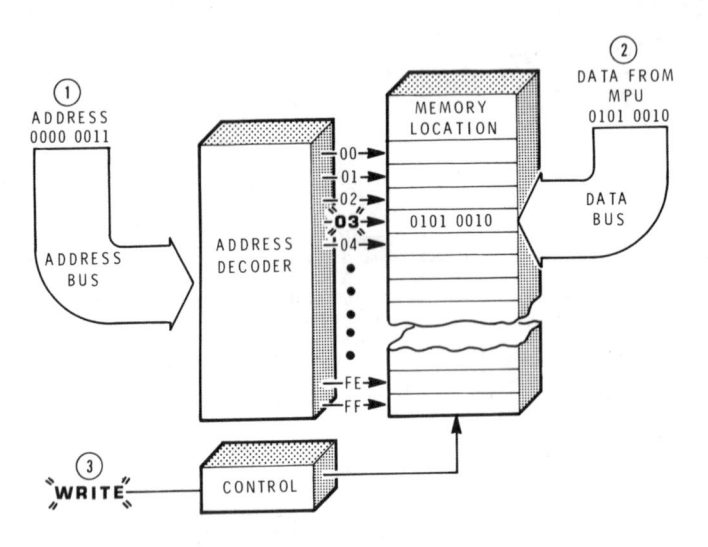

Figure 2-8
Writing into Memory.

The accepted name for a memory of this type is **Random Access Memory** (RAM). "Random access' means that all memory locations are equally accessible. However, in recent years RAM has come to mean a random access **read/write** memory. As you will see later, there is another type of memory called a read only memory (ROM). It is also randomly accessible, but it does not have a write capability. Today, the accepted definition of RAM is a random access **read/write** memory. A read only memory, although it is randomly accessible, is called a ROM and never a RAM.

Fetch-Execute Sequence

When the microcomputer is executing a program, it goes through a fundamental sequence that is repeated over and over again. Recall that a program consists of instructions that tell the microcomputer exactly what operations to perform. These instructions must be stored in an orderly manner in memory. Instructions must be fetched, one at a time, from memory by the MPU. The instruction is then executed by the MPU.

The operation of the microcomputer can be broken down into two phases, as shown in Figure 2-9. When the microprocessor is initially started, it enters the **fetch phase**. During the fetch phase, an instruction is taken from memory and decoded by the MPU. Once the instruction is decoded, the MPU switches to the **execute phase**. During this phase, the MPU carries out the operation dictated by the instruction.

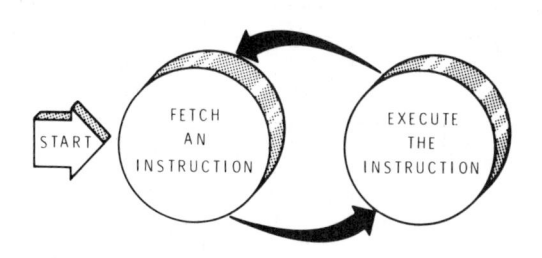

Figure 2-9
The Fetch-Execute Sequence.

The fetch phase always consists of the same series of operations. Thus, it always takes the same amount of time. However, the execute phase will consist of different sequences of events, depending on what type of instruction is being executed. Thus, the time of the execute phase may vary considerably from one instruction to the next.

A Sample Program

Now that you have a general idea of the registers and circuits found in a microcomputer, we will examine how all these circuits work together to execute a simple program. At this point, we are primarily interested in showing you how the microcomputer operates. Therefore, the program will be a very trivial one.

Let's see how the computer goes about solving a problem like 7 + 10 = ? While this seems like an incredibly easy problem, the computer, if left to its own resources, does not have the foggiest notion of how to solve it. You must tell the computer how to solve the problem right down to the smallest detail. You do this by writing a program.

Before you can write the program you must know what instructions are available to you and the computer. Every microprocessor comes with a listing of its instruction set. Assume that, after looking over the list, you decide that three instructions are necessary to solve the problem. These three instructions and a description of what they do are shown in Figure 2-10.

NAME	MNEMONIC	OPCODE	DESCRIPTION
Load Accumulator	LDA	$1000\ 0110_2$ or 86_{16}	Load the contents of the next memory location into the accumulator.
Add	ADD	$1000\ 1011_2$ or $8B_{16}$	Add the contents of the next memory location to the present contents of the accumulator. Place the sum in the accumulator.
Halt	HLT	$0011\ 1110_2$ or $3E_{16}$	Stop all operations.

Figure 2-10

Instructions Used in the Sample Program.

The first column in the table gives the name of the instruction. When writing programs, it is often inconvenient to write out the entire name. For this reason, each instruction is given an abbreviation or a memory aid called a **mnemonic**. The mnemonics are given in the second column. The third column is called the operation code or **opcode**. This is the binary number that the computer and the programmer use to represent the instruction. The opcode is given in both binary and hexadecimal form. The final column describes exactly what operation is performed when the instruction is executed. Study this table carefully; you will be using these instructions over and over again.

Assume that you wish to add 7 to 10_{10} and place the sum in the accumulator. The program is an elementary one. First you will load 7 into the accumulator with the LDA instruction. Next, you will add 10_{10} to the accumulator using the ADD instruction. Finally, you will stop the computer with the HLT instruction.

Using the mnemonics and the decimal representation of the numbers to be added, the program looks like this:

>LDA 7
>ADD 10
>HLT

Unfortunately, the basic microcomputer cannot understand mnemonics or decimal numbers. It can interpret binary numbers and nothing else. Thus, you must write the program as a sequence of binary numbers. You can do this by replacing each mnemonic with its corresponding opcode and each decimal number with its binary counterpart.

That is:

LDA 7	becomes	1000 0110	0000 0111
		opcode from	binary representation
		Figure 2-10	for 7

And:

ADD 10	becomes	1000 1011	0000 1010
		opcode from	binary representation
		Figure 2-10	for 10_{10}

Finally,

HLT	becomes	0011 1110
		opcode from
		Figure 2-10

Notice that the program consists of three instructions. The first two instructions have two parts: an 8-bit opcode followed by an 8-bit operand. The operands are the two numbers that are to be added (7 and 10_{10}).

Recall that the microprocessor and memory work with 8-bit words or bytes. Because the first two instructions consist of 16-bits of information, they must be broken into two 8-bit bytes before they can be stored in memory. Thus, when the program is stored in memory, it will look like this:

1st Instruction	{	1000 0110		Opcode for LDA
	{	0000 0111		Operand (7)
2nd Instruction	{	1000 1011		Opcode for ADD
	{	0000 1010		Operand (10_{10})
3rd Instruction		0011 1110		Opcode for HLT

Five bytes of memory are required. You can store this 5-byte program any place in memory you like. Assuming you store it at the first five memory locations, the memory can be diagrammed as shown in Figure 2-11.

ADDRESS		MEMORY	MNEMONICS/CONTENTS
HEX	BINARY	BINARY CONTENTS	
00	0000 0000	1000 0110	LDA
01	0000 0001	0000 0111	7
02	0000 0010	1000 1011	ADD
03	0000 0011	0000 1010	10_{10}
04	0000 0100	0011 1110	HLT
⋮			
FD	1111 1101		
FE	1111 1110		
FF	1111 1111		

Figure 2-11
The Program in Memory.

Notice that each memory location has two 8-bit binary numbers associated with it. One is its address, the other is its contents. Be careful not to confuse these two numbers. The address is fixed. It is established when the microcomputer is built. However, the contents may be changed at any time by storing new data.

Before you see how this program is executed, let's review the material covered in this section.

Self-Test Review

12. The circuit in the microprocessor that performs arithmetic and logic operations is called the _____.

13. The numbers that are operated upon by the computer are called _____.

14. Where are the two operands held as they are transferred to the ALU?

15. Where is the result held after an arithmetic operation?

16. Which register in the MPU holds the instruction while the opcode is being decoded?

17. Which circuit in the MPU determines the memory location from which the next byte of information will be taken?

18. Which register holds the address while it is being decoded?

19. How many memory locations can be specified by an 8-bit address?

20. Explain the 3-step procedure for writing the number 34_{16} into memory location 9.

21. Define mnemonic.

22. Define opcode.

23. Define RAM.

24. An instruction is retrieved from memory and decoded during the _____ phase.

25. The operation indicated by the instruction is carried out during the _____ phase.

26. In our hypothetical microcomputer, the mnemonic for the load accumulator instruction is _____.

27. The opcode for the halt instruction is _____.

28. When the ADD instruction is executed, where is the SUM stored?

29. How many memory locations are required to store the following program?

    LDA 13_{10}
    ADD 17_{10}
    ADD 10_{10}
    HLT

30. What will be the contents of the accumulator after this program is executed?

Answers

12. Arithmetic logic unit (ALU).

13. Operands.

14. One is held in the accumulator; the other in the data register.

15. In the accumulator.

16. Data register.

17. The program counter.

18. The address register.

19. $2^8 = 256_{10}$.

20. Step 1. The address 9 is placed on the address bus.

    Step 2. The data 34_{16} is placed on the data bus.

    Step 3. The read/write line is switched to the write state.

21. A mnemonic is an abbreviation or memory aid.

22. An opcode is a binary number that tells the microprocessor which instruction to execute.

23. RAM has come to mean a random access read/write memory.

24. Fetch.

25. Execute.

26. LDA.

27. $0011\ 1110_2$.

28. In the accumulator.

29. Seven.

30. 40_{10} or 101000_2.

EXECUTING A PROGRAM

Before a program can be run, it must be placed in memory. Later, you will see how this is done. For now, assume that we have already loaded the program developed in the previous section.

The important registers of the microcomputer are shown in Figure 2-12. Notice that our 5-byte program for adding 7 and 10_{10} is shown in memory. The following paragraphs will take you through the step-by-step procedure by which the computer executes this program.

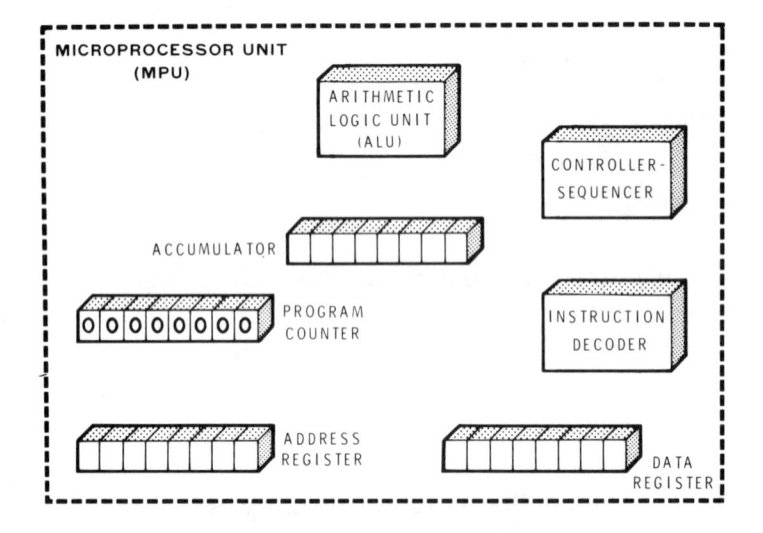

ADDRESS	BINARY CONTENTS	MNEMONICS/ DECIMAL CONTENTS
0000 0000	1000 0110	LDA
0000 0001	0000 0111	7
0000 0010	1000 1011	ADD
0000 0011	0000 1010	10
0000 0100	0011 1110	HLT

Figure 2-12
The Program Counter is Set to the Address of the First Instruction.

To begin executing the program, the program counter must be set to the address of the first instruction. In this case, the first instruction is in memory location 0000 0000, so the program counter is set accordingly. The procedure for setting the program counter to the proper address will be discussed later.

The Fetch Phase

The first step is to fetch the first instruction from memory. The sequence of events that happen during the fetch phase is controlled by the controller-sequencer. It produces a number of control signals which will cause the events illustrated in Figure 2-13 through 2-17 to occur.

First the contents of the program counter are transferred to the address register as shown in Figure 2-13. Recall that this is the address of the first instruction.

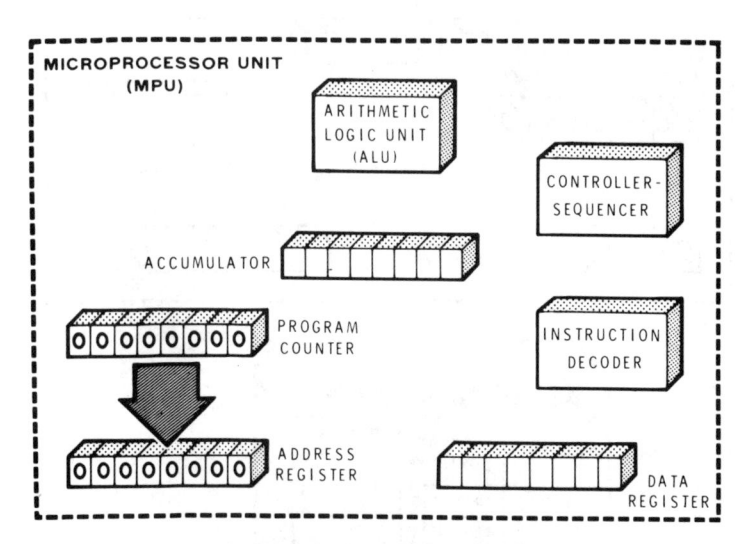

ADDRESS	BINARY CONTENTS	MNEMONICS/DECIMAL CONTENTS
0000 0000	1000 0110	LDA
0000 0001	0000 0111	7
0000 0010	1000 1011	ADD
0000 0011	0000 1010	10
0000 0100	0011 1110	HLT

Figure 2-13
The Contents of the Program Counter are Transferred to the Address Register.

Once the address is safely in the address register, the program counter is incremented by one. That is, its contents change from 0000 0000 to 0000 0001 (Figure 2-14). Notice that this does not change the contents of the address register in any way.

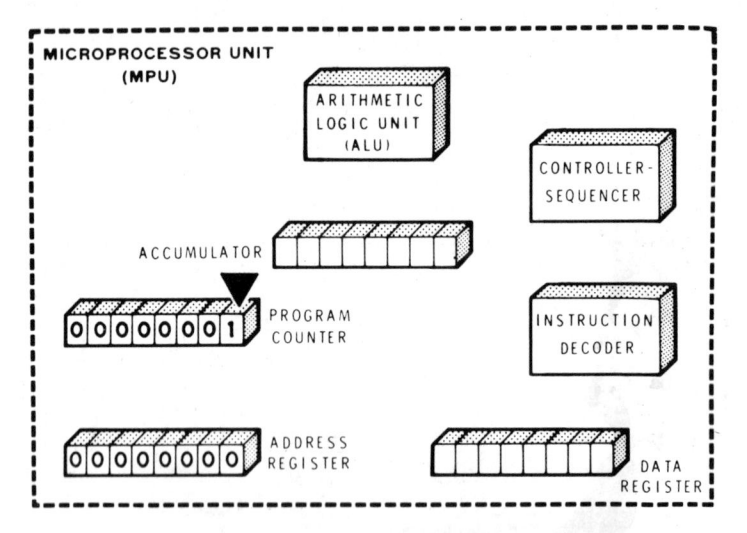

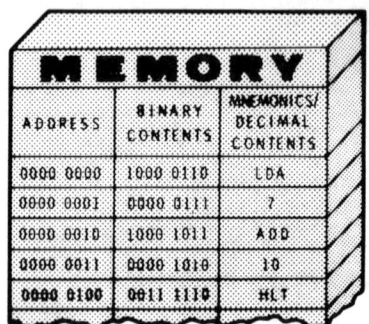

Figure 2-14
The Program Counter is Incremented.

MICROPROCESSORS

Next, the contents of the address register (0000 0000) are placed on the address bus (Figure 2-15). The memory circuits decode the address and select memory location 0000 0000.

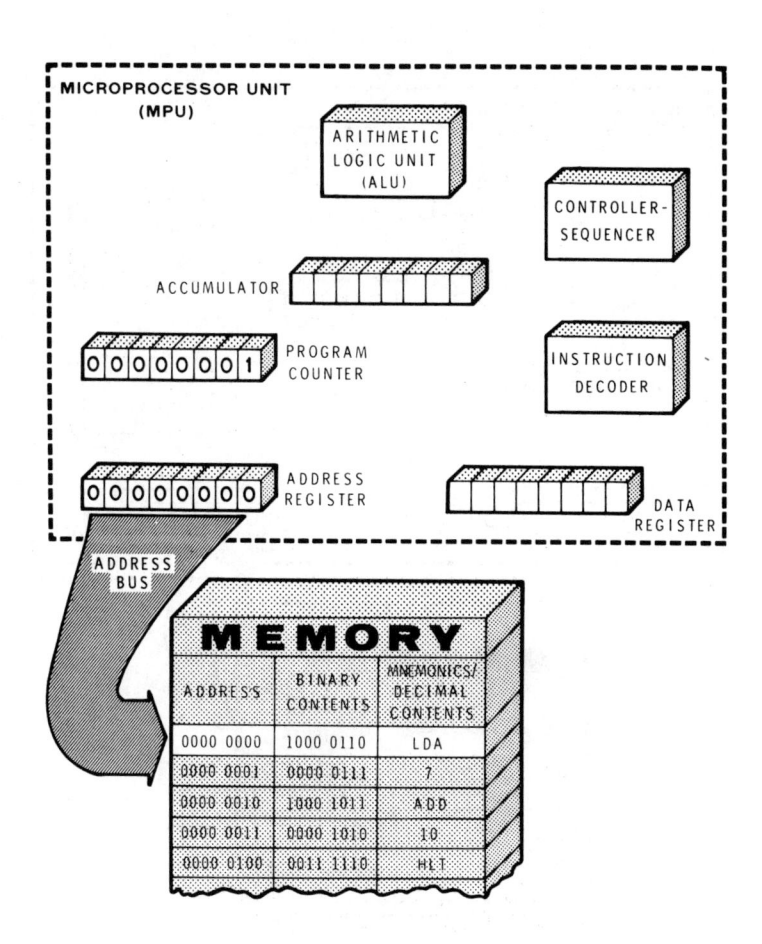

Figure 2-15
The Address of the First Instruction is
Placed on the Address Bus.

The contents of the selected memory location are placed on the data bus and transferred to the data register in the MPU. After this operation, the opcode for the LDA instruction will be in the data register as shown in Figure 2-16.

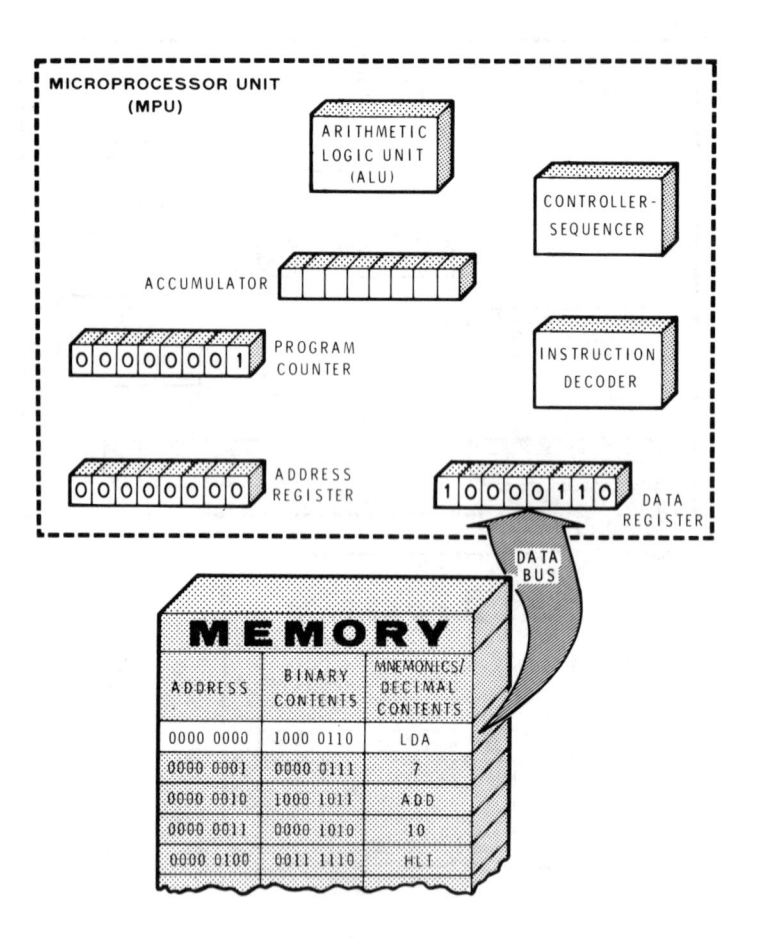

Figure 2-16
The Opcode of the First Instruction is Placed on the Data Bus.

The next step is to decode the instruction (Figure 2-17). The opcode is transferred to the instruction decoder. This circuit recognizes that the opcode is that of an LDA instruction. It informs the controller-sequencer of this fact and the sequencer produces the necessary control pulses to carry out the instruction. This completes the fetch phase of the first instruction.

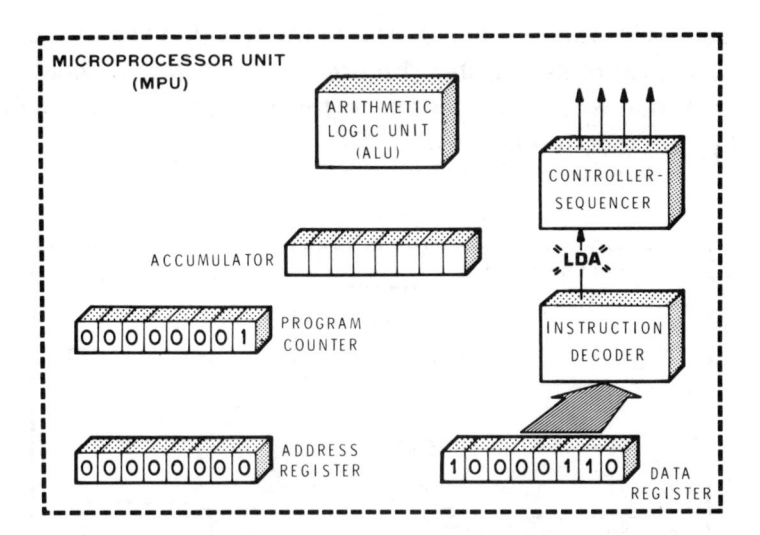

Figure 2-17
The Opcode is Decoded.

The Execute Phase

The first instruction was fetched from memory and decoded during the fetch phase. The MPU now knows that this is an LDA instruction. During the execute phase, it must carry out this instruction by reading out the next byte of memory and placing it in the accumulator.

The first step is to transfer the address of the next byte from the program counter to the address register (Figure 2-18). You will recall that the program counter was incremented to the proper address (0000 0001) during the previous fetch phase.

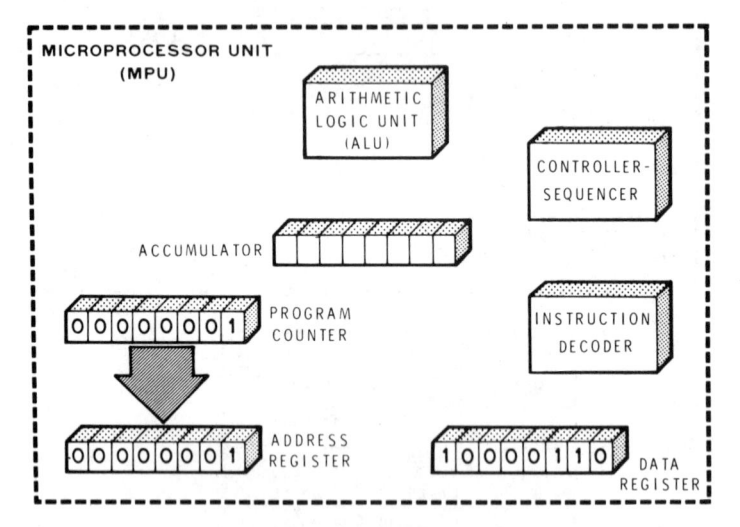

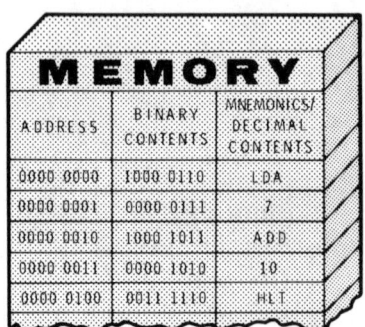

Figure 2-18
The Contents of the Program Counter are Transferred to the Address Register.

MICROPROCESSORS

The next two operations are shown in Figure 2-19. First, the program counter is incremented to 0000 0010 in anticipation of the next fetch phase. Second, the contents of the address register (000 0001) are placed on the address bus.

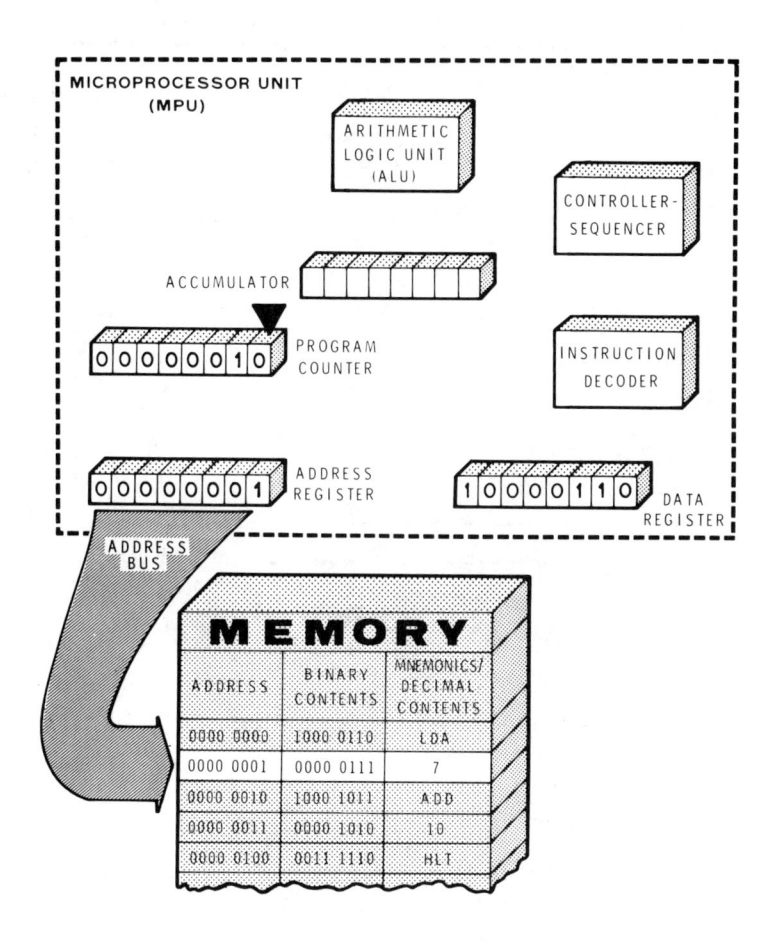

Figure 2-19
The Program Counter is Incremented;
the Contents of the Address Register
are Placed on the Address Bus.

The address is decoded and the contents of memory location 0000 0001 are loaded into the data register as shown in Figure 2-20. Recall that this is the number 7. An instant later, the number is transferred to the accumulator. Thus, the first execute phase ends with the number 7 in the accumulator.

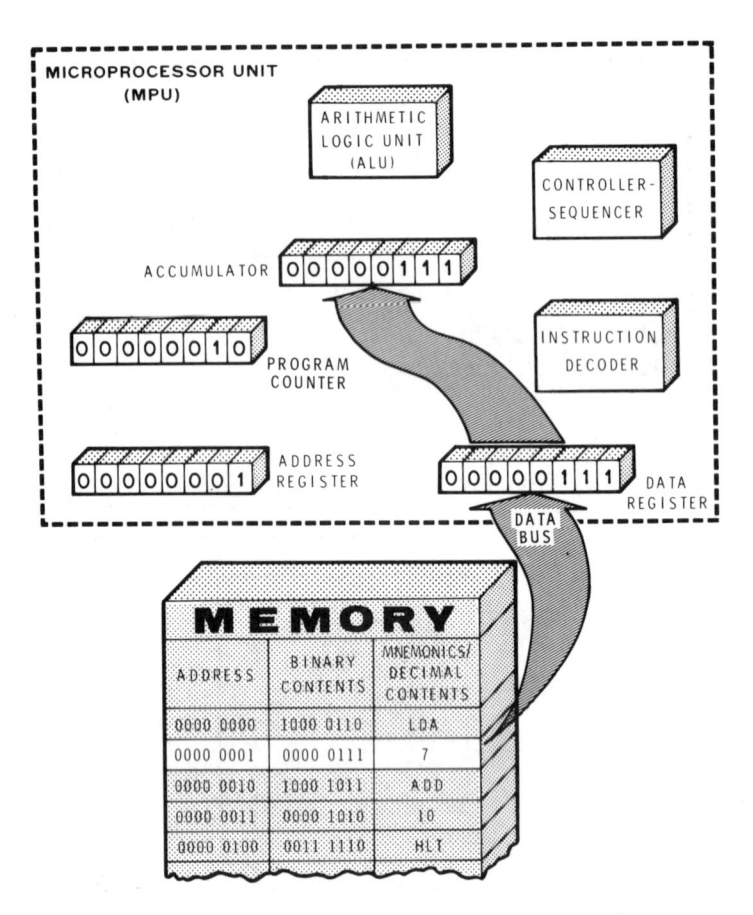

Figure 2-20
The First Operand is Transferred to the Accumulator Via the Data Register.

Fetching the Add Instruction

The next instruction in our program is the ADD instruction. It is fetched from memory using the same procedure outlined above. Figure 2-21 illustrates this five-step procedure:

1. The contents of the program counter (0000 0010) are transferred to the address register.

MICROPROCESSORS

2. The program counter is incremented to 0000 0011.

3. The address is placed on the address bus.

4. The contents of the selected memory location are transferred to the data register.

5. The contents of the data register are decoded by the instruction decoder.

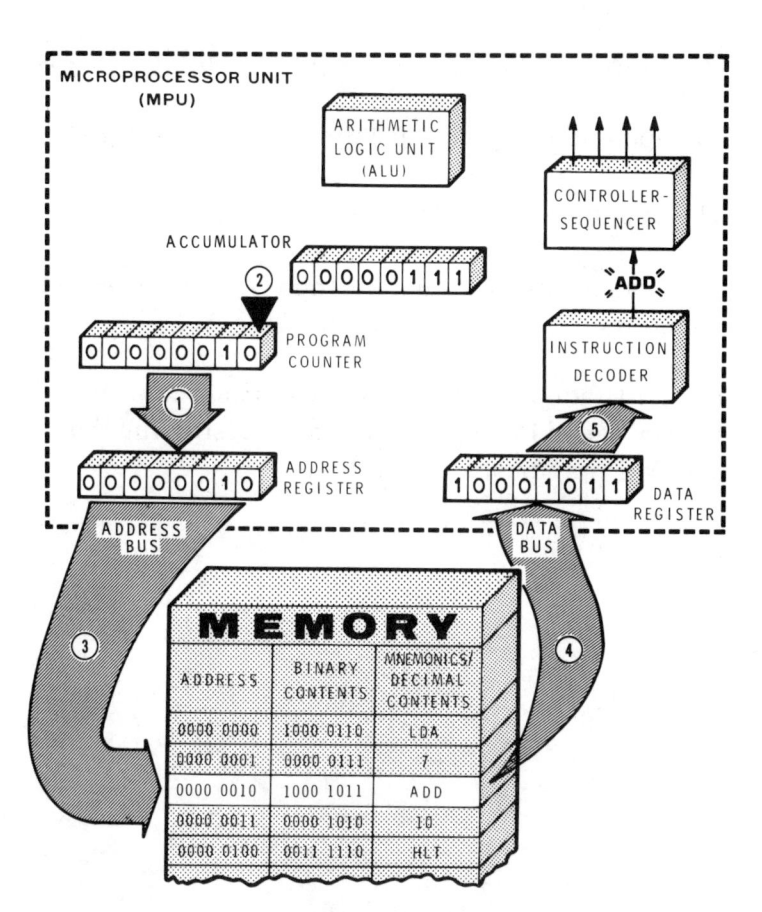

Figure 2-21
Fetching the ADD Instruction.

The data word fetched from memory is the opcode for the ADD instruction. Thus, the controller-sequencer produces the necessary control pulses to execute this instruction.

Executing the Add Instruction

The execution of the ADD instruction is a six-step procedure. This procedure is illustrated in Figure 2-22.

1. The contents of the program counter (0000 0011) are transferred to the address register.

2. The program counter is incremented to 0000 0100 in anticipation of the next fetch phase.

3. The address of the operand is placed on the address bus.

4. The operand (10_{10}) is transferred to the data register.

5A. The operand (10_{10}) is transferred into one input of the ALU.

5B. Simultaneously, the other operand (7) is transferred from the accumulator to the other input of the ALU.

6. The ALU adds the two operands. Their sum ($0001\ 0001_2$ or 17_{10}) is loaded into the accumulator, destroying the number (7) that was previously stored there.

MICROPROCESSORS

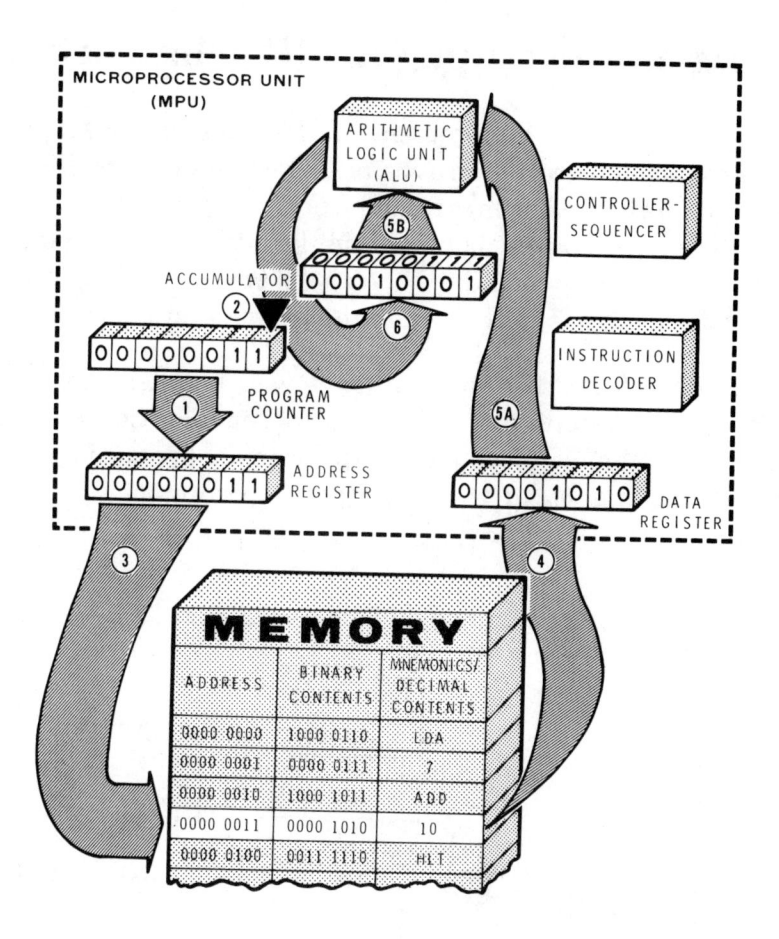

Figure 2-22
Executing the ADD Instruction.

The computation portion of our program ends with the sum of the two operands in the accumulator. However, the program is not finished until it tells the computer to stop executing instructions.

Fetching and Executing the HLT Instruction

The final instruction in the program is a HLT instruction. It is fetched using the same fetch procedure as before. The five steps are illustrated in Figure 2-23. The address comes from the program counter via the address register. When this address is placed on the address bus, memory location 0000 0100 is read out and the opcode for HLT is loaded into the data register. The opcode is decoded and the instruction is executed.

The execution of the HLT instruction is very simple. The controller-sequencer simply stops producing control signals. Consequently, all computer operations stop. Notice that the program has accomplished our objective of adding 7_{10} to 10_{10}. The resulting sum, 17_{10}, is in the accumulator.

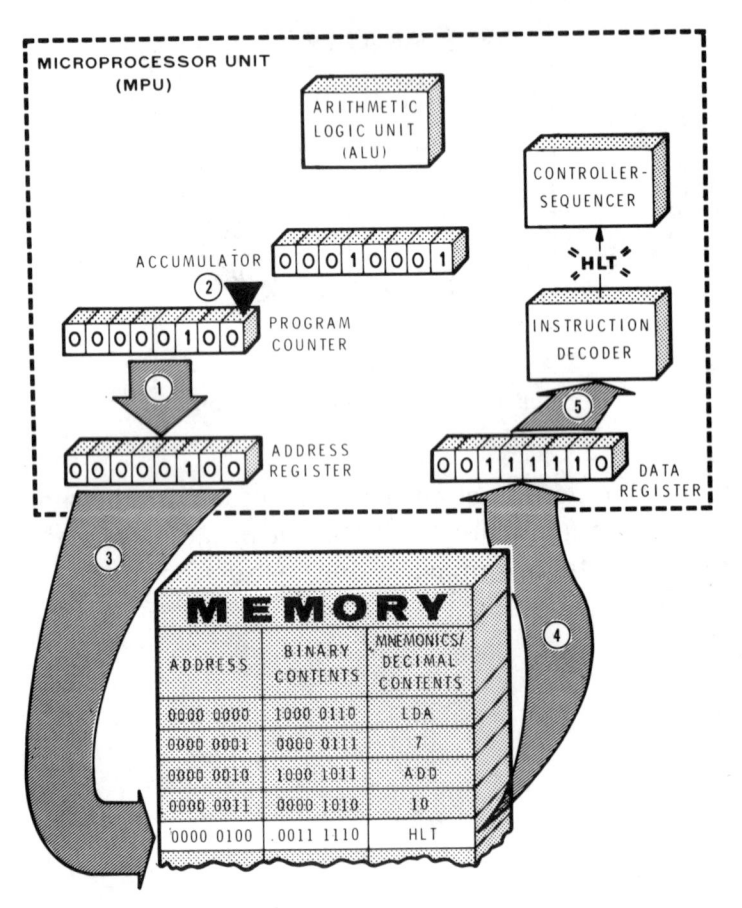

Figure 2-23
Fetching and Executing the HLT Instruction.

Self-Test Review

Examine this sample program carefully and answer the questions below:

```
LDA  8
ADD  7
ADD  4
HLT
```

31. During the first fetch phase, what binary number is loaded into the data register?

32. During the first execute phase the number 0000 1000$_2$ is loaded into the _____.

33. During the second fetch phase, what binary number is loaded into the data register?

34. If the first byte of the program is placed in address 0000 0000, what is the address of the first ADD instruction?

35. How many bytes of memory are taken up by the program?

36. What number is in the accumulator during the third fetch phase?

37. When the program is finished running, what number is in the accumulator?

38. What is the final number in the program counter?

39. What are the final contents of the address register?

40. What are the final contents of the data register?

Answers

31. The opcode for the LDA instruction, $1000\ 0110_2$.

32. Accumulator.

33. The opcode for ADD, 1000 1011.

34. $0000\ 0010_2$.

35. Seven.

36. 15_{10} or $0000\ 1111_2$.

37. 19_{10} or $0001\ 0011_2$.

38. 7_{10} or $0000\ 0111_2$.

39. 6_{10} or $0000\ 0110_2$.

40. The opcode for the HLT instruction, $0011\ 1110_2$.

ADDRESSING MODES

If you examine the program discussed in the previous section, you will find that it uses two distinctly different types of instructions. One type of instruction requires an operand. LDA and ADD are examples of this type. These are two-byte instructions. The first byte is the opcode; the second is the operand.

Microprocessors also have single-byte instructions. HLT is a good example. This instruction requires no operand; thus, it can be implemented with a single byte.

Instructions can be classified in several different ways. One of the most basic distinctions is their addressing mode. The addressing mode refers to the method by which an instruction addresses its operand.

Inherent or Implied Addressing

Single-byte instructions have no operand or the operand is implied by the opcode itself. For example, the HLT instruction has no operand at all. However, some single-byte instructions may have an implied operand. An example is the "increment accumulator" instruction. The number that is operated upon (incremented) is the number in the accumulator. This instruction simply adds one to the contents of the accumulator. This type of addressing will be referred to in this course as **implied addressing** or **inherent addressing**. The operations performed during an instruction of this type are illustrated in Figure 2-24.

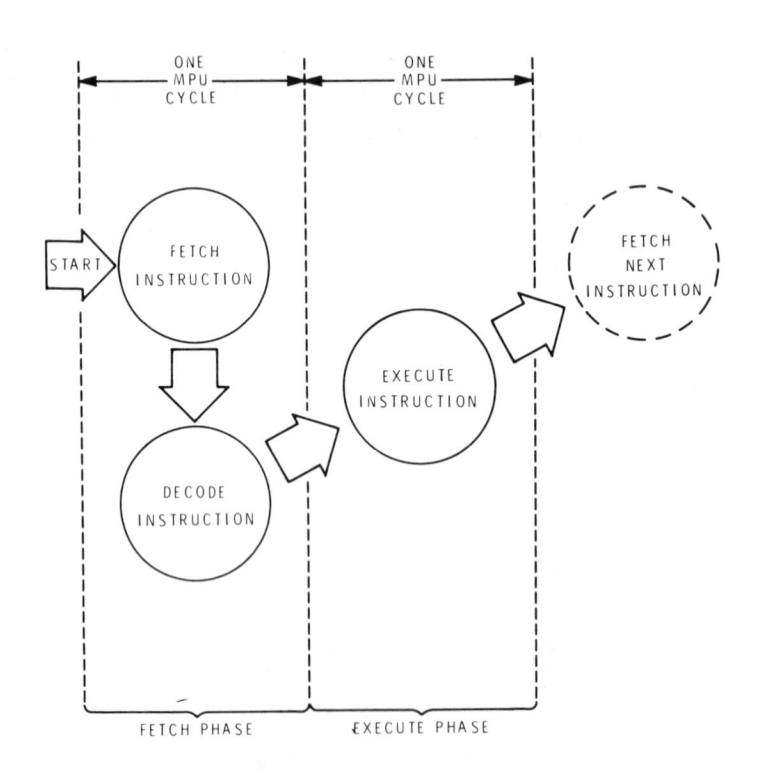

Figure 2-24
Operations Performed in the Inherent
or Implied Addressing Mode.

Immediate Addressing

In our previous program, the two-byte instructions use the **immediate addressing** mode. In this mode, the operand is the byte immediately following the opcode. That is, the byte of data that is to be operated upon is the second byte of the instruction. When these two-byte instructions are stored in memory, the address of the operand is the memory location following the opcode. The operations performed during this type of instruction are illustrated in Figure 2-25.

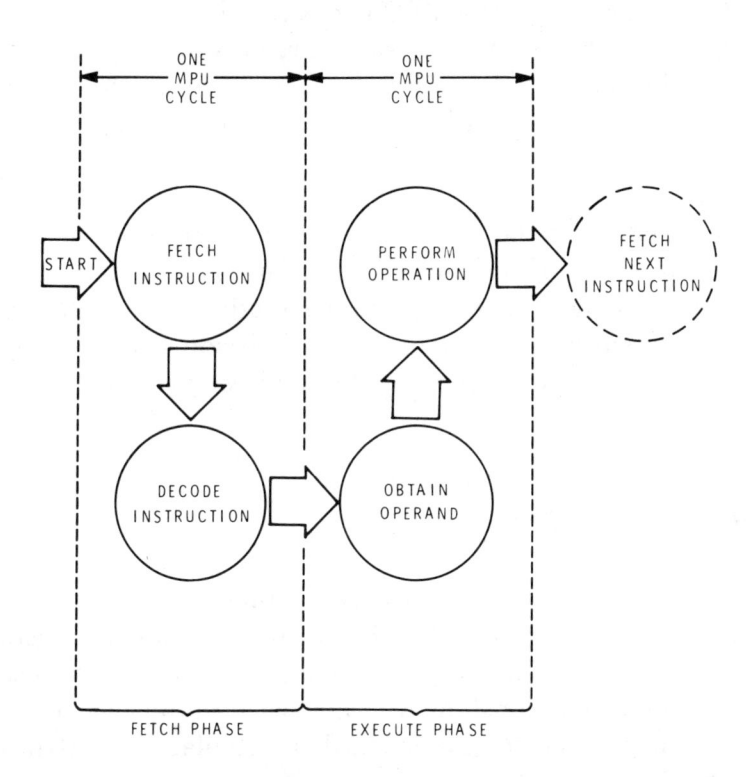

Figure 2-25
Operations Performed in the Immediate Addressing Mode.

The inherent and immediate addressing modes have two advantages. First, they require little memory space; one and two bytes respectively. This is important because memory locations cost money. Generally, the less memory space taken by a program, the better off we are. Second, these addressing modes require a minimum of execution time. The execution time can become important in long programs.

The time required for an instruction to be fetched and executed is often given in **MPU cycles**. We will define an MPU cycle as the minimum time required to fetch a data byte from memory. Thus, the fetch phase of an instruction requires one MPU cycle. In inherent and immediate addressing modes, the execute phase also requires one MPU cycle. Therefore, the **minimum** time required to fetch and execute any instruction is two MPU cycles. As you will see later, other addressing modes will require more MPU cycles.

Because of their fast execution time and their efficient use of memory, the inherent and immediate modes of addressing should be used wherever possible. However, there are many situations in which these addressing modes are simply not suitable. For this reason, every microprocessor will have instructions which use other addressing modes.

Direct Addressing

Most computer operations involve an operand. To realize its full potential, the computer must be able to manipulate the operand in many different ways. Immediate addressing of an operand is most useful when the operand is a constant that is used by only one instruction in the program. In this case, the operand can be placed immediately after that instruction's opcode.

However, there are many cases in which the operand is a variable which may be operated upon by many different instructions. In these cases, the immediate addressing mode is simply not practical and a more sophisticated form of addressing is necessary.

One way of solving this problem is to use the **direct addressing mode**. In this mode, an instruction requires two bytes of memory. The first byte is the opcode of the instruction just as before. However, the second byte is **not** the operand. Instead, the second byte is the **address** of the operand. The format of the instruction as it appears in memory is shown in Figure 2-26.

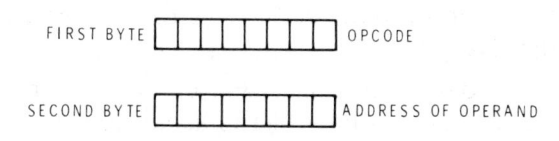

```
FIRST BYTE  [        ] OPCODE

SECOND BYTE [        ] ADDRESS OF OPERAND
```

Figure 2-26
Format of an Instruction which uses
the Direct Addressing Mode.

Three typical direct-addressing-mode instructions are listed in Figure 2-27. The first is the load accumulator instruction (LDA). Read the description carefully and note the difference between this instruction and the LDA immediate instruction discussed earlier. An example of each may help. In the **immediate addressing** mode, the instruction

$$LDA \quad 50_{10}$$

means "load 50_{10} into the accumulator." But in the **direct addressing** mode, the same instruction means "load the number at memory location 50_{10} into the accumulator."

NAME	MNEMONIC	OPCODE	DESCRIPTION
Load Accumulator	LDA	$1001\ 0110_2$ or 96_{16}	Load the contents of the memory location whose address is given by the next byte into the accumulator.
Add	ADD	$1001\ 1011_2$ or $9B_{16}$	Add the contents of the memory location whose address is given by the next byte to the present contents of the accumulator. Place the sum in the accumulator.
Store Accumulator	STA	$1001\ 0111_2$ or 97_{16}	Store the contents of the accumulator in the memory location whose address is given by the next byte.

Figure 2-27
Direct Addressing Mode Instructions.

You may have noticed that this instruction has a different opcode from the LDA immediate instruction. This is necessary to tell the MPU the exact nature of the instruction. That is, the opcode tells the MPU the addressing mode as well as the operation that is to be performed.

The ADD instruction also has a slightly different meaning in the direct addressing mode. Recall that, in the **immediate** addressing mode,

$$\text{ADD} \quad 10_{10}$$

means "add 10_{10} to the contents of the accumulator." However, in the **direct** addressing mode.

$$\text{ADD} \quad 10_{10}$$

means "add the contents of memory location 10_{10} to the contents of the accumulator." Once again, the opcode tells the MPU the addressing mode. An opcode of $8B_{16}$ means ADD immediate whereas an opcode of $9B_{16}$ means ADD direct.

The last instruction shown is a store accumulator (STA) instruction. It tells the MPU to store the contents of the accumulator in the address indicated by the second byte of the instruction.

For example:

$$\text{STA} \quad 20_{10}$$

means "store the contents of the accumulator in memory location 20_{10}." Because the second byte of the instruction must be an address, there is no STA immediate instruction.

The direct addressing mode instructions require one or more additional MPU cycles to execute. A typical fetch-execute sequence is illustrated in Figure 2-28. The instruction fetch is the same regardless of the addressing mode. However, the execution phase is extended since the MPU must first obtain the address of the operand from memory and then retrieve the operand itself from memory.

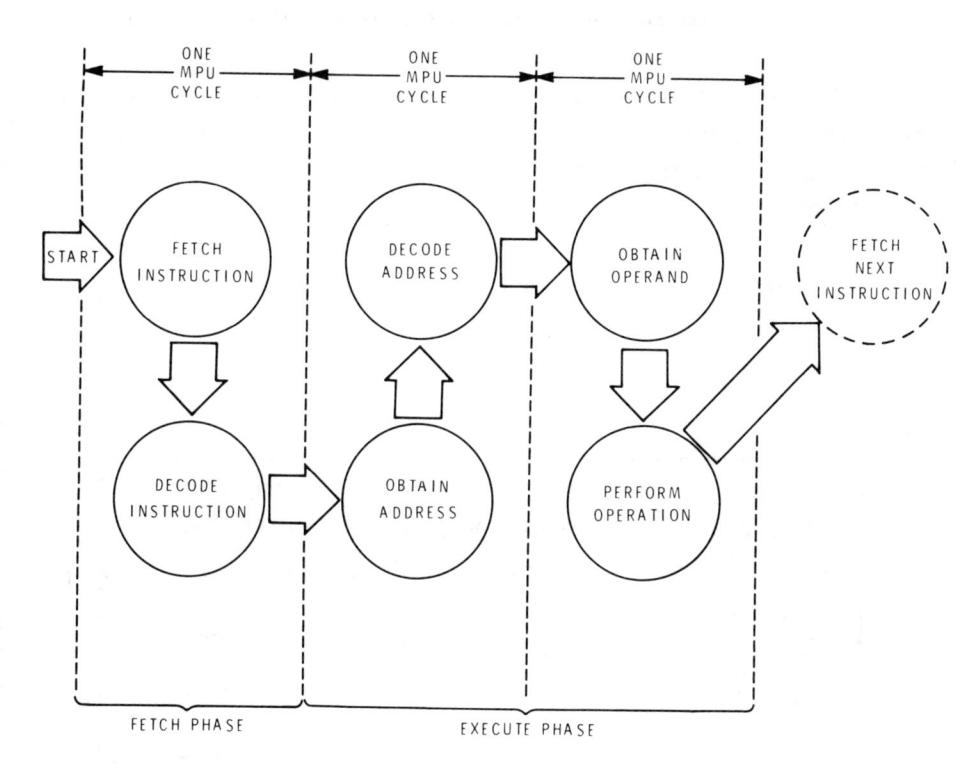

Figure 2-28
Most Direct Addressing Mode Instructions Require Three MPU Cycles.

Direct addressing generally requires more memory and longer execution times. However, there are many cases in which the added flexibility makes direct addressing worthwhile in spite of these disadvantages.

Sample Program Using Direct Addressing

The differences between direct and immediate addressing can be illustrated by a sample program. Earlier we examined a program which added two numbers (7 and 10). The sum was placed in the accumulator. Now let's look at the same program using direct addressing, only this time the sum will be stored in memory.

Figure 2-29 shows the program as it would look when stored in memory. Assume that we have arbitrarily stored the program starting at memory location or address $0001\ 0000_2$ (16_{10}). Addresses 16_{10} and 17_{10} contain the first instruction:

$$\text{LDA } 23_{10}$$

BINARY ADDRESS	BINARY CONTENTS	MNEMONICS/CONTENTS	
0001 0000	1001 0110	LDA	1st Instruction
0001 0001	0001 0111	23_{10}	
0001 0010	1001 1011	ADD	2nd Instruction
0001 0011	0001 1000	24_{10}	
0001 0100	1001 0111	STA	3rd Instruction
0001 0101	0001 1001	25_{10}	
0001 0110	0011 1110	HLT	4th Instruction
0001 0111	0000 0111	7_{10}	Data
0001 1000	0000 1010	10_{10}	
0001 1001	0000 0000	Reserved for sum	

Figure 2-29
Sample Program Using Direct Addressing.

This instruction tells the MPU to load the contents of memory location 23_{10} into the accumulator. Looking down to address 23_{10} ($0001\ 0111_2$), you see that it contains the operand 7. Thus, the first instruction causes 7 to be loaded into the accumulator.

The second instruction is in memory locations 18_{10} and 19_{10}. It is:

    ADD 24_{10}

This tells the MPU to add the number at address 24_{10} to the number in the accumulator. Address 24_{10} ($0001\ 1000_2$) contains the number 10_{10}. Therefore, the second instruction causes 10_{10} to be added to the contents of the accumulator. The sum (17_{10}) is placed back in the accumulator.

The third instruction, in locations 20_{10} and 21_{10}, is:

    STA 25_{10}

This tells the MPU to store the contents of the accumulator in memory location 25_{10}. After this instruction is executed, the number 17_{10} will appear in location 25_{10}.

The final instruction tells the MPU to halt. The program illustrates the value of the HLT instruction. Let's assume that the HLT instruction is inadvertently omitted. In this case, the MPU would fetch the next byte in sequence and attempt to execute it as if it were an instruction. The next byte is the number 7_{10}. This is a data word and was never intended to be an instruction. Nevertheless, the MPU probably has an instruction with an opcode of 7_{10}. After executing this instruction, the MPU will continue to fetch and execute whatever it finds in the remaining memory locations. Without a HLT instruction, it has no way of knowing where the instructions end and data begins.

Executing the Sample Program

The data flow within the microcomputer is slightly different for the direct addressing mode. Figure 2-30 shows several of the data paths within the microcomputer. Using this type of diagram, let's examine the data manipulations that occur during the execution of our sample program.

Notice that our program is loaded in memory starting at address 16_{10}. The program counter is set to 16_{10}, so the MPU is ready to begin executing the program.

The first fetch phase is illustrated in Figure 2-30. During this phase:

1. The contents of the program counter are loaded into the address register.

2. The program counter is incremented to 17_{10}.

3. The contents of the address register are placed on the address bus.

4. The contents of the selected memory location are transferred via the data bus to the data register.

5. The contents of the data register are decoded.

6. The MPU recognizes that an LDA direct operation is indicated. This concludes the fetch phase.

MICROPROCESSORS

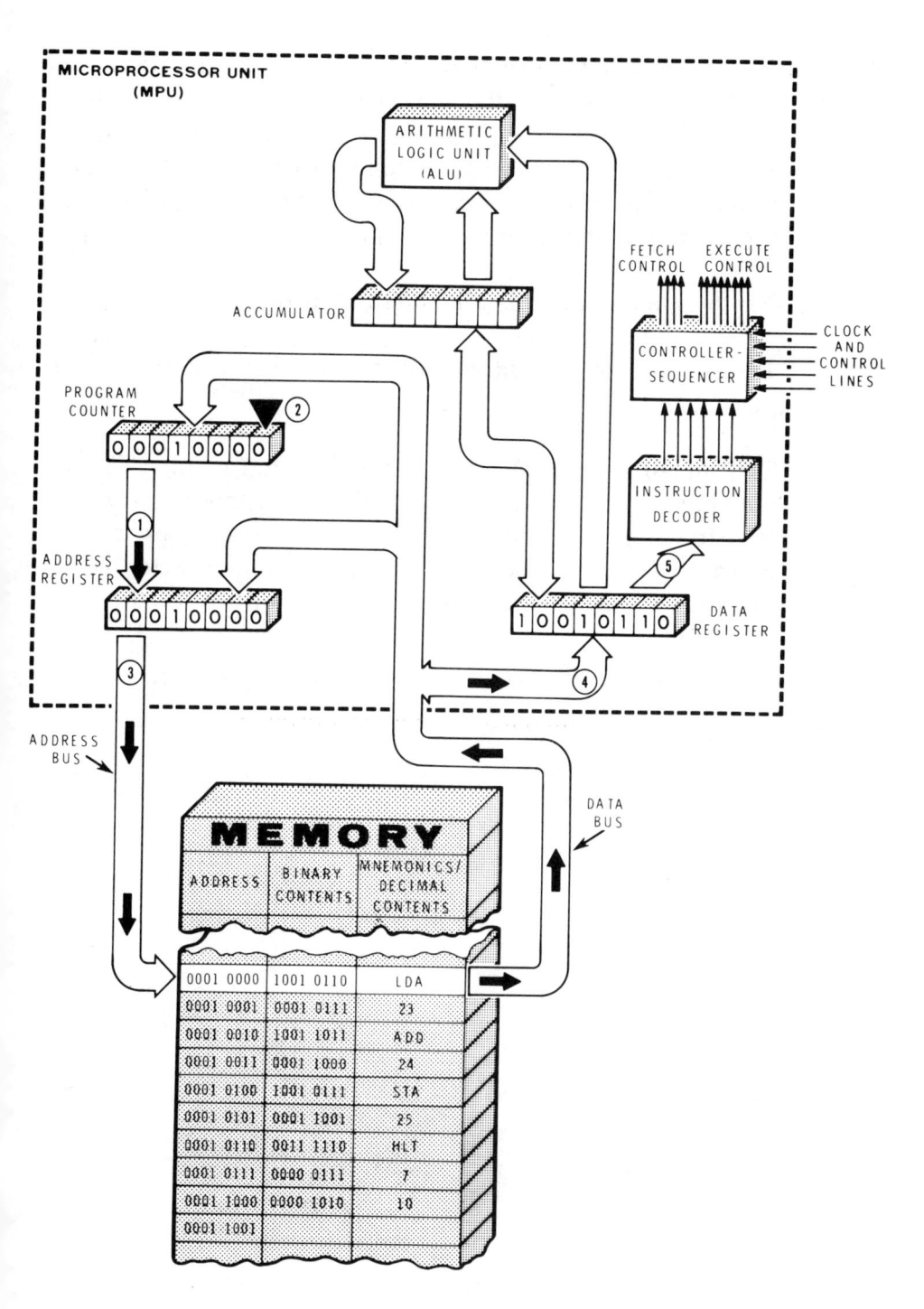

Microcomputer Basics | **2-51**

Figure 2-30
Fetching the Opcode of the First Instruction.

The execute phase has two parts when direct addressing is indicated. Figure 2-31 illustrates the first half of the execute phase. During this half:

1. The contents of the program counter are transferred to the address register. This number is the memory location that holds the address of the operand.

2. The program counter is incremented to 18_{10}.

3. The contents of the address register are placed on the address bus.

4. The contents of the selected memory location are placed on the data bus. However, in the direct addressing mode, this data is transferred to the address register. Thus, 23_{10} goes into the address register, replacing the previous contents. After this cycle, the address register will appear as shown in Figure 2-32.

MICROPROCESSORS

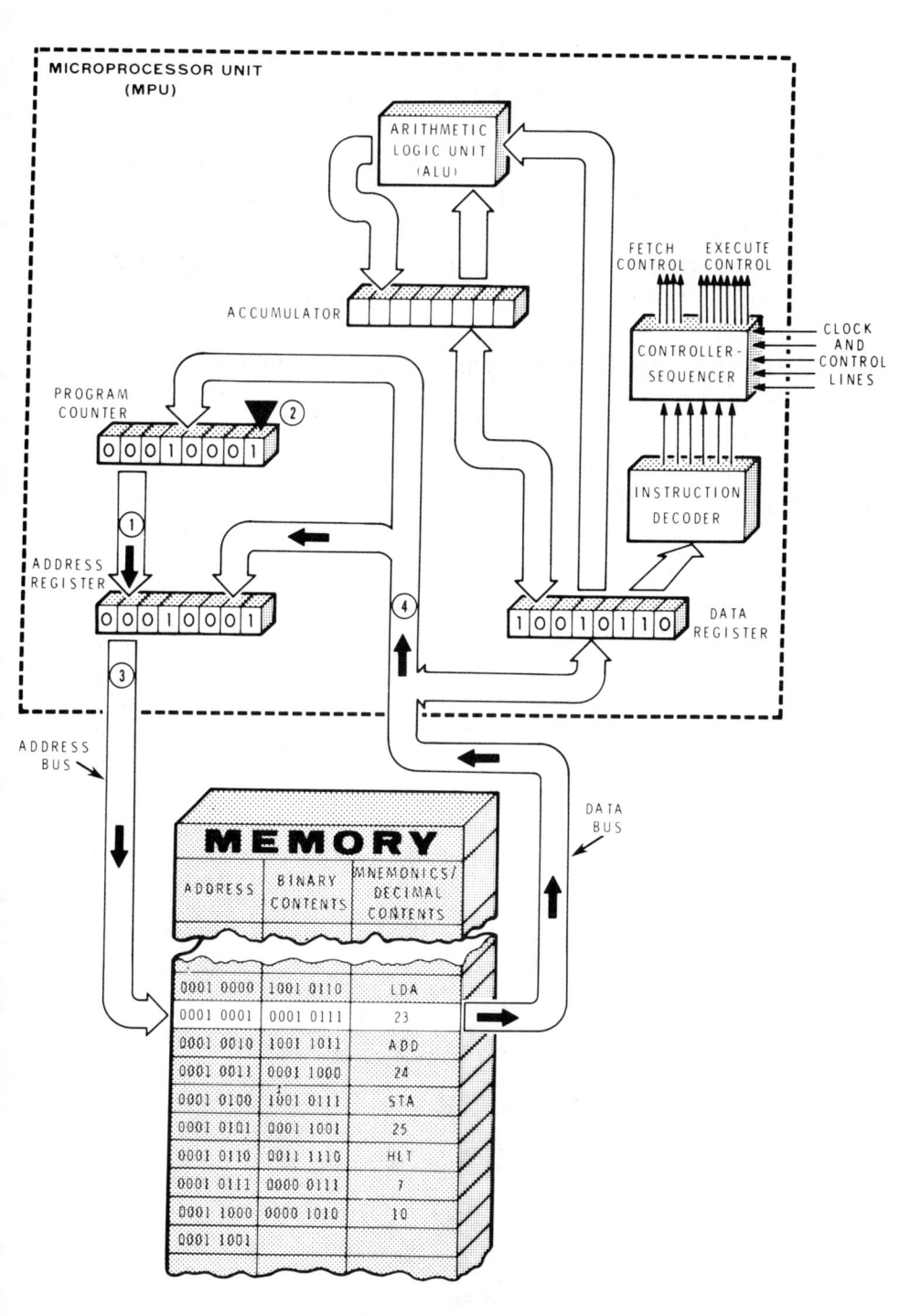

Microcomputer Basics | 2-53

Figure 2-31
Fetching the Address of the First Operand

During the second half of the execute phase, the operand is loaded into the accumulator as shown in Figure 2-32. The procedure is:

1. The address of the operand which is in the address register is placed on the address bus.

2. The operand is read out of memory location 23_{10} and is transferred via the data bus to the data register.

3. The operand is transferred from the data register to the accumulator.

This completes the execution of the first instruction. Notice that the first operand (7_{10}) is now in the accumulator.

MICROPROCESSORS

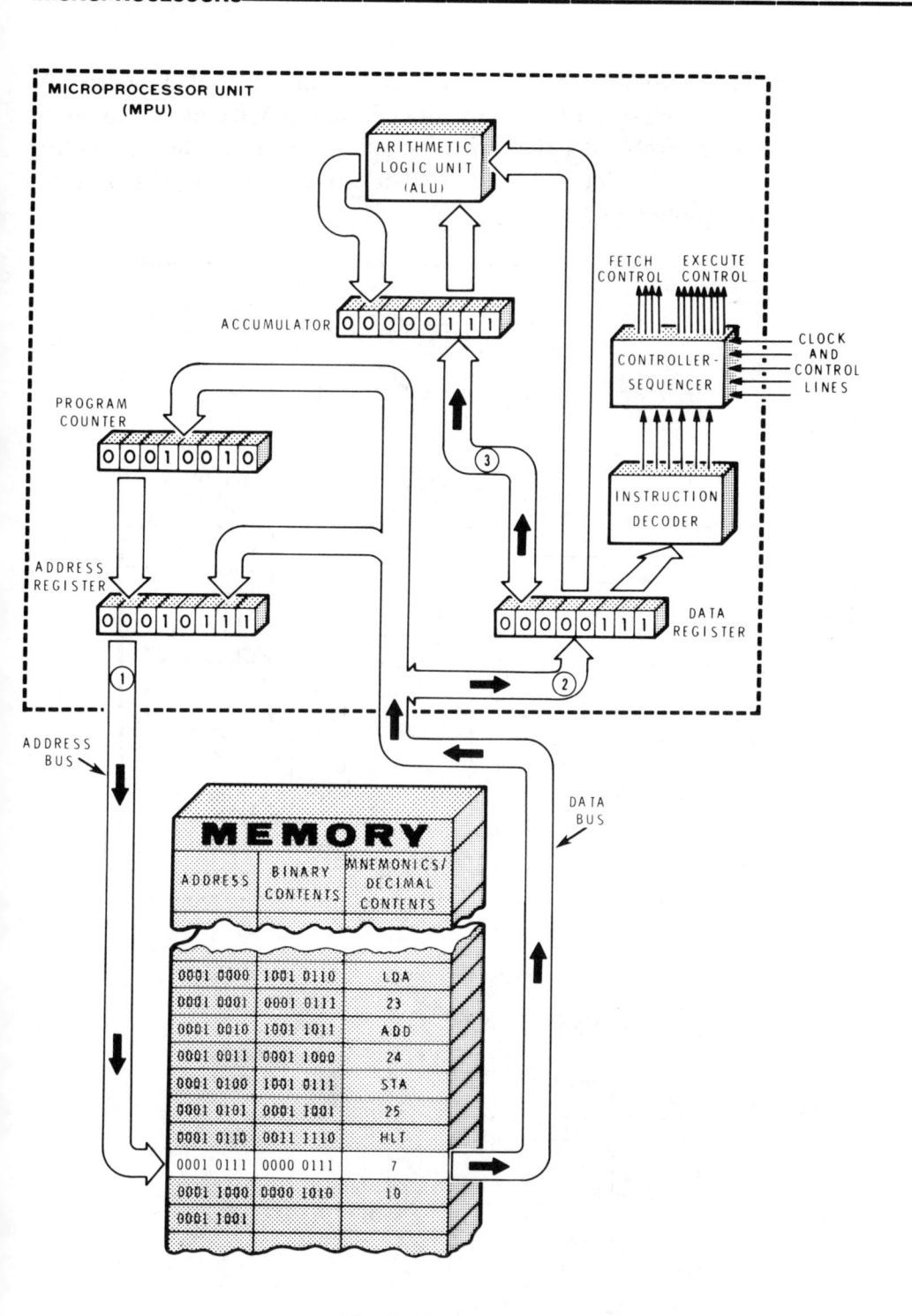

Microcomputer Basics | **2-55**

Figure 2-32
Fetching the First Operand.

The fetch phase for the second instruction is similar to that of the first. As shown in Figure 2-33, it causes the opcode of the ADD instruction to be read out of address 18_{10}. The opcode is transferred to the instruction decoder via the data bus and data register. In the process, the program counter is incremented to 19_{10}.

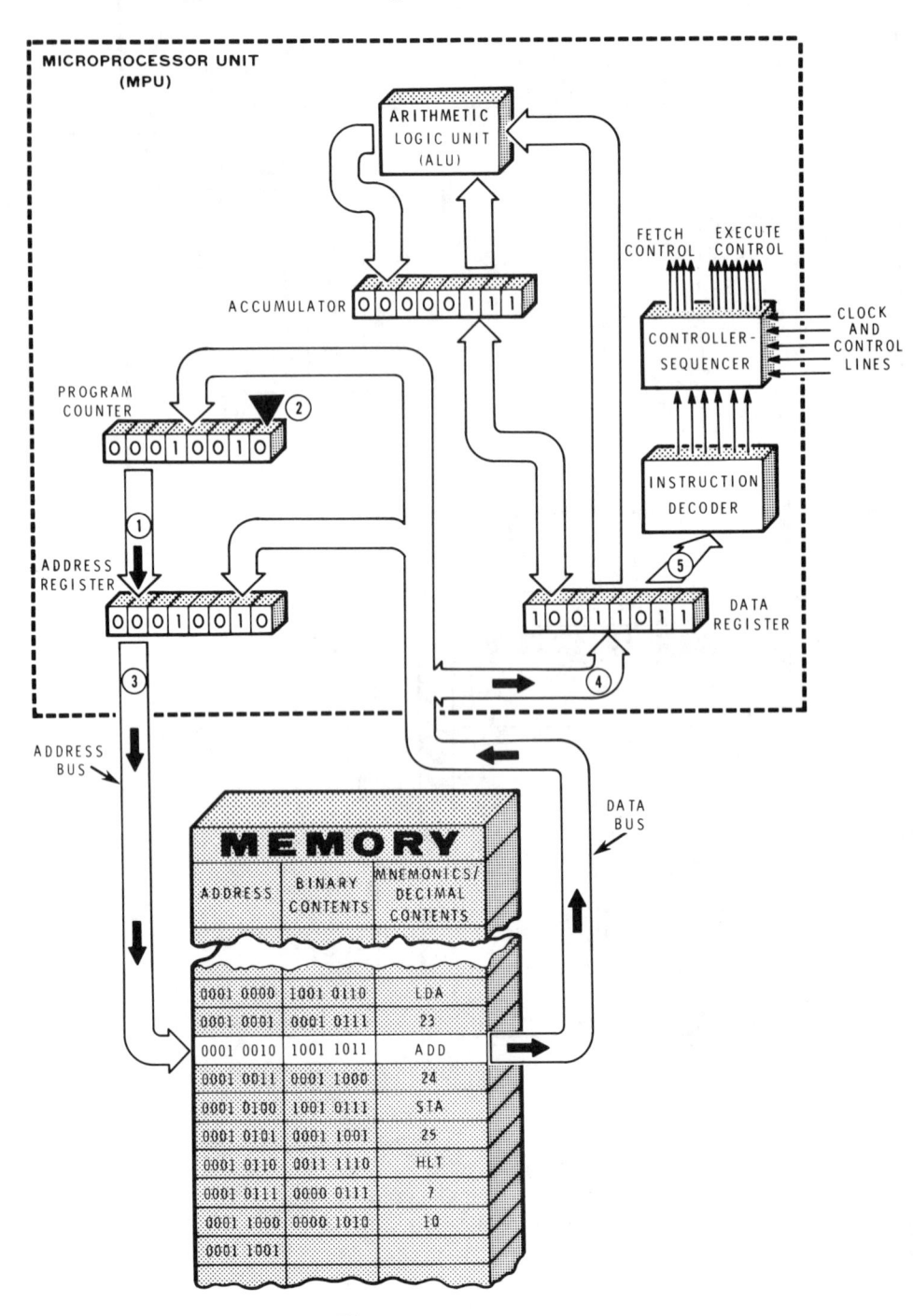

Figure 2-33
Fetching the Opcode of the Second Instruction.

MICROPROCESSORS

Microcomputer Basics **2-57**

The first half of the execute phase is illustrated in Figure 2-34. Here, the address of the second operand is read out of memory location 19_{10} and is placed in the address register.

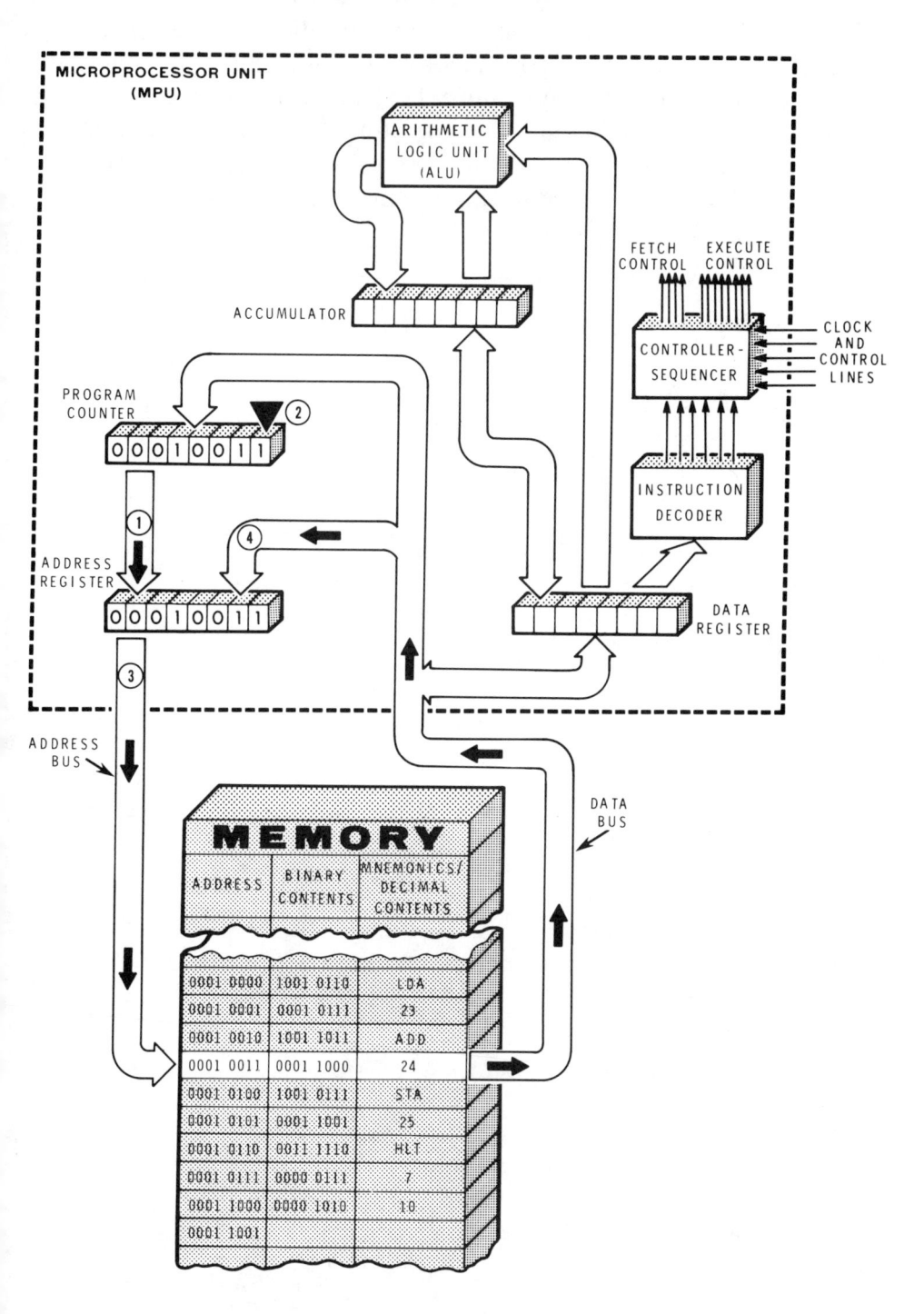

Figure 2-34
Fetching the Address of the Second Operand.

Figure 2-35 illustrates the second cycle of the execute phase. Here the address of the second operand is transferred from the address register to the address bus. The address is 24_{10}. Therefore, the contents of location 24_{10} are placed on the data bus and transferred to the data register. That is, the second operand 10_{10} is loaded into the data register. Then, the operand from the data register is made available at one input to the ALU. Simultaneously, the first operand which has been waiting in the accumulator is made available at the other input to the ALU. The ALU adds the two operands together, producing a result of 17_{10}. This sum is put back in the accumulator, replacing the previous number.

MICROPROCESSORS

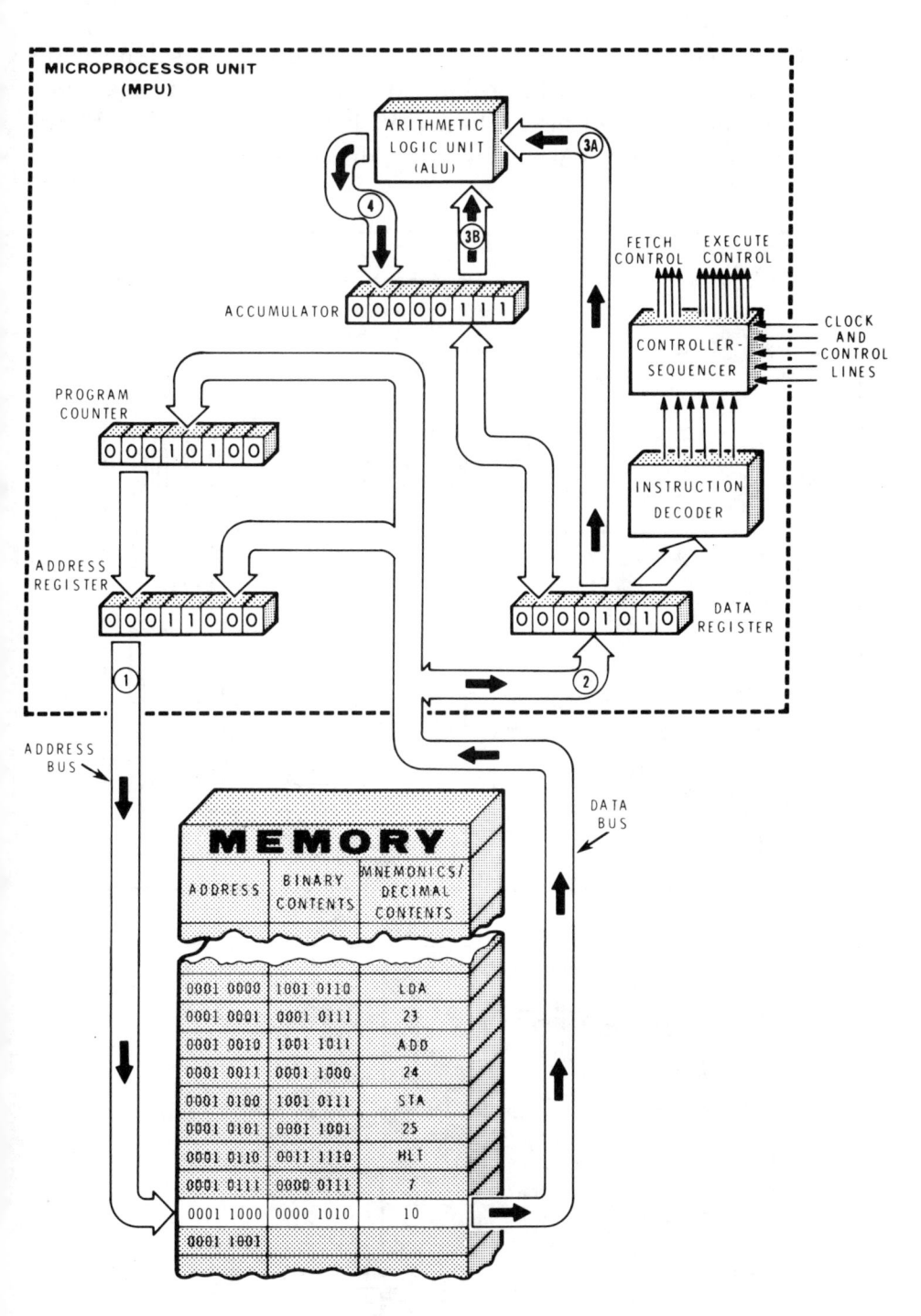

Microcomputer Basics | **2-59**

Figure 2-35
Adding the Two Operands.

Now all that remains is to place the sum in memory. This is done by the STA 25$_{10}$ instruction. Since this is the next instruction in sequence, it will be fetched and executed next. The fetch phase is illustrated in Figure 2-36. It ends with the STA opcode being decoded.

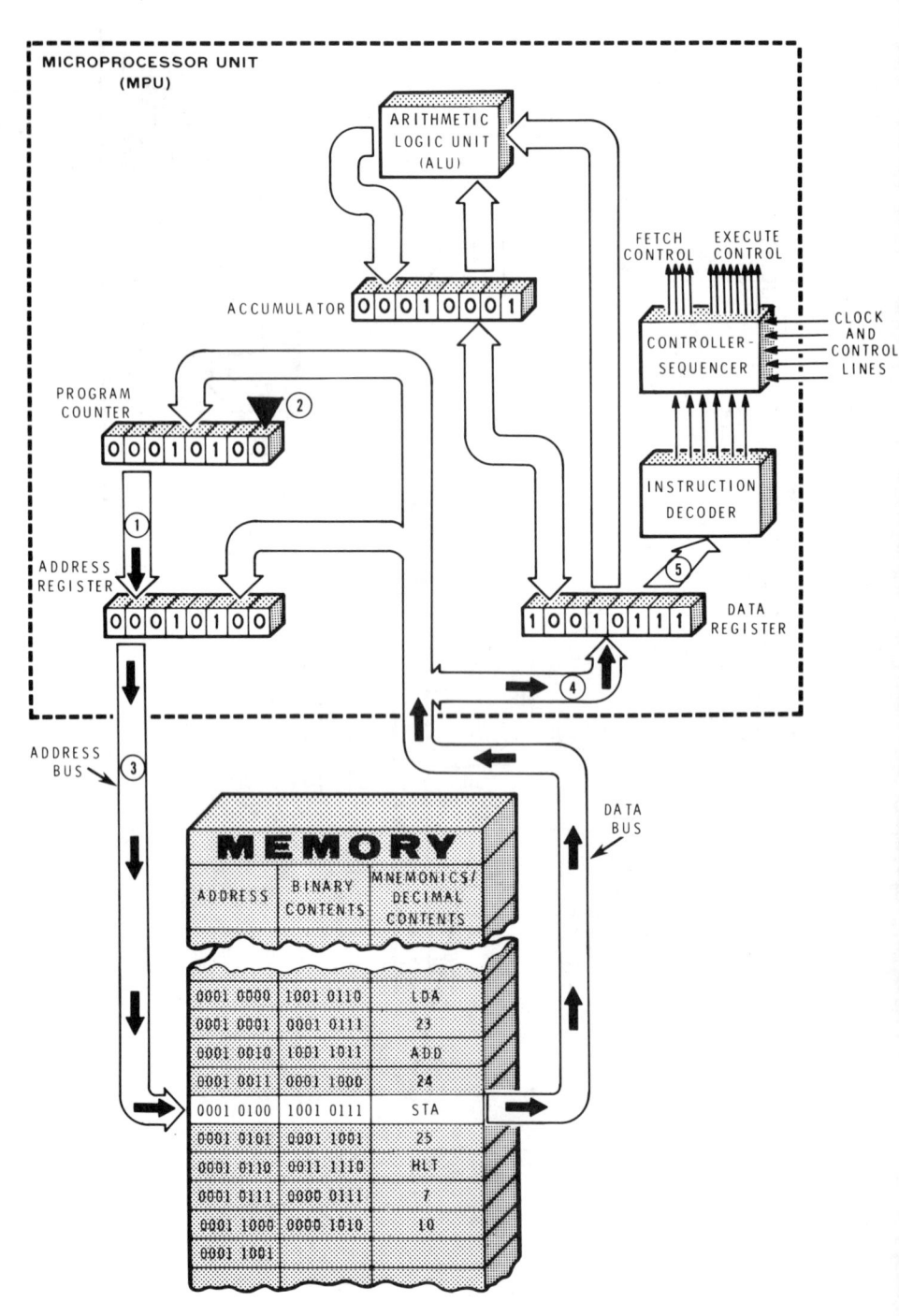

Figure 2-36
Fetching the Third Opcode.

MICROPROCESSORS

Microcomputer Basics **2-61**

The first half of the execution phase of the STA instruction involves loading the address of the storage location into the address register. Figure 2-37 illustrates that this four-step procedure is identical to that performed for the previous two instructions. It ends with the address 25_{10} in the address register.

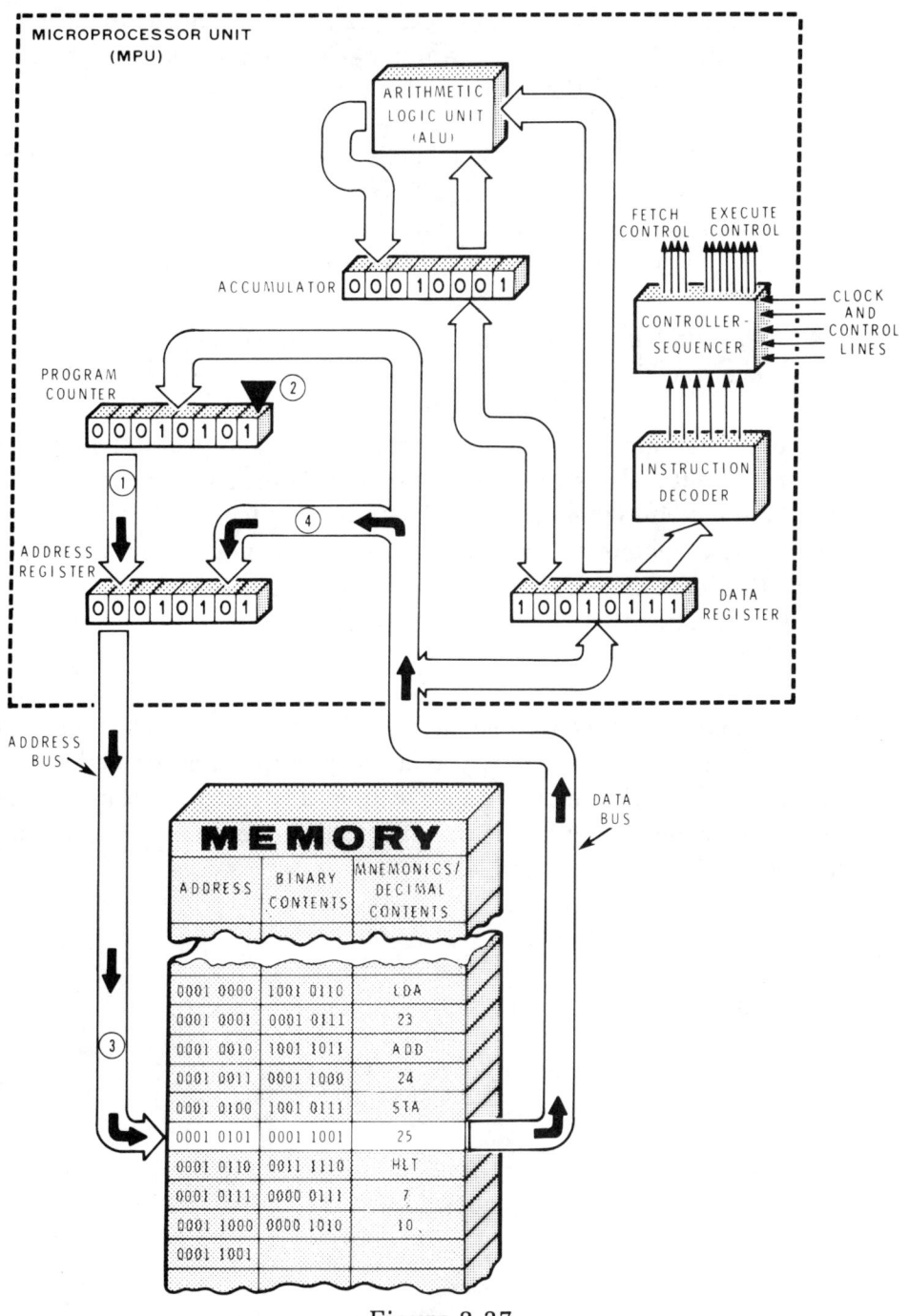

Figure 2-37
Fetching the Third Address.

During the final half of the execute phase, the contents of the accumulator are transferred to the data register and are then stored in the selected memory location. We have not yet discussed this operation in detail. Therefore, the step-by-step procedure is presented below. Refer to Figure 2-38 for the following steps:

1. The contents of the accumulator (17_{10}) are transferred to the data register. At this point, the number 17_{10} exists in both the accumulator and the data register.

2. The address at which this data is to be stored is placed on the address bus.

3. The contents of the data register are placed on the data bus.

4. The number on the data bus is written into the selected memory location. That is, 17_{10} is written into memory location 25_{10}.

Notice that, after this operation, the number 17_{10} appears at memory location 25_{10}, but it also appears in the accumulator. Thus, the number is merely "copied" into memory. It is also important to note that the previous contents of memory location 25_{10} are lost whenever you write new data into this location. For this reason, you must be certain that you do not write into a location that contains an instruction or some byte of data that you will need later.

The program has now accomplished its goal. It has added 10 to 7 and has stored the sum back in memory. The last step in the program is the HLT instruction. The MPU fetches and executes this instruction next. The fetch and execute sequence for this instruction were discussed earlier and need not be repeated here.

MICROPROCESSORS

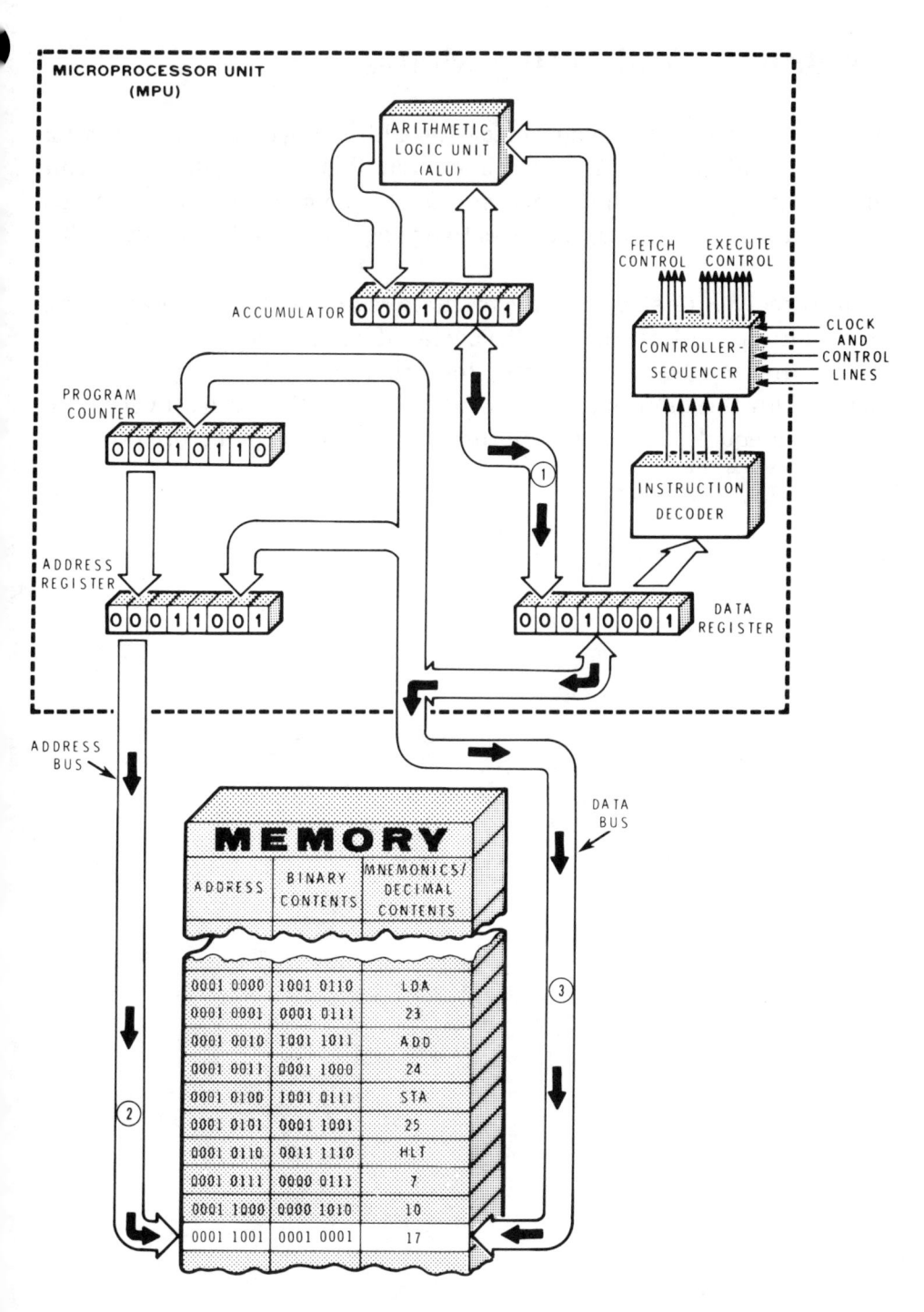

Microcomputer Basics | **2-63**

Figure 2-38
Storing the Sum.

Combining Addressing Modes

When writing programs, you can use the addressing mode that best suits your application. For example, the program that was just discussed can be shortened by using the immediate addressing mode with the first two instructions. Figure 2-39 compares two programs that do the same job.

Using direct addressing only, the program required ten bytes of memory. Its execution requires eleven MPU cycles. If you use immediate addressing for the first two instructions, the program requires eight bytes of memory. Furthermore, it can be executed in nine MPU cycles. Everything else being equal, the second approach would probably be preferred.

A. USING DIRECT ADDRESSING

HEX ADDRESS	HEX CONTENTS	MNEMONICS/ CONTENTS	COMMENTS
00	96	LDA	Load accumulator direct with operand 1
01	07	07_{10}	which is stored at this address.
02	9B	ADD	Add to accumulator direct with operand 2
03	08	08_{10}	which is stored at this address.
04	97	STA	Store the sum
05	09	09_{10}	at this address.
06	3E	HLT	Stop
07	21	33_{10}	Operand 1
08	17	23_{10}	Operand 2
09	—	—	Reserved for sum.

B. COMBINING ADDRESSING MODES

HEX ADDRESS	HEX CONTENTS	MNEMONICS/ CONTENTS	COMMENTS
00	86	LDA	Load accumulator immediately with
01	21	33_{10}	Operand 1.
02	8B	ADD	Add to accumulator immediately with
03	17	23_{10}	Operand 2.
04	97	STA	Store the sum
05	07	07_{10}	at this address.
06	3E	HLT	Stop
07	—	—	Reserved for sum.

Figure 2-39
By Combining the Addressing Modes, We Can Save Memory Space And Computer Time.

Self-Test Review

41. What addressing mode is used by single byte instructions?

42. In the immediate addressing mode, what is the second byte of the instruction?

43. In the direct addressing mode, what is the second byte of the instruction?

44. In all addressing modes, what is the first byte of the instruction?

45. Define MPU cycle.

46. Which of the three addressing modes discussed so far requires the longest execution time?

47. Refer to Figure 2-39A. What number is loaded into the accumulator by the first instruction?

48. What number is added to the accumulator by the second instruction?

49. When the computer halts, what number will be in memory location 09?

50. Refer to Figure 2-39B. When the computer halts, what number will be in memory location 07?

Answers

41. Inherent or implied.

42. The operand.

43. The address of the operand.

44. The opcode.

45. An MPU cycle is the time required to fetch a byte from memory.

46. The direct addressing mode.

47. 21_{16} or 33_{10}.

48. 17_{16} or 23_{10}.

49. 38_{16} or 56_{10}.

50. 38_{16} or 56_{10}.

UNIT 2 SUMMARY

1. A microprocessor is a logic device that is used in digital electronic systems.

2. The microprocessor is the "brains" of the microcomputer. It performs arithmetic, logic, and control operations.

3. The microcomputer is composed of RAM, ROM, a clock, and an I/O interface.

4. Parallel conductors within the microcomputer that carry address and data information are called a bus.

5. The microcomputer communicates with the "outside world" through one or more I/O ports.

6. The operation of the microprocessor is controlled by a list of instructions called a program.

7. One who writes these instructions is called a programmer.

8. The computer program is stored outside of the computer and later loaded into memory when needed to perform an operation. This is known as the stored program concept.

9. A computer word is a group of binary bits. It is the fundamental unit of information used in the computer.

10. The most common word length is eight bits. Thus, an 8-bit binary word can have any one of 256_{10} unique values. It can also represent any of the 128 ASCII code characters.

11. Some microprocessors use a 4-bit word length, while others may use a 12- or 16-bit word length.

12. A 16-bit word can represent $65,536_{10}$ unique values.

13. The 8-bit word length defines the size of many different components in the microprocessor/microcomputer system. Many important microprocessor registers have an 8-bit capacity, and the bus which is used to transfer data words consists of eight parallel conductors.

14. Microprocessors that use 16-bit words also use 8-bit segments of data. These 8-bit segments are called bytes.

15. A 16-bit word is composed of two 8-bit bytes. The first eight bits in a 16-bit word is called the low byte, while the last eight bits is called the high byte.

16. The bits in an 8-bit byte or word are numbered from 0 through 7, with 0 being the least significant bit. In a 16-bit word, the bits are numbered from 0 through 15.

17. The microprocessor (MPU) contains many specialized circuits. They include the data register, the instruction decoder, the controller-sequencer, arithmetic logic unit (ALU), program counter, address register, and accumulator.

18. The ALU performs arithmetic or logic operations on the data supplied to the MPU. The data supplied to the ALU are called operands.

19. The accumulator is a specialized register that performs two functions. First, it is used to hold an operand before it is processed by the ALU. Second, it is used to store the result of the ALU process.

20. Specific MPU instructions load data into the accumulator from memory and store data from the accumulator into memory.

21. The data register is a temporary storage location for data going to or coming from the data bus.

22. The address register is a temporary storage location that holds the address of the memory location or I/O port that is used in the operation that is presently being performed.

23. The program counter controls the sequence the instructions in a program are executed.

24. The instruction decoder decodes the instruction pulled from memory to determine the operation the MPU will perform.

25. The controller-sequencer determines the sequence of events necessary to complete the operation described by the program instruction.

MICROPROCESSORS
Microcomputer Basics 2-71

26. Memory is a series of locations outside the MPU where program data and instructions are stored. If the MPU operates on 8-bit words, each memory location contains storage for eight bits of data.

27. Memory size is identified by the number of storage locations and the number of data bits that can be stored in one location. A 256 × 8 memory contains 256_{10} storage locations, each eight bits wide.

28. Two buses connect memory to the MPU. One bus is used to transfer data to and from the MPU, the other is used by the MPU to address a specific memory location.

29. Reading the contents of a memory will not destroy the contents of that memory location. This is known and nondestructive read-out (NDRO).

30. You can read from or write to random access memory (RAM).

31. You can only read from read only memory (ROM).

32. When executing a program, the MPU goes through a fundamental sequence of steps or phases called the fetch-execute sequence.

33. In the fetch phase, the MPU reads and decodes an instruction from memory.

34. In the execute phase, the MPU performs the operation described by the instruction. The time to perform the operation will vary with the operation.

35. A mnemonic is an abbreviation or memory aid used by a programmer for identifying an instruction.

36. An opcode is the number or value assigned to mnemonic. Each mnemonic has its own opcode. This is the information that is decoded by the MPU.

37. An instruction operand is the data that the MPU will process during the execution of an instruction.

38. The time required for an instruction to be fetched and executed is often given in MPU cycles.

39. An instruction addressing mode refers to the method the MPU uses to address an instruction's operand.

40. In the inherent or implied addressing mode, the instruction has no operand or the operand is implied by the instruction opcode.

41. In the immediate addressing mode, the operand is stored in the next sequential memory location following the instruction opcode.

42. In the direct addressing mode, the next sequential memory location does not contain the operand. Rather, it contains the address of the operand, or the address of the memory location where the operand will be stored.

43. Many instructions can be written using different addressing modes. That is, you can use immediate addressing to add a value to the accumulator or you can use direct addressing to add a value to the accumulator.

Perform Experiment 3 at the end of Book 2.

Unit 3

COMPUTER ARITHMETIC

INTRODUCTION

In this Unit you will complete your study of the binary number system. Since microprocessors use binary numbers for data and control, it is important that you become familiar with them.

Computer arithmetic involves many forms of number manipulation. In the pages that follow you will be given the fundamentals of binary mathematics, addition, subtraction, multiplication, and division. Then you will learn to perform two's complement arithmetic using binary numbers. Finally, you will be shown how the microprocessor performs the four basic Boolean logic operations. These logical operations include AND, OR, exclusive OR, and invert.

UNIT OBJECTIVES

When you complete this Unit you will be able to:

1. Add two binary numbers.

2. Subtract one binary number from another.

3. Multiply one binary number by another.

4. Divide one binary number by another.

5. Derive the one's complement of a binary number.

6. Derive the two's complement of a binary number.

7. Add binary numbers using two's complement arithmetic.

8. Manipulate binary numbers using the AND operation.

9. Manipulate binary numbers using the OR operation.

10. Manipulate binary numbers using the exclusive OR operation.

11. Logically invert binary numbers.

BINARY ARITHMETIC

A number system can be used to perform two basic operations: addition and subtraction. But by using addition and subtraction, you can then perform multiplication, division, and any other numerical operation. In this section, binary arithmetic (addition, subtraction, multiplication, and division) will be examined, using decimal arithmetic as a guide.

Binary Addition

Binary addition is performed somewhat like decimal addition. If two decimal numbers, 56719 and 31863, are added together, the sum 88582 is obtained. You could analyze the details of this operation in the following manner.

> NOTE: In the following explanations, the term "first column" refers to the first column of figures you work with in the problem — the column on the right (9, 3, and 2 in the following example). The term "second column" refers to the second column you work with, etc.

Carry:	00101
Addend:	56719
Augend:	+ 31863
Sum:	88582

Adding the first column, decimal numbers 9 and 3, gives the sum of 12. This is expressed in the sum as the digit 2 with a carry of 1. The carry is then added to the next column. Adding the second column decimal numbers 1 and 6, and the carry from the first column, gives the sum of 8, with no carry. This process continues until all of the columns (including carries) have been added. The sum represents the numeric value of the addend and augend. (The **addend** is the number to be added to another number, while the **augend** is the number to which the addend is added.)

MICROPROCESSORS — Computer Arithmetic 3-5

REVIEW

When you add two binary numbers, you perform the same operation. Figure 3-1 summarizes the four rules of addition with binary numbers.

1. $0 + 0 = 0$

2. $0 + 1 = 1$

3. $1 + 1 = 0$ with a carry of 1.

4. $1 + 1 + 1 = 1$ with a carry of 1.

Figure 3-1
Rules for binary addition.

To illustrate the process of binary addition, let's add 1101 to 1101.

```
Carry:        1101
Addend:       1101
Augend:     + 1101
Sum:         11010
```

In the first column, 1 plus 1 equals 0 with a carry of 1 to the second column. This agrees with rule 3. In the second column, 0 plus 0 equals 0 with no carry. To this sum, the carry from the first column is added. Thus, 0 plus 1 equals 1 with no carry. These two additions in the second column give a total sum of 1 with a carry of 0. Rules 1 and 2 were used to obtain the sum.

In column three, 1 plus 1 equals 0 with a carry of 1. To this sum, the second column carry is added. This yields a third column sum of 0 with a carry of 1 to column four. Rules 3 and 1 were used to obtain the sum.

In column four, 1 plus 1 equals 0 with a carry of 1. To this sum, the third column carry is added. This yields a fourth column sum of 1 with a carry to the fifth column. Rule 4 allows you to add three binary 1's and obtain 1 with a carry of 1.

In column five, there is no addend or augend. Therefore, you can assume rule 2 and add the carry to 0 to obtain the sum of 1. Thus, the sum of 1101_2 plus 1101_2 equals 11010_2. You can verify this by converting the binary numbers to decimal numbers.

Now study the following two examples of binary addition, where 10001111_2 is added to 10110101_2 and 111011_2 is added to 11001100_2.

```
Carry:       10111111
Addend:      10110101
Augend:    + 10001111
Sum:        101000100


Carry:       11111000
Addend:      11001100
Augend:    + 00111011
Sum:        100000111
```

When binary addition is performed with a microprocessor, 8-bit numbers are generally used. As shown in the last example, two zeros were added after the MSB of the augend to produce an 8-bit number. After addition, a 1 in the ninth bit is represented as the "carry" bit by the microprocessor. This will be explained in a later unit.

Binary Subtraction

Binary subtraction is performed exactly like decimal subtraction. Therefore, before binary subtraction can be attempted, decimal subtraction should be reexamined. You know that if decimal 5486 is subtracted from 8303, the difference 2817 is obtained.

```
Minuend after borrow:    7 12 9 13
Minuend:                 8  3 0  3
Subtrahend:             -5  4 8  6
Difference:              2  8 1  7
```

Because the digit 6 in the subtrahend is larger than the digit 3 in the minuend, a 1 is borrowed from the next higher-order digit in the minuend. If that digit is 0, as in this example, 1 is borrowed from the next higher-order digit that contains a number other than 0. That digit is reduced by 1 (from 3 to 2 in this example) and the digits skipped in the minuend are given the value 9. This is equivalent to removing 1 from 30 with the result of 29, as in this example. In the decimal system, the digit borrowed has the value of ten. Therefore, the minuend digit now has the value 13, and 6 from 13 equals 7.

In the second column, 8 from 9 equals 1. Since the subtrahend is larger than the minuend in the third column, 1 is borrowed from the next higher-order digit. This raises the minuend value from 2 to 12, and 4 from 12 equals 8. In the fourth column, the minuend was reduced from 8 to 7 because of the previous borrow, and 5 from 7 equals 2.

Whenever 1 is borrowed from a higher-order digit, the borrow is equal in value to the radix or base of the number system. Therefore, a borrow in the decimal number system equals ten, while a borrow in the binary number system equals two.

When you subtract one binary number from another, you use the same method described for decimal subtraction. Figure 3-2 summarizes the four rules for binary subtraction.

    1.   0 − 0 = 0

    2.   1 − 1 = 0

    3.   1 − 0 = 1

    4.   0 − 1 = 1   with a borrow of 1.

Figure 3-2
Rules for binary subtraction.

To illustrate the process of binary subtraction, let's subtract 1101 from 11011.

```
Minuend after borrow:    0 10 10 1 1
Minuend:                   1  1 0 1 1
Subtrahend:              −    1 1 0 1
Difference:                   1 1 1 0
```

The "minuend after borrow" now shows the value of each minuend digit after a borrow occurs. Remember that binary 10 equals decimal 2.

In the first column, 1 from 1 equals 0 (rule 2). Then, 0 from 1 in the second column equals 1 (rule 3). In the third column, 1 from 0 requires a borrow from the fourth column. Thus, 1 from 10_2 equals 1 (rule 4). The minuend in the fourth column is now 0, from the previous borrow. Therefore, a borrow is required from the fifth column, so that 1 from 10_2 in the fourth column equals 1 (rule 4). Because of the previous borrow, the minuend in the fifth column is now 0 and the subtrahend is 0 (nonexistant), so that 0 from 0 equals 0 (rule 1). The 0 in the fifth column is not shown in the difference because it is not a significant bit. Thus, the difference between 11011_2 and 1101_2 is 1110_2. You can verify this by converting the binary numbers to decimal numbers.

As a further example of binary subtraction, subtract 00100101_2 from 11000100_2, as shown below. Then proceed to the next example and subtract 10111010_2 from 11101110_2.

Minuend after borrow:	1 0 1 1 1 10 1 10
Minuend:	1 1 0 0 0 1 0 0
Subtrahend:	−0 0 1 0 0 1 0 1
Difference:	1 0 0 1 1 1 1 1

Minuend after borrow:	0 0 10 10 1 1 1 0
Minuend:	1 1 1 0 1 1 1 0
Subtrahend:	−1 0 1 1 1 0 1 0
Difference:	0 0 1 1 0 1 0 0

When a borrow is required in the minuend, 1 is obtained from the next high-order bit that contains a 1. That bit then becomes 0, and all bits skipped (0 value bits) are given the value 1. This is equivalent to removing 1 from 1000_2 with the result of 0111_2.

As with binary addition, microprocessors generally perform subtraction on 8-bit number groups. In the previous example, the answer contained only six significant bits, but two 0 bits were added to maintain the 8-bit grouping. This would also be true for the minuend and subtrahend.

Subtraction of a large number from a smaller number will be described in a later section of this Unit.

Binary Multiplication

Multiplication is a short method of adding a number to itself as many times as it is specified by the multiplier. However, if you were to multiply 324_{10} by 223_{10}, you would probably use the following method.

Multiplicand:	324
Multiplier:	× 223
First partial product:	972
Second partial product:	648
Third partial product:	648
Carry:	0121
Final product:	72252

Using this short form of multiplication, you multiply the multiplicand by each digit of the multiplier and then sum the partial products to obtain the final product. Note that, for convenience, the additive carries are set-down under the partial products rather than over them as in normal addition.

Binary multiplication follows the same general principles as decimal multiplication. However, with only two possible multiplier bits (1 or 0), binary multiplication is a much simpler process. Figure 3-3 lists the rules of binary multiplication. These rules are used to multiply 1111_2 by 1101_2 on the next page.

1. $0 \times 0 = 0$

2. $0 \times 1 = 0$

3. $1 \times 0 = 0$

4. $1 \times 1 = 1$

Figure 3-3
Rules for binary multiplication.

Multiplicand:	1111
Multiplier:	×1101
First partial product:	1111
Second partial product:	0000
Carry:	0000
Sum of partial products:	1111
Third partial product:	1111
Carry:	111100
Sum of partial products:	1001011
Fourth partial product:	1111
Carry:	1111000
Final product:	11000011

As with decimal multiplication, you multiply the multiplicand by each bit in the multiplier and add the partial sums. First you multiply 1111_2 by the least significant multiplier bit (1) and set down the partial product so the least significant bit (LSB) is under the multiplier bit. Then you multiply the multiplicand by the next multiplier bit (0) and set down the partial product so the LSB is under the multiplier bit. Now that there are two partial products, they should be added. Although it is possible to add more than two binary numbers, keeping track of the multiple carries may become confusing. Therefore, for these examples, add only two partial products at a time.

Notice that the first partial product is identical to the multiplicand. The second partial product is all zeros. Since the binary number system contains only ones and zeros, the partial product will always equal either the multiplicand or zero. Because of this, you can obtain the third partial product by copying the multiplicand. Begin with the LSB under the third multiplier bit. Add this value to the previous partial sum. Now obtain the fourth partial product by copying the multiplicand. Begin with the LSB under the fourth multiplier bit. Add this value to the previous partial sum. This is the final product. You can verify the result by converting the binary numbers to decimal.

Reexamine the illustration for the previous multiplication example. Notice that binary multiplication is a process of shift and add. For each 1 bit in the multiplier you copy down the multiplicand, beginning with the LSB under the bit. You can ignore any zeros in the multiplier. But do not make the mistake of setting down the multiplicand under the 0 bit.

MICROPROCESSORS — Computer Arithmetic 3-11

To make sure you fully understand binary multiplication, multiply 1001_2 by 1100_2 and then multiply 1101_2 by 1111_2.

Multiplicand:	1001
Multiplier:	×1100
First partial product:	0000
Second partial product:	0000
Carry:	0000
Sum of partial products:	00000
Third partial product:	1001
Carry:	00000
Sum of partial products:	100100
Fourth partial product:	1001
Carry:	000000
Final product:	1101100

Multiplicand:	1101
Multiplier:	×1111
First partial product:	1101
Second partial product:	1101
Carry:	11000
Sum of partial products:	100111
Third partial product:	1101
Carry:	100100
Sum of partial products:	1011011
Fourth partial product:	1101
Carry:	1111000
Final product:	11000011

In the first of these last two examples, the two zeros in the multiplier were included in the multiplication process. This was to insure that the multiplicand was copied down under the proper multiplier bits. The multiplication process could have been represented in this manner:

Multiplicand:	1001
Multiplier:	×1100
Third partial product:	100100
Fourth partial product:	1001
Carry:	000000
Final product:	1101100

Remember, just as in decimal multiplication, you must keep track of any zeros by setting a zero in the product under the 0 bit in the multiplier. This is very important when the zero occupies the LSB.

Binary Division

Division is the reverse of multiplication. Therefore, it is a procedure for determining how many times one number can be subtracted from another. The process you are probably familiar with is called "long" division. If you were to divide decimal 181 by 45, you would obtain the quotient, 4-1/45, as follows:

```
                 004        Quotient
    Divisor  45 ) 181       Dividend
                 180
                   1        Remainder
```

Using long division, you would examine the most significant digit in the dividend and determine if the divisor was smaller in value. In this example the divisor is larger, so the quotient is zero. Next, you examine the two most significant digits. Again the divisor is larger, so the quotient is again zero. Finally, you examine the whole dividend and discover it is approximately four times the divisor in value. Therefore, you give the quotient a value of 4. Next, you subtract the product of 45 and 4 (180) from the dividend. The difference of one represents a fraction of the divisor. This fraction is added to the quotient to produce the correct answer of 4-1/45.

Binary division is performed in a similar manner. However, binary division is a simpler process since the number base is two rather than ten. First, let's divide 100011_2 by 101_2.

```
                    000111       Quotient
    Divisor:  101 ) 100011       Dividend
                    101
                    111          Remainder
                    101
                    101          Remainder
                    101
                      0          Remainder
```

Using long division, you examine the dividend beginning with the MSB and determine the number of bits required to exceed the value of the divisor. When you find this value, place a one in the quotient and subtract the divisor from the selected dividend value. Then carry the next least significant bit in the dividend down to the remainder. If you can subtract the divisor from the new remainder, place a one in the quotient. Then subtract the divisor from the remainder and carry the next least significant bit in the dividend (LSB in this example) down to the remainder. If the divisor can be subtracted from the new remainder, place a one in the quotient and subtract the divisor from the remainder. Continue the process until all of the dividend bits have been carried down. Then express any remainder as a fraction of the divisor in the quotient. Thus, 100011_2 divided by 101_2 equals 111_2. You can verify the answer by converting the binary numbers to decimal.

To make sure you fully understand binary division, work out the following examples of long division. Divide 101000_2 by 1000_2 and then divide 100111_2 by 110_2.

```
                       000101      Quotient
        Divisor   1000 ) 101000    Dividend
                        1000
                        1000       Remainder
                        1000
                           0       Remainder
```

```
                       000110.1    Quotient
        Divisor:   110 ) 100111.0  Dividend
                        110
                         111       Remainder
                         110
                          110      Remainder
                          110
                            0      Remainder
```

In the second example, the quotient was not a whole number, but rather a whole number plus a fraction (remainder divided by the divisor). The answer 110-11/110 is correct. You could have left the answer in this form or, as in the example, continue the division process until the remainder was zero. This is made possible by adding a sufficient number of zeros after the binary point to permit division by the divisor. In the previous example, only one zero was added after the binary point. As you learned in Unit 1, adding zeros after the binary point will not affect the value of the number. Note that some numbers cannot be solved in this manner (e.g., decimal 1/3).

Representing Negative Numbers

Until now, we have been examining binary arithmetic using unsigned numbers. However, when you perform some arithmetic operations with a microprocessor, you must be able to express both positive and negative (signed) numbers. Over the years three methods have been developed for representing signed numbers. Of these, only one method has survived. The two older methods will be examined first, and then the system that is used today.

SIGN AND MAGNITUDE. Using this system, a binary number contained both the sign (+ or −) and the value of the number. Therefore, positive and negative values were expressed as follows:

$$+45_{10} = 0010 1101_2$$

SIGN   MAGNITUDE

$$-45_{10} = 1010 1101_2$$

The MSB of the binary number indicated the sign, while the remaining bits contained the value of the number. As you can see, a zero sign bit indicated a positive value, while a one sign bit indicated a negative value.

While this method of representing negative numbers may seem logical, its popularity was short-lived. Because it required complex and slow arithmetic circuitry, it was abandoned long before microprocessors were invented.

ONE'S COMPLEMENT. Another method of representing negative numbers became popular in the early days of computers. It was called the one's complement method. Using this system, positive numbers were represented in the same way as in the sign-magnitude system. That is, the MSB in any number was considered to be a sign bit. A sign bit of 0 represented positive. Using 8-bit numbers, positive values were represented like this:

$$+ 4_{10} = \underline{0\ 0000100}$$
$$+ 17_{10} = \underline{0\ 0010001}$$
$$+127_{10} = \underline{0\ 1111111}$$

Sign bit   Binary value

Negative numbers were represented by the **one's complement** of the positive value. The one's complement of a number is formed by changing all 0's to 1's and all 1's to 0's. As shown above, $+4_{10}$ is represented as $\underline{0\ 0000100}_2$. By changing all 0's to 1's and all 1's to 0's, the representation for -4_{10} was formed. In this case:

$$-4_{10} = \underline{1\ 1111011}_2$$

Notice that all the bits, including the sign bit, were inverted. In the same way:

$$-17_{10} = \underline{1\ 1101110}_2$$
$$-127_{10} = \underline{1\ 0000000}_2$$

The one's complement method is not used for representing signed numbers in microprocessors. However, as you will see later, you may still be called upon to find the one's complement of a number. Remember, you do this by simply changing all 0's to 1's and all 1's to 0's.

Figure 3-4 shows an interesting relationship. In the first column, 8-bit patterns of 0's and 1's are shown. The second column shows the decimal number that each pattern represents if you consider the pattern to be an unsigned binary number. Notice that an 8-bit pattern can represent unsigned numbers between 0 and 255_{10}.

The third column shows the decimal number that each pattern represents if you consider the pattern to be a one's complement binary number. Notice that the range of numbers is from -127_{10} to $+127_{10}$. Notice also that there are two representations of zero. The pattern $0000\ 0000_2$ represents $+0$ while its one's complement ($1111\ 1111_2$) represents -0.

TWO'S COMPLEMENT. The method used to represent signed numbers in microprocessors is called two's complement. In this system, positive numbers are represented just as they were with the sign-and-magnitude method and the one's complement method. That is, it uses the same bit pattern for all positive values up to $+127_{10}$. However, negative numbers are represented as the two's complement of positive numbers.

The two's complement of a number is formed by taking the one's complement and then adding 1. For example if you work with 8-bit numbers and use the two's complement system, $+4_{10}$ is represented by 00000100_2. To find -4_{10}, you must take the two's complement of this number. You do this by first taking the one's complement, which is 11111011_2. Next, add 1 to form the two's complement:

$$\begin{array}{r} 11111011_2 \\ +1 \\ \hline 11111100_2 \end{array}$$

Thus, the two's complement representation of -4_{10} is 11111100_2.

To be sure you have the idea, look at a second example: how do you express -17_{10} as an 8-bit two's complement number? Start with the two's complement representation of $+17_{10}$, which is 00010001_2. Take the one's complement by changing all 0's to 1's and 1's to 0's. Thus, the one's complement of $+17_{10}$ is 11101110_2. Next, find the two's complement by adding 1:

$$\begin{array}{r} 11101110_2 \\ +1 \\ \hline 11101111_2 \end{array}$$

BIT PATTERN	UNSIGNED BINARY	1's COMPLEMENT
00000000	0	+0
00000001	1	+1
00000010	2	+2
00000011	3	+3
.	.	.
.	.	.
.	.	.
.	.	.
01111100	124	+124
01111101	125	+125
01111110	126	+126
01111111	127	+127
10000000	128	−127
10000001	129	−126
10000010	130	−125
10000011	131	−124
.	.	.
.	.	.
.	.	.
.	.	.
11111100	252	−3
11111101	253	−2
11111110	254	−1
11111111	255	−0

Figure 3-4
Table of bit pattern values for unsigned binary numbers and 1's complement numbers.

Figure 3-5 compares unsigned, two's complement, and one's complement numbers. Several 8-bit patterns are shown on the left. The other three columns show the decimal number represented by these patterns.

Notice that the range of 8-bit two's complement numbers is from -128_{10} to $+127_{10}$. Notice also that there is only one representation for 0.

If this table included all 256_{10} possible 8-bit patterns, you could look up any pattern to see what number it represents. The patterns which have 0 as their MSB are easy to determine without a table. The pattern represents the binary number directly. But what decimal number is represented by the two's complement number 11110011? You should know that this represents some negative number because the MSB is a 1.

Actually, you can determine the value very easily by simply taking the two's complement to find the equivalent positive number. Remember, you find the two's complement, by taking the one's complement and adding 1. The one's complement is 00001100_2. Thus, the two's complement is:

$$\begin{array}{r} 00001100_2 \\ +1 \\ \hline 00001101_2 \end{array} \quad \text{or } +13_{10}$$

Since the two's complement of 11110011_2 represents $+13_{10}$, then 11110011_2 must equal -13_{10}.

BIT PATTERN	UNSIGNED BINARY	2's COMPLEMENT	1's COMPLEMENT
00000000	0	0	+0
00000001	1	+1	+1
00000010	2	+2	+2
00000011	3	+3	+3
⋮	⋮	⋮	⋮
01111100	124	+124	+124
01111101	125	+125	+125
01111110	126	+126	+126
01111111	127	+127	+127
10000000	128	−128	−127
10000001	129	−127	−126
10000010	130	−126	−125
10000011	131	−125	−124
⋮	⋮	⋮	⋮
11111100	252	−4	−3
11111101	253	−3	−2
11111110	254	−2	−1
11111111	255	−1	−0

Figure 3-5
Table of bit pattern values for unsigned binary, 2's complement and 1's complement numbers.

Self-Test Review

1. _____ and _____ are the two basic operations that can be performed with a number system.

2. Add the following binary numbers.

   A.   10011011   B.   11000110   C.   10000110
        +00010111   +00110001   +00110110

3. Subtract the following binary numbers.

   A.   11011011   B.   10001011   C.   11011001
        −10110010   −10000001   −00111011

4. Multiply the following binary numbers.

   A.   1011   B.   1101   C.   1100
       ×1101   ×1001   ×1100

5. Solve for the quotient in the following groups.

   A.   101) 1001011   B.   11) 111001   C.   1101) 11110111

6. 10001111_2 represents decimal _____ in sign/magnitude notation.

7. The 1's complement of 00010110_2 is _____.

8. The 2's complement of 00010110_2 is _____.

9. The 2's complement number 11100110 represents the decimal number _____.

10. Find the signed decimal equivalents of the following two's complement numbers.

Two's Complement Number	Decimal Number
00000111	
10000111	
11111111	
01110000	
10000000	

11. Find the two's complement representation for the following signed decimal numbers.

Decimal Number	Two's Complement Number
+32	
−32	
+73	
− 7	
−120	

Answers

1. Addition, subtraction.

2. A.
Carry:	00011111
Addend:	10011011
Augend:	+ 00010111
Sum:	10110010

   B. 11110111.

   C. 10111100.

3. A.
Minuend after borrow:	1 0 10 1 1 0 1 1
Minuend:	1 1 0 1 1 0 1 1
Subtrahend:	− 1 0 1 1 0 0 1 0
Difference:	1 0 1 0 0 1

   B. 1010.

   C. 10011110.

4. A.
Multiplicand:	1011
Multiplier:	× 1101
First partial product:	1011
Second partial product:	00000
Carry:	0000
Sum of partial products:	01011
Third partial product:	101100
Carry:	01000
Sum of partial products:	110111
Fourth partial product:	1011000
Carry:	1110000
Final product:	10001111

   B. 1110101.

   C. 10010000

MICROPROCESSORS — Computer Arithmetic 3-23

5. A. Divisor: 101) 1001011   Quotient: 0001111   Dividend

    ```
              0001111    Quotient
        101 )1001011    Dividend
              101
              1000      Remainder
               101
                111     Remainder
                101
                101     Remainder
                101
                  0     Remainder
    ```

    B. 10011.

    C. 10011.

6. −15.

7. 11101001_2.

8. 11101010_2.

9. First, find the two's complement of 11100110 by changing 1's to 0's; 0's to 1's; and adding 1:

    ```
    00011001
           1
    00011010
    ```

    Since this number represents $+26_{10}$, the original number must have represented -26_{10}.

10.
Two's Complement Number	Decimal Number
00000111	+7
10000111	−121
11111111	−1
01110000	+112
10000000	−128

11.
Decimal Number	Two's Complement Number
+32	00100000
−32	11100000
+73	01001001
−7	11111001
−120	10001000

TWO'S COMPLEMENT ARITHMETIC

In the previous section, you saw that signed numbers are represented in microprocessors in two's complement form. In this section you will see why.

In digital electronic devices such as computers, simple circuits cost less and operate faster than more complex ones. Two's complement numbers are used with arithmetic because they allow the simplest, cheapest, and fastest circuits.

A characteristic of the two's complement system is that both signed and unsigned numbers can be added by the same circuit. For example, suppose you wish to add the **unsigned** numbers 132_{10} and 14_{10}. The addition looks like this:

Addend:	10000100_2	132_{10}
Augend:	00001110_2	$+ 14_{10}$
Sum:	10010010_2	146_{10}

As you saw in the previous unit, the microprocessor has an ALU circuit that can add unsigned binary numbers in this way. The adder in the ALU is designed so that when the bit pattern 10000100 appears at one input and 00001110 appears at the other, the bit pattern 10010010 appears at the output.

The question arises, "How does the ALU know that the bit patterns at the inputs represent unsigned numbers and not two's complement numbers?" The answer is "it doesn't." The ALU always adds as if the inputs were unsigned binary numbers. Nevertheless, it still produces the correct sum even if the inputs are signed two's complement numbers.

Look at the example given above. If you assume that the inputs are two's complement signed numbers, then the addend, augend, and sum are:

Addend:	10000100_2	-124_{10}
Augend:	00001110_2	$+ 14_{10}$
Sum:	10010010_2	-110_{10}

Notice that the bit patterns are the same. Only the meaning of the bit patterns has changed. In the first example, we assumed that the bit patterns represented unsigned numbers and the adder produced the proper unsigned result. In the second example, we assumed that the bit patterns represented signed numbers. Again, the adder produced the proper signed result.

This proves a very important point. The adder in the ALU always adds bit patterns as if they are unsigned binary numbers. It is our interpretation of these bit patterns that decides if unsigned or signed numbers are indicated. The beauty of two's complement is that the bit patterns can be interpreted either way. This allows us to work with either signed or unsigned numbers without requiring different circuits for each.

Two's complement arithmetic also simplifies the arithmetic logic unit in another way. All microprocessors have a subtract instruction. Thus, the ALU must be able to subtract one number from another. However, if this required a separate subtraction circuit, the complexity and cost of the ALU would be increased. Fortunately, two's complement arithmetic allows the ALU to perform a subtract operation using an adder circuit. That is, the MPU uses the same circuit for both addition and subtraction.

The MPU performs subtraction by a binary addition process. To see why this works, it may be helpful to look at a similar process with the decimal number system. The decimal equivalent of two's complement is called ten's complement. Since you are more familiar with the decimal number system, briefly examine ten's complement arithmetic.

Ten's Complement Arithmetic

An easy way to illustrate ten's complement is to consider an analogy. Visualize the odometer or mileage indicator on your car. Generally, this is a six-digit device that indicates mileage between 00,000.0 and 99,999.9 miles. Let's ignore the tenths digit and concentrate on the other five.

In an automobile, the register generally operates in only one direction (forward). However, consider what happens if it is turned backwards instead. Starting at +3 miles, the count proceeds backwards as follows:

$$
\begin{array}{c}
00,003 \\
00,002 \\
00,001 \\
00,000 \\
99,999 \\
99,998 \\
99,997 \\
\text{etc.}
\end{array}
$$

It is easy to visualize that 99,999 represents −1 mile. Also, 99,998 represents −2 miles; 99,997 represents −3 miles; etc. This is how signed numbers are represented in ten's complement form.

Once you accept this system for representing positive and negative numbers, you can perform arithmetic with these signed numbers. For example, if you add +3 and −2, the result should be +1. Using the system developed above, +3 is represented by 00003 while −2 is represented by 99,998. Thus, the addition looks like this:

$$\begin{array}{rr} 00003 & +3 \\ +99998 & -2 \\ \hline 100001 & +1 \end{array}$$

↑—Discard final carry.

If you now discard the final carry on the left in the sum, the answer is 00001, the representation of +1. You can also find the ten's complement of a digit by subtracting the digit from ten. For example, the ten's complement of 6 is 4 since 10−6 = 4. To complement a number containing more than one digit, raise ten to a power equal to the total number of digits, then subtract the number from it. For example, to obtain the ten's complement of 654_{10}, first raise ten to the third power since there are three digits in the number. Then, subtract 654 from the result.

$$\begin{array}{r} 10^3 = 1000 \\ -654 \\ \hline 346 \end{array}$$

Thus, the ten's complement of 654_{10} is 346_{10}.

Once you find the ten's complement, you can subtract one number from another by an indirect method using only addition. Since childhood you have subtracted like this:

$$\begin{array}{lr} \text{Minuend:} & 973 \\ \text{Subtrahend:} & -654 \\ \hline \text{Difference:} & 319 \end{array}$$

However, you can arrive at the same answer by using the ten's complement of the subtrahend and adding. Recall that the ten's complement of 654_{10} is 346_{10}. Let's compare these two methods of subtraction:

STANDARD METHOD			TEN'S COMPLEMENT METHOD	
Minuend	973	973	Minuend
Subtrahend	−654	+346	Ten's complement of subtrahend
Difference	319	1319	Difference

↑ Discard final carry

Notice that when you use the ten's complement method, the answer is too large by 1000_{10}. However, you can still arrive at the correct answer by simply discarding the final carry.

While the ten's complement method of subtraction works, it is not used because it is more complex than the standard method. In fact, it does not eliminate subtraction entirely since the ten's complement itself is found by subtraction.

The binary equivalent of ten's complement is two's complement. It overcomes the disadvantage of ten's complement in that the two's complement can be formed without any subtraction at all. Recall that you can form the two's complement of a binary number by changing all 0's to 1's, all 1's to 0's and then adding 1. Let's examine two's complement arithmetic in more detail.

Two's Complement Subtraction

As in ten's complement arithmetic, you can form the two's complement by subtracting from a power of the base (two). However, because the MPU cannot subtract directly, it uses the method given earlier for finding the two's complement. Once the two's complement is formed, the MPU can perform subtraction indirectly by adding the two's complement of the subtrahend to the minuend.

To illustrate this point, look at the following two ways of subtracting 26_{10} from 69_{10}. The two numbers are expressed as they would appear to an 8-bit microprocessor. The standard method of subtraction looks like this:

Minuend:	01000101_2	69
Subtrahend:	-00011010_2	−26
Difference:	00101011_2	43

While this method works fine on paper, it's of little use to the microprocessor since the MPU has no subtract circuitry. However, the MPU can still perform subtraction by the indirect method of adding the two's complement of the subtrahend to the minuend:

Two's complement of
Minuend: 01000101
Subtrahend: +11100110
Difference: 100101011
              ↑
              └─ Discard final carry

This illustrates a major reason for using the two's complement system to represent signed numbers. It allows the MPU to perform subtraction and addition with the same circuit.

The method that the MPU uses to perform subtraction is of little importance to the user of microprocessors. Most microprocessors have a subtract instruction. This instruction is used like any other without regard for how the operation is implemented internally. When the subtract instruction is implemented, the MPU automatically takes care of operations like complementing the subtrahend, adding, and discarding the carry. The procedure has been explained here so you can appreciate the importance of two's complement arithmetic.

Arithmetic With Signed Numbers

There are many applications in which the microprocessor must work with signed numbers. In these cases, signed numbers are represented in two's complement form. While this greatly simplifies the circuitry of the MPU, it places an extra burden on the user. The programmer must ensure that all signed numbers are entered into the microprocessor in two's complement form. Also, the resulting data produced by the MPU may be in two's complement form. Here's how an 8-bit MPU handles signed numbers.

Adding Positive Numbers. Assume that the MPU is to add the two positive numbers +7 and +3. Since an 8-bit MPU is assumed, the arithmetic operation looks like this:

```
 00000111    + 7
+00000011    + 3
 00001010    +10
```

The sign bits are underlined. Remember, when representing signed numbers, that the MSB is the sign bit. A 0 represents "+" and a 1 represents "−." In this example, you added +7 and +3 to form a sum of $+10_{10}$. You know that all three numbers are positive since the MSB's are all 0's.

While this operation seems straightforward enough, it is easy for the unwary to make an error when adding positive numbers. Remember, the highest 8-bit positive number you can represent in two's complement form is $+127_{10}$. If the sum exceeds this value, an error occurs. For example, suppose you attempt to add $+65_{10}$ to $+67_{10}$. The MPU adds the numbers as if they are unsigned binary:

$$\underline{0}1000001$$
$$\underline{0}1000011$$
$$\overline{\underline{1}0000100}$$

If the answer is interpreted as a two's complement number, an error has occurred. You have added two positive numbers and yet the answer appears to be negative since the MSB of the sum is 1. This is called a two's complement overflow. It occurs when the sum exceeds $+127_{10}$. Many microprocessors have a way of detecting this condition. We will discuss this in more detail in a future unit.

Adding Positive and Negative Numbers. The real beauty of the two's complement system is illustrated when you add numbers with unlike signs. For example, assume that an 8-bit microprocessor is to add +7 and −3. Remember, since these are signed numbers, they must be represented in two's complement form. That is, +7 is represented as 00000111_2 while −3 is represented as 11111101_2. If these two numbers are added, the sum will be:

Addend:	00000111	(+7)
Augend:	+11111101	+(−3)
Sum:	100000100	(+4)

↑ Discard final carry

Notice that the sum is correct if you ignore the final carry bit. Keep in mind that the MPU adds the two numbers as if they were unsigned binary numbers. It is merely our interpretation of the answer that makes the system work for signed numbers.

The system also works when the negative number is larger. For example, when −9 is added to +8 the result should be −1. Remember, the signed numbers must be represented in two's complement form:

$$
\begin{array}{lll}
\text{Addend:} & 11110111 & (-9) \\
\text{Augend:} & \underline{00001000} & \underline{+(+8)} \\
\text{Sum:} & 11111111 & -1
\end{array}
$$

Notice that the sum is the two's complement representation for −1.

Adding Negative Numbers. The final case involves two negative numbers. If both numbers are negative, then the sum should also be negative.

For example, suppose the MPU is to add −3 to −4. Obviously, the result should be −7. The two signed numbers must be represented in two's complement form. That is, −3 must be represented as 11111101_2 while −4 must be represented as 11111100_2. The MPU adds these two bit patterns as if they were unsigned binary numbers. Thus the result is:

$$
\begin{array}{lll}
\text{Addend:} & 11111101 & (-3) \\
\text{Augend:} & \underline{+11111100} & \underline{+(-4)} \\
\text{Sum:} & 111111001 & (-7)
\end{array}
$$

— Discard final carry

Once again, the answer is correct if you ignore the final carry bit.

When you add two negative numbers, you must remember the capacity of the MPU. The largest negative number that can be represented by eight bits is -128_{10}. If the sum exceeds this value, the sum will appear to be in error. For example, suppose you add -120_{10} to -18_{10}.

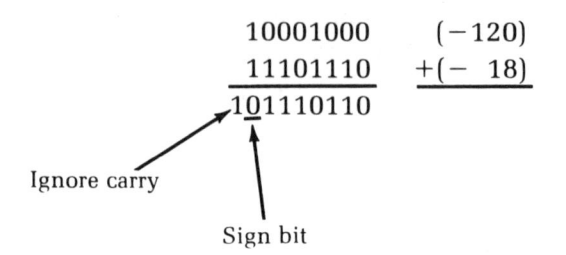

$$
\begin{array}{ll}
10001000 & (-120) \\
\underline{11101110} & \underline{+(-\ 18)} \\
101110110 &
\end{array}
$$

Ignore carry

Sign bit

Notice that the sign bit in the sum is 0, representing a positive number. Thus, the MPU has added two negative numbers and has produced a positive result. This apparent error is caused by exceeding the 8-bit capacity. This is another example of two's complement overflow.

Self-Test Review

12. In microprocessors, signed numbers are represented in _____ _____ form.

13. The ALU adds bit patterns as if they represent _____ binary numbers.

14. When a microprocessor executes a subtract instruction, what operations are actually performed inside the MPU?

15. What is the largest 8-bit positive number that can be represented in two's complement form?

16. When you are adding two positive numbers, what is meant by two's complement overflow?

17. If $+19_{10}$ and -21_{10} are added by an 8-bit microprocessor, the two's complement result will be _____.

18. Can two's complement overflow occur when two negative numbers are added?

19. A microprocessor adds 10001110_2 to 00010001_2. If these are unsigned binary numbers, the resulting bit pattern will be _____. If these are two's complement numbers, the resulting bit pattern will be _____.

20. If the bit patterns in question 19 represent unsigned numbers, the resulting bit pattern represents decimal _____.

21. If the bit patterns in question 19 represent two's complement numbers, the resulting bit pattern represents decimal _____.

Answers

12. Two's complement.

13. Unsigned.

14. The following operations occur:

    1. The MPU complements the subtrahend by changing 0's to 1's and 1's to 0's.

    2. One is added to the complemented subtrahend to form the two's complement.

    3. The two's complement of the subtrahend is added to the minuend.

15. 01111111_2 or $+127_{10}$.

16. When you add positive numbers, two's complement overflow occurs when the sum exceeds $+127_{10}$.

17. 11111110_2 or -2_{10}.

18. Yes. When you add negative numbers, two's complement overflow occurs when the sum exceeds -128_{10}.

19. In either case, the resulting bit pattern will be 10011111.

20. 159_{10}.

21. -97_{10}.

BOOLEAN OPERATIONS

Along with the basic mathematical processes examined earlier, the microprocessor can manipulate binary numbers logically. This system was conceived using the theorems developed by the mathematician George Boole. As a result, this branch of binary mathematics is given the name Boolean Algebra. In this section, the Boolean operations performed by the microprocessor will be examined. A more detailed description of Boolean Algebra is provided in the Heathkit Continuing Education Series course titled "Digital Techniques."

AND Operation

The AND function produces the logical product of two or more logic variables. That is, the logical product of an AND operation is logic 1 if all of the variable inputs are logic 1. If any of the input variables are logic 0, the logical product is 0. This process can be represented by the formula A · B = C, where A and B represent input variables (logic 1 or 0) and C represents the output or logical product of the AND operation. The AND function is designated by a dot between the variables. Do not confuse it with the mathematical multiplication sign.

Figure 3-6 is a "truth" table for a two-variable AND function. The 1's and 0's represent all of the possible logic combinations. Thus, you can see that the AND function is a sort of "all or nothing" operation. Unless all the input variables are logic 1, the output cannot be logic 1.

INPUTS		OUTPUT
A	B	C
0	0	0
0	1	0
1	0	0
1	1	1

Figure 3-6
Truth Table for an AND function.

When the microprocessor implements the logic AND operation, one 8-bit binary number is ANDed with a second 8-bit binary number. Refer to Figure 3-7 for an illustration of this process.

```
           8-BIT         8-BIT         RESULT OF
           NUMBER        NUMBER        AND OPERATION

    MSB    1       •     1       =     1    MSB
           0       •     0       =     0
           0       •     1       =     0
           1       •     0       =     0
           1       •     1       =     1
           0       •     1       =     0
           1       •     0       =     0
    LSB    0       •     0       =     0    LSB
```

Figure 3-7
8-bit logic AND operation.

Although more than two logic variables can be ANDed together, the microprocessor operates on only two variables at a time. Now try one more example of the AND operation. AND 10011101 with 11000110.

$$1 \cdot 1 = 1 \quad \text{MSB}$$
$$0 \cdot 1 = 0$$
$$0 \cdot 0 = 0$$
$$1 \cdot 0 = 0$$
$$1 \cdot 0 = 0$$
$$1 \cdot 1 = 1$$
$$0 \cdot 1 = 0$$
$$1 \cdot 0 = 0 \quad \text{LSB}$$

OR Operation

The OR (sometimes known as inclusive OR) function produces the logical sum of two or more logic variables. That is, the logical sum of an OR operation is logic 1 if either input is logic 1. The logical sum is 0 if **all** of the input variables are logic 0. This process can be represented by the formula A + B = C, where A and B represent input variables and C represents the output or logical sum of the OR operation. The OR function is designated by a plus sign (or a circled dot ⊙) between the variables. Do not confuse the plus sign with the mathematical add sign.

Figure 3-8 is a "truth" table for a two-variable OR function. The 1's and 0's represent all of the possible logic combinations. Thus, you can see that the OR function is a sort of "either or both" operation. If either or both input variables are logic 1, the output must be logic 1.

INPUTS		OUTPUT
A	B	C
0	0	0
1	0	1
0	1	1
1	1	1

Figure 3-8
Truth Table for an OR function.

When the microprocessor implements the logic OR operation, one 8-bit binary number is ORed with a second 8-bit binary number. Refer to Figure 3-9 for an illustration of this process.

	8-BIT NUMBER		8-BIT NUMBER		RESULT OF OR OPERATION	
MSB	1	+	1	=	1	MSB
	0	+	0	=	0	
	0	+	1	=	1	
	1	+	0	=	1	
	1	+	1	=	1	
	0	+	1	=	1	
	1	+	0	=	1	
LSB	0	+	0	=	0	LSB

Figure 3-9
8-bit logic OR operation.

As with the AND function, two or more logic variables can be ORed together. However, the microprocessor operates on only two variables at a time. Now try one more example of the OR operation. OR 10011101 with 11000101.

$$\begin{aligned}1 + 1 &= 1 \quad \text{MSB}\\0 + 1 &= 1\\0 + 0 &= 0\\1 + 0 &= 1\\1 + 0 &= 1\\1 + 1 &= 1\\0 + 0 &= 0\\1 + 1 &= 1 \quad \text{LSB}\end{aligned}$$

Exclusive OR Operation

The Exclusive OR (EOR or XOR) function performs a logical test for "equalness" between two logic variables. That is, if two variable inputs are equal (both logic 1 or 0), the output or result of the EOR operation is logic 0. If the inputs are not equal (one is logic 1, the other logic 0) the output is logic 1. This can be represented by the formula $A \oplus B = C$, where A and B represent input variables and C represents the output or result. The EOR function is designated by a circled plus sign between the variables.

Figure 3-10 is a "truth" table for the EOR function. The 1's and 0's represent all of the possible logic combinations. You can see that the EOR function is a sort of "either but not both" operation. That is, either input can be logic 1 or 0, but not both for a logic 1 output.

INPUTS		OUTPUT
A	B	C
0	0	0
0	1	1
1	0	1
1	1	0

Figure 3-10
Truth Table for an EOR function.

MICROPROCESSORS
Computer Arithmetic 3-37

When the microprocessor implements the logic EOR operation, one 8-bit binary number is exclusively ORed with a second 8-bit number. Refer to Figure 3-11 for an illustration of this process.

	8-BIT NUMBER		8-BIT NUMBER		RESULT OF EOR OPERATION	
MSB	1	⊕	1	=	0	MSB
	0	⊕	0	=	0	
	0	⊕	1	=	1	
	1	⊕	0	=	1	
	1	⊕	1	=	0	
	0	⊕	1	=	1	
	1	⊕	0	=	1	
LSB	0	⊕	0	=	0	LSB

Figure 3-11
8-bit logic EOR operation.

Now try one more example of the EOR operation. EOR 10011101_2 with 11000101_2.

$$1 \oplus 1 = 0 \quad \text{MSB}$$
$$0 \oplus 1 = 1$$
$$0 \oplus 0 = 0$$
$$1 \oplus 0 = 1$$
$$1 \oplus 0 = 1$$
$$1 \oplus 1 = 0$$
$$0 \oplus 0 = 0$$
$$1 \oplus 1 = 0 \quad \text{LSB}$$

Invert Operation

The invert operation performs a direct complement of a single input variable. That is, a logic 1 input will produce a logic 0 output. This process can be represented by the truth table in Figure 3-12.

INPUT	OUTPUT
A	$\overline{A}$
1	0
0	1

Figure 3-12
Truth Table for an invert function.

Note that the complement of **A** is $\overline{A}$. The bar above the **A** indicates that **A** has been inverted, and is read "not **A**." Therefore, the complement of **A** is "not **A**" ($\overline{A}$).

When the microprocessor implements the logic invert operation, the 8-bit binary number is complemented. This operation is also known as 1's complement. Thus, the complement of 11010110_2 is 00101001_2. As with the previous logic operations, the invert function operates on each individual bit of the 8-bit number.

Self-Test Review

22. The result of an AND operation is binary 1 when:

    A. All inputs are binary 0.

    B. Any one input is binary 0.

    C. All inputs are binary 1.

    D. Any one input is binary 1.

23. Perform the AND operation on the following 8-bit number pairs.

    A. 11010110 and 10000111.

    B. 00110011 and 11110000.

    C. 10101010 and 11011011.

24. The result of an OR operation is binary 0 when:

    A. All inputs are binary 1.

    B. All inputs are binary 0.

    C. Any one input is binary 1.

    D. Any one input is binary 0.

25. Perform the OR operation on the following 8-bit number pairs.

    A. 11010110 and 10000111.

    B. 00110011 and 11110000.

    C. 10101010 and 11011011.

26. The result of an XOR operation is binary 0 if the inputs are:

    A. Equal.

    B. Not equal.

27. The symbol for the EOR operation is:

    A. •

    B. +

    C. ⊕

    D. ×

28. Perform the EOR operation on the following 8-bit number pairs.

    A. 11010110 and 10000111.

    B. 00110011 and 11110000.

    C. 10101010 and 11011011.

29. $\overline{A}$ represents the _____ of **A**.

    A. Sum.

    B. Product.

    C. Complement.

    D. Supplement.

30. Perform the invert operation on the following 8-bit numbers.

    A. 11010110.

    B. 00110011.

    C. 10101010.

Answers

22. C. All inputs are binary 1.

23. A. 1 • 1 = 1
        1 • 0 = 0
        0 • 0 = 0
        1 • 0 = 0
        0 • 0 = 0
        1 • 1 = 1
        1 • 1 = 1
        0 • 1 = 0

    B. 00110000.

    C. 10001010.

24. B. All inputs are binary 0.

25. A. 1 + 1 = 1
        1 + 0 = 1
        0 + 0 = 0
        1 + 0 = 1
        0 + 0 = 0
        1 + 1 = 1
        1 + 1 = 1
        0 + 1 = 1

    B. 11110011.

    C. 11111011.

26. A. Equal.

27. C. $\oplus$

28. A. $1 \oplus 1 = 0$
         $1 \oplus 0 = 1$
         $0 \oplus 0 = 0$
         $1 \oplus 0 = 1$
         $0 \oplus 0 = 0$
         $1 \oplus 1 = 0$
         $1 \oplus 1 = 0$
         $0 \oplus 1 = 1$

     B.   11000011.

     C.   01110001.

29. C. Complement.

30. A.   00101001.

     B.   11001100.

     C.   01010101.

UNIT 3 SUMMARY

1. A number system can be used to perform two basic operations: addition and subtraction. From these, you can then perform multiplication, division, and any other numerical operation.

2. The addend is the number that is added to another number.

3. The augend is the number that is added to the addend.

4. The sum the result of adding the addend to the augend.

5. When performing decimal addition, you add the addend to the augend in each column of numbers beginning with the column that contains the LSD. If the sum of any column produces a value greater than nine, you add the carry to the next column on the left.

6. Binary addition is similar to decimal addition. There are four rules you should follow:

    A. Adding zero to zero produces the sum of zero.
    B. Adding zero to one produces the sum of one.
    C. Adding one to one produces the sum of zero with a carry of one.
    D. Adding one to one to one produces the sum of one with a carry of one.

7. The subtrahend is the number that is subtracted from another number.

8. The minuend is the number from which the subtrahend is subtracted.

9. The difference is the result of subtracting the subtrahend from the minuend.

10. When performing decimal subtraction, you subtract the subtrahend from the minuend in each column of numbers beginning with the column that contains the LSD. If the minuend of any column is smaller than the subtrahend, one is borrowed from the minuend in the column on the left, reducing that minuend by one, and ten is added to the minuend that required the borrow.

11. Binary subtraction is similar to decimal subtraction. There are four rules you should follow:

    A. Subtracting zero from zero produces the difference of zero.
    B. Subtracting one from one produces the difference of zero.
    C. Subtracting zero from one produces the difference of one.
    D. Subtracting one from zero produces the difference of one with a borrow of one.

12. The multiplicand is the number that is added to itself.

13. The multiplier is the number that specifies how many times the multiplicand is added to itself.

14. The product is the result of the multiplication.

15. Multiplication is a short method for adding a multiplicand to itself as many times as it is specified by the multiplier.

16. Binary multiplication is a process of shift left and add.

17. There are four rules you must follow when multiplying binary numbers:

    A. Multiplying zero times zero gives the product zero.
    B. Multiplying zero times one gives the product zero.
    C. Multiplying one times zero gives the product zero.
    D. Multiplying one times one gives the product one.

18. The dividend is the number that is divided in a division operation.

19. The divisor is the number that is used to divide the dividend.

20. The quotient is the number of times the divisor will divide into the dividend.

21. The remainder is what is left of the dividend after the last division.

22. Division is a short method for subtracting a divisor from a dividend until what is left of the dividend is less than the divisor or zero. The number of subtractions is recorded as the quotient. The value remaining after the subtraction is the remainder.

MICROPROCESSORS — Computer Arithmetic 3-45

23. Binary division is a process of shift right and add.

24. The rules of binary division are the same as the rules for binary subtraction.

25. The sign and magnitude of a number can be represented in binary.

26. A signed binary number is normally eight bits in length. The sign of the number is represented by the MSB. This is called the sign bit.

27. In the sign and magnitude method of representing a value, the sign bit is zero for positive and one for negative. The remaining seven bits represent the magnitude of the value.

28. In the one's complement method of representing a signed value, the positive values are the same as in the sign and magnitude method. Negative values are represented by first presenting the value as a positive value, and then inverting all of the bits, including the sign bit.

29. In the two's complement method of representing a signed value, the positive values are the same as in the one's complement method. Negative values are represented by first obtaining the one's complement of the value, and then adding one to the value. This is the method used by the microprocessor to represent a signed value.

30. The maximum value that can be represented by a two's complement binary number is $+127_{10}$ or -128_{10}.

31. The microprocessor can only add binary numbers. To subtract one number from another, the subtrahend must be converted to its negative two's complement form. Then the minuend is added to the subtrahend. Any carries into the ninth bit are discarded.

32. Boolean operations include AND, OR, Exclusive OR, and Invert.

33. The AND operation produces the logical product of two or more binary variables. The possible results are:

    A. Zero AND zero equals zero.
    B. Zero AND one equals zero.
    C. One AND zero equals zero.
    D. One AND one equals one.

34. The OR operation produces the logical sum of two or more binary variables. The possible results are:

    A. Zero OR zero equals zero.
    B. Zero OR one equals one.
    C. One OR zero equals one.
    D. One OR one equals one.

35. The Exclusive OR (EOR or XOR) operation produces the logical test for "equalness" between two binary variables. The possible results are:

    A. Zero XOR zero equals zero.
    B. Zero XOR one equals one.
    C. One XOR zero equals one.
    D. One XOR one equals zero.

36. The Invert operation performs a direct complement of a single binary variable.

Perform Experiment 4 at the end of Book 2.

Unit 4

INTRODUCTION TO PROGRAMMING

INTRODUCTION

In the final analysis there are only two things you can do with a microprocessor. You can program it and you can interface it with the outside world. In this course, you learn to program the microprocessor first. This unit, along with the associated experiments, will serve as an introduction to programming.

The programs you encounter in this unit are simple enough that anyone can understand them, and yet they illustrate many important concepts. By studying these programs, you will develop an understanding of how the microprocessor handles complex tasks. At the same time, you will gain practice using the instruction set.

UNIT OBJECTIVES

When you have completed this unit, you will be able to:

1. Draw the symbols used in flow charting and explain the purpose of each.

2. Develop flow charts that illustrate step-by-step procedures for solving simple problems.

3. Explain the purpose of conditional and unconditional branching.

4. Using the block diagram of the hypothetical microprocessor, trace the data flow during the execution of a branch instruction.

5. Compute the proper relative address for branching forward or backward from one point to another in a program.

6. Explain the purpose of the carry, negative, zero, and overflow flags. Give an example of a situation that can cause each to be set and another example that will cause each to clear. List eight instructions that test one of these flags.

7. Write programs that can: multiply by repeated addition; divide by repeated subtraction; convert binary to BCD; convert BCD to binary; add multiple-precision numbers; subtract multiple-precision numbers; add BCD numbers.

BRANCHING

The programs discussed earlier were all "straight line" programs; the instructions were executed one after another in the order in which they were written. Programs of this type are extremely limited because they use only a fraction of the microprocessor's power.

The real power of the microprocessor comes from its ability to execute a section of a program over and over again. In an earlier program we saw that two numbers could be multiplied by repeated addition. As long as the numbers are very small and we know the value of the two numbers, we can write a "straight line" program to multiply the numbers. For example, 5 could be multiplied by 4 with the following program:

Address	Instruction/Data	Comments
00	LDA 09	Load direct
02	ADD 09	Add direct
04	ADD 09	Add direct
06	ADD 09	Add direct
08	HLT	
09	05	

This technique is very crude for a number of reasons. If the two numbers are large, such as 98 and 112, the number of ADD instructions becomes excessive. Moreover, the values of the two numbers to be multiplied are generally not known. Therefore, even if we were willing to write enough ADD instructions, we simply would not know how many to write. Obviously, some better technique must be available.

A technique that is used in virtually every program is called **looping**. This allows a section of the program to be run as often as needed. Every microprocessor has a group of instructions called JUMP or BRANCH instructions that allow it to execute these program loops. These allow the microprocessor to escape the normal instruction sequence.

The microprocessor discussed in this course has both jump and branch instructions. In this unit, we will confine our discussion to the branch instructions. In a later unit we will discuss the jump instructions.

Before discussing the types of branch instructions, we must first discuss a new addressing mode called relative addressing.

Relative Addressing

In previous units, we discussed immediate addressing and direct addressing. Recall that in the immediate addressing mode no address is specified. The data is assumed to be the byte following the opcode. In direct addressing, an address is given. The data is assumed to be at that address.

Branch instructions are somewhat different from the instructions discussed earlier. While the branch instruction has an address associated with it, the address does not indicate the location of data. Instead, the address indicates the location of the next instruction that is to be executed.

The format of the branch instruction is shown in Figure 4-1. All branch instructions are 2-byte instructions. The first byte is the 8-bit opcode. This code identifies the particular type of branch instruction. As you will see later, a microprocessor may have a dozen or more different branch instructions. Each has its own opcode that uniquely identifies it.

FIRST BYTE ☐☐☐☐☐☐☐☐ OPCODE

SECOND BYTE ☐☐☐☐☐☐☐☐ RELATIVE ADDRESS OF NEXT INSTRUCTION TO BE EXECUTED.

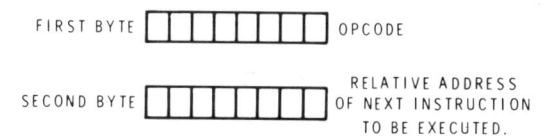

Figure 4-1
Format of the branch instruction.

The second byte of the branch instruction indicates the point to which the program is to branch. That is, it specifies the address of the next instruction that is to be executed.

In some microprocessors, the address is absolute. That is, the address is the memory location that holds the next instruction. In this case, the instruction BRANCH 30_{16} would mean that the instruction to be executed next is at address 30_{16}. In other words, some microprocessors use direct addressing when branching.

Our hypothetical microprocessor uses a different technique called relative addressing. In this addressing mode, the byte following the opcode does not represent an absolute address. Instead, it is a number that must be added to the program counter to form the new address. Consider the instruction:

BRANCH 30_{16}

Using relative addressing, this does not mean that the next instruction is to be taken from memory location 30_{16}. Rather, it means that 30_{16} must be added to the present contents of the program counter. Thus, if the program counter is at 08_{16} when the BRANCH 30_{16} instruction is executed, the next instruction will be fetched from location $08_{16} + 30_{16} = 38_{16}$.

By the same token, if the contents of the program counter is FA_{16} when a BRANCH 03 is encountered, the next instruction will be fetched from location $FA_{16} + 03 = FD_{16}$. Notice that this allows the MPU to jump over the instructions at addresses FB_{16} and FC_{16}.

Executing a Branch Instruction

Determining the relative address to use as the second byte of the branch instruction can be confusing unless you keep in mind the method by which the MPU executes a program. Therefore, let's go through the manipulations that take place within the MPU during the execution of the branch instruction.

Figure 4-2 shows sections of a program stored in memory. Let's assume that the MPU has been executing this program. Let's further assume that the MPU just completed the execution of the LDA 05 instruction at addresses 12_{16} and 13_{16}. The address register still holds the address of the last byte that was read from memory. The accumulator and data register hold the contents (05) of the last location that was read out.

Notice that the program counter contains the address of the next instruction to be executed. This address points to the branch instruction in memory location 14_{16}. Let's pick up the action at this point.

MICROPROCESSORS

Introduction to Programming | **4-7**

Figure 4-2
Status of the MPU registers after executing the LDA 05 instruction.

MPU Registers:
- Accumulator: 0000 0101
- Program Counter: 0001 0100
- Address Register: 0001 0011
- Data Register: 0000 0101

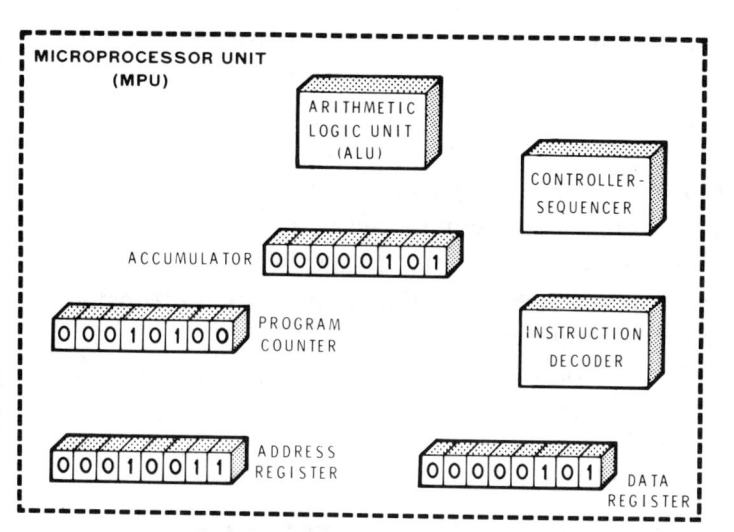

Memory:

ADDRESS	BINARY CONTENTS	MNEMONICS/ CONTENTS
0001 0010	1000 0110	LDA
0001 0011	0000 0101	05_{16}
0001 0100	0010 0000	BRA
0001 0101	0000 0111	07_{16}
0001 0110	——	——
0001 1100	——	——
0001 1101	1000 1011	ADD
0001 1110	0000 0110	06_{16}
0001 1111	——	——

Figure 4-3 shows how the first byte of the branch instruction is fetched. This is the standard fetch operation that was discussed earlier:

1. The address (14_{16}) is transferred from the program counter to the address register.
2. The program counter is incremented to 15_{16}.
3. The address is strobed onto the address bus.
4. The contents of the selected memory location are transferred via the data bus to the data register.
5. The instruction decoder examines this opcode and finds it to be a branch instruction.

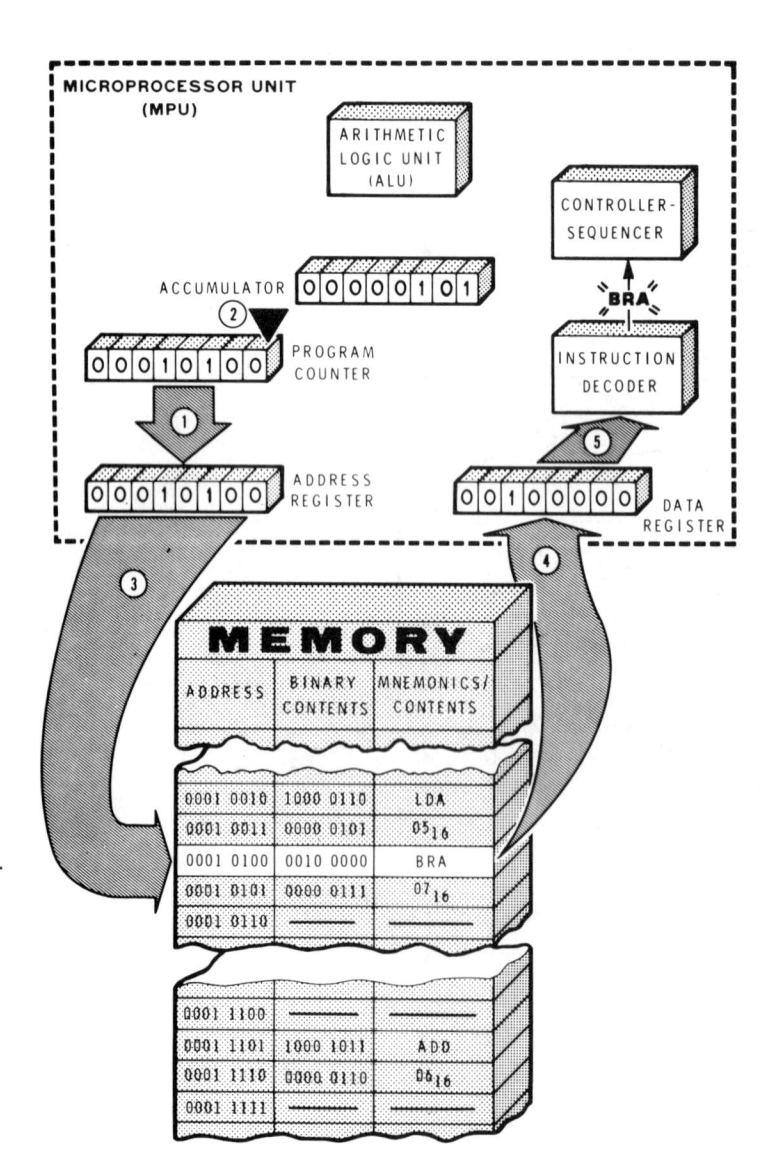

Figure 4-3
Fetching the BRA instruction.

Therefore, the controller-sequencer starts the procedure for executing a branch instruction.

During the next machine cycle, the relative address is fetched. This procedure is shown in Figure 4-4. The major events are:

1. The address (15_{16}) is transferred from the program counter to the address register.
2. The program counter is incremented to 16_{16}.
3. The address (15_{16}) is strobed onto the address bus.
4. The contents of location 15_{16} are transferred to the data register via the data bus.

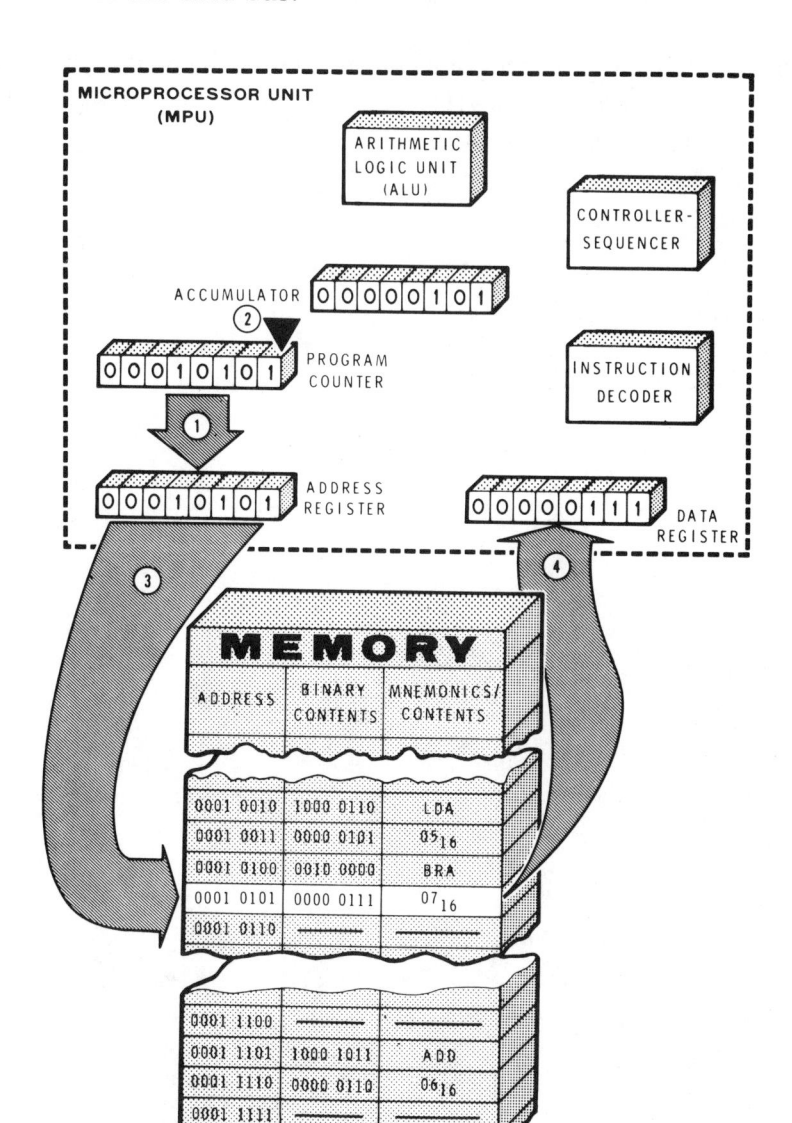

Figure 4-4
Fetching the relative address.

Figure 4-5 shows the state of the various registers after the relative address is fetched. The relative address (07_{16}) is in the data register. Now look at the program counter. Notice that it points to address 16_{16}. However, the MPU has not yet finished executing the branch instruction. It must now compute the new address by adding the relative address to the program count. It uses the addition capabilities of the ALU to perform this function. That is, the program count and relative address are strobed into the ALU. The ALU adds the two together and produces a sum of

```
0001  0110    program count
0000  0111    relative address
0001  1101    new program count
```

This sum is loaded into the program counter. Thus, the next instruction is fetched from memory location $1D_{16}$. That is, the next instruction to be executed is the ADD 06_{16} instruction.

MICROPROCESSORS

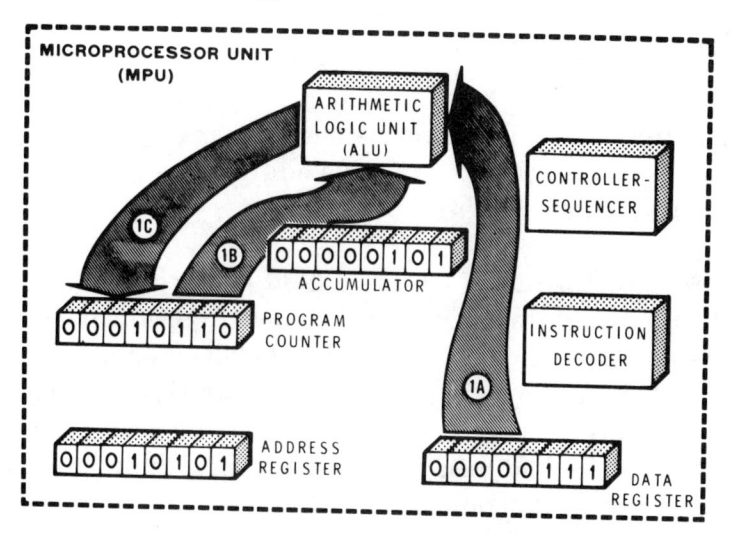

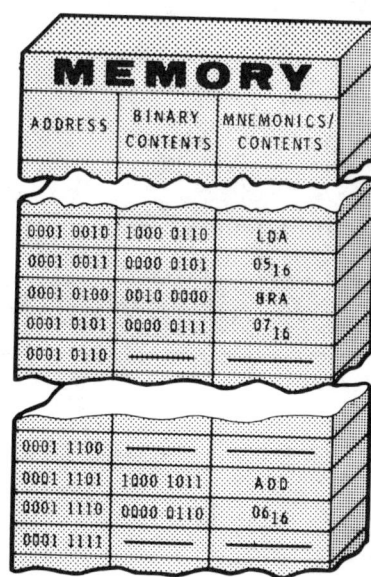

Introduction to Programming **4-11**

Figure 4-5
Computing the address of the next instruction.

Branching Forward

Branching in the forward direction is a simple task if you know the value of the program count when the relative address is added. A couple of examples will illustrate the procedure.

In Figure 4-6A, the BRANCH 03 instruction is placed in locations 32_{16} and 33_{16}. Assuming this instruction is executed, from which location will the next instruction be fetched? Remember that the program counter will always point to the next byte in sequence. Since the last byte fetched was the relative address from location 33_{16}, the program counter must be at 34_{16} when the relative address is added. Adding the relative address produces a new program count of

$$\begin{array}{r} 34_{16} \\ +\ 3_{16} \\ \hline 37_{16} \end{array}$$

Thus, the next instruction will be fetched from location 37_{16}.

HEX ADDRESS	HEX CONTENTS	MNEMONICS/ HEX CONTENTS
32	20	BRA
33	03	03
34	—	—
35	—	—
36	—	—
37	—	—
38	—	—

A

Program will branch to here

HEX ADDRESS	HEX CONTENTS	MNEMONICS/ HEX CONTENTS
18	20	BRA
19	??	??
1A		
1B	Originating Address	
1C		
1D		
1E		
1F		
20		
21		
22		
23	Destination Address	
24		

B

We wish to Branch to here

Figure 4-6
Branching forward.

MICROPROCESSORS
Introduction to Programming | 4-15

HEX ADDRESS	HEX CONTENTS	MNEMONICS/ HEX CONTENTS
56	—	—
57	—	—
58	—	—
59	—	—
5A	—	—
5B	—	—
5C	—	—
5D	20	BRA
5E	F9	F9
5F	—	—

Program branches to here → 58

A

HEX ADDRESS	HEX CONTENTS	MNEMONICS/ HEX CONTENTS
A0	—	—
A1	—	—
A2	—	—
A3	—	—
A4	—	—
A5	—	—
A6	—	—
A7	—	—
A8	—	—
A9	—	—
AA	—	—
AB	—	—
AC	—	—
AD	—	—
AE	—	—
AF	—	—
B0	20	BRA
B1	??	??
B2	—	—

We wish to branch to here → A0

B

Figure 4-7
Branching backwards.

In our example, the program count will be advanced to $B2_{16}$ after the relative address is fetched. This is our originating address. The point to which we wish to branch is $A0_{16}$. This is our destination address. Subtracting yields a difference of

$$
\begin{array}{rll}
1011\ 0010_2 & B2_{16} & \text{Originating address} \\
-\ 1010\ 0000_2 & A0_{16} & \text{Destination address} \\
\hline
0001\ 0010_2 & 12_{16} & \text{Difference}
\end{array}
$$

Next you compute the relative address by taking the two's complement of the difference. The two's complement of $0001\ 0010_2$ is $1110\ 1110_2$. In hexadecimal this is EE_{16}. Thus, the required relative address is EE_{16}.

Self-Test Review

1. What addressing mode is used by the branch instruction?

2. What does the second byte of a branch instruction indicate?

3. What happens in the MPU during the execution of the branch instruction?

4. What type of relative address causes a branch forward?

5. What type of relative address causes a branch backwards?

6. What is the maximum number of memory locations that can be branched over during a forward branch?

7. What is the maximum number of memory locations that can be branched over during a backward branch?

8. The opcode for the branch instruction is at address 20_{16}. The relative address is 06_{16}. After the branch instruction is executed, from what address will the next opcode be fetched?

9. The opcode for the branch instruction is at address 20_{16}. The relative address is $F1_{16}$. After the branch instruction is executed, from what address will the next opcode be fetched?

Answers

1. Relative addressing.

2. The second byte of the branch instruction is the relative address. This number is added to the contents of the program counter to form the absolute address.

3. The relative address is retrieved from memory and is added to the program count. The new program count goes into the program counter.

4. A positive two's complement number.

5. A negative two's complement number.

6. $0111\ 1111_2$ or $+127_{10}$.

7. $1000\ 0000_2$ or -128_{10}.

8. 28_{16}. Recall that during the execution of the branch instruction, the program counter will be incremented twice to 22_{16}. Thus, when the relative address (06_{16}) is added, the new address becomes 28_{16}.

9. As in answer 8, the program counter is automatically advanced to 22_{16} ($0010\ 0010_2$) before the relative address is added. $F1_{16}$ is equal to $1111\ 0001_2$. When this is added to the program count, the new address becomes

	0010	0010_2	Old program count
	1111	0001_2	Relative address
1	0001	0011_2	New program count

   Ignore carry ⬆

Thus, the next opcode will be fetched from address 13_{16}.

CONDITIONAL BRANCHING

The branch instruction allows the MPU to jump forward over a block of data or over a portion of a program. It also allows the MPU to jump backwards so a group of instructions can be repeated.

Until now we have been discussing the **unconditional** branch instruction. This type of instruction always results in a program branch. For this reason, it is called the **BR**anch **A**lways instruction. Its mnemonic is BRA.

There are other types of branch instructions that greatly expand the versatility of the MPU. These are called **conditional** branch instructions. Unlike BRA, these instructions cause a branch only if some specified condition is met.

A good example of a conditional branch instruction is the Branch If Minus (BMI). This instruction may or may not initiate a branch operation, depending on the result of some previous arithmetic or logic operation. This instruction might be placed after a subtract instruction. If the result of the subtraction is a negative number, the branch would be implemented. Otherwise, the MPU would continue to fetch and execute instructions in numerical order. An example may help to illustrate this.

Figure 4-8 shows part of a program that uses the branch if minus (BMI) instruction. Let's start with the instruction at address 95_{16}. This instruction causes the contents of location $B0_{16}$ to be loaded into the accumulator. Next, the SUB instruction subtracts the contents of location $B1_{16}$ from the number in the accumulator. The next instruction (BMI) examines the result of the subtraction. If the result was a minus number, the program will branch over the next three bytes. That is, the next instruction to be executed is the STA instruction at address $9E_{16}$. Thus, the resulting number in the accumulator is stored in location $B3_{16}$ and the MPU halts.

If the result of the subtraction is not minus, the BMI instruction has no effect. That is, the BMI instruction is fetched and executed but no branch occurs because the specified condition is not met. In this case, the next instruction to be executed is the STA instruction at address $9B_{16}$. Thus, the result of the subtraction will be stored in location $B2_{16}$.

MICROPROCESSORS

HEX ADDRESS	HEX CONTENTS	MNEMONIC/HEX CONTENTS	COMMENTS
95	96	LDA	Load accumulator direct
96	B0	B0	with contents of this address.
97	90	SUB	Subtract
98	B1	B1	the contents of this address.
99	2B	BMI	If result is minus
9A	03	03	branch this far.
9B	97	STA	If result is not minus, store
9C	B2	B2	at this address;
9D	3E	HLT	then halt.
9E	97	STA	If result is minus, store
9F	B3	B3	it at this address;
A0	3E	HLT	then halt.

Figure 4-8
This program uses the BMI instruction
to make a simple decision.

Notice that the program flow can take one of two paths, depending on the result of the subtraction. The BMI instruction gives the MPU this capability. The conditional branch instructions are sometimes called "decision making instructions." The reason for this becomes obvious if you consider the implications of our sample program. Here the MPU decides if the number at address $B1_{16}$ is larger than that at $B0_{16}$. The program path is determined by the outcome of this decision. If the number in $B1_{16}$ is larger, the result of the subtraction is a negative number. In this case, the result is stored in location $B3_{16}$. Otherwise, the resulting difference is stored in location $B2_{16}$.

Virtually all programs must make some type of decision. Some frequently encountered decisions are:

"Which of two numbers is larger?"

"Does this byte represent a letter of the alphabet or a numeral?"

"Are these two numbers equal?"

"Is this an even number?"

"Has the program loop been repeated the proper number of times?"

Conditional branch instructions are used in making all of these decisions.

Condition Codes

As the name implies, a conditional branch instruction causes a program branch only if some specified condition is met. Some commonly monitored conditions are:

1. Did a previous operation result in a negative number in the accumulator?
2. Did a previous operation result in zero in the accumulator?
3. Did a previous operation result in a carry from bit 7 of the accumulator?

To keep track of these conditions, most microprocessors have a group of single bit registers called condition code registers. Three of these registers are shown in Figure 4-9. They are the Negative (N) Register, the Zero (Z) Register, and the Carry (C) Register.

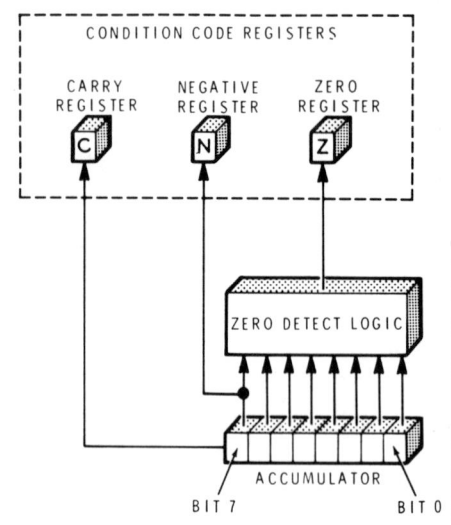

Figure 4-9
Condition code registers monitor the operations in the accumulator.

Negative (N) Register Recall that negative numbers are expressed in two's complement form. Using this system, the most significant bit determines whether or not the number is negative. In an 8-bit byte, bit 7 is a 1 if the two's complement number is negative. Thus, the N register monitors bit 7 of the accumulator. Immediately after an operation that involves the accumulator, the N register looks at bit 7 to see if the number is negative. If so, the N register is set to 1. If the number in the accumulator is not negative, the N register is reset to 0.

Most operations that involve the accumulator affect the N register in this way — **but not all**. In a later unit we will point out how this register is affected by each instruction. In this unit, we will assume that the N register is affected as outlined above any time a number is added to, subtracted from, loaded into, or stored from the accumulator.

Another name for a condition code is a flag. Thus, the N register is sometimes called the N flag or the negative flag.

Zero (Z) Register This register monitors the accumulator looking for all zeros. Immediately after an operation that involves the accumulator, the zero-detect circuit looks at the resulting number. If all 8 bits are 0, the Z register is set to 1. Otherwise, the Z register is reset to 0. Most operations that involve the accumulator affect the Z register in this way.

Carry (C) Register The C register acts somewhat like an extension of the accumulator. You have seen that when two unsigned 8-bit numbers are added, the sum is frequently a 9-bit number. For example:

```
      1001  0010    8-bit addend
  +   1100  0110    8-bit augend
    1 0101  1000    9-bit sum
    ↑
carry ┘
```

Since the accumulator is an 8-bit register, the sum will not fit. The most significant bit (the carry) would be lost if you did not have another 1-bit register to hold it. This is the purpose of the C register. Any operation that causes a carry out of bit 7 will set the carry register to 1. Arithmetic operations that do not result in a carry will reset this register to 0.

The carry register is also used to keep track of "borrows" during subtract operations. If a subtraction requires a borrow for bit 7, the carry flag will also be set. For example, suppose you subtract an unsigned, binary number from a smaller unsigned binary number. The result will, of course, be a negative number. Moreover, bit 7 will have to "borrow" a bit to complete the subtraction. As a simple example, let's subtract 2 from 1. The subtraction looks like this

```
Borrow →  1
          0000  0001    Minuend
      -   0000  0010    Subtrahend
          1111  1111    Difference
```

The carry bit is set to 1 to indicate that a borrow operation occurred. Many subtraction operations do not require borrows. In these cases, the carry bit is reset to 0 to indicate that no borrow occurred.

Notice that the carry code can have different meanings, depending on the operation involved. That is, a 1 can mean either that a carry occurred or that a borrow occurred. The precise meaning of the 1 depends on whether the operation was an addition or a subtraction. We will discuss some additional aspects of the carry register in a later unit.

Overflow (V) Register The final condition code that is to be considered in this unit keeps track of two's complement overflow. Figure 4-10 shows how this register is connected in the MPU. A special circuit detects an overflow condition by monitoring bit 7 of the ALU's input and output lines. This circuit sets the V flag when an overflow occurs but clears it if no overflow occurs.

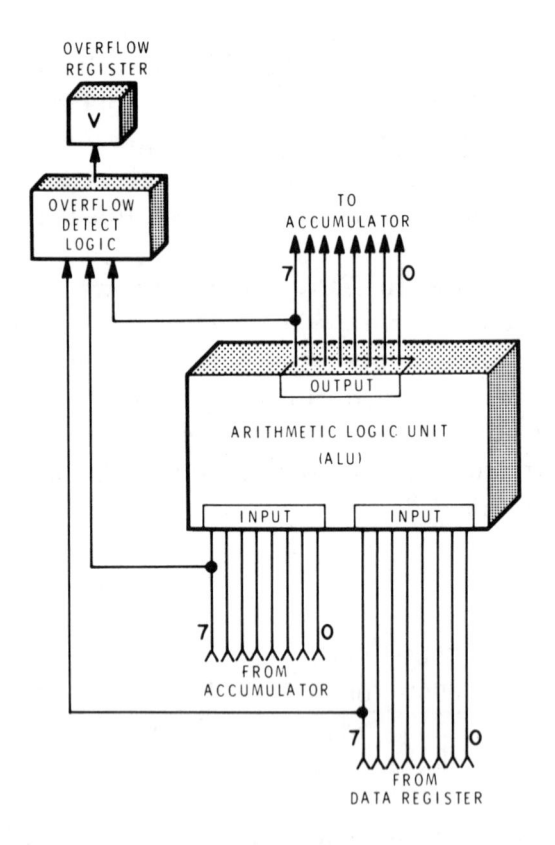

Figure 4-10
The overflow register monitors bit 7 of the ALU's input and output lines.

Let's see what is meant by two's complement overflow. Recall that the ALU adds numbers as if they were unsigned binary numbers. Even so, it can handle signed binary numbers if the proper bit patterns represent the negative numbers. This is the reason that the two's complement method of representing signed numbers has become so popular. A disadvantage of this system is that the magnitude of the number must be represented by 7 bits, since the eighth bit is used as the sign. Remember that a 1 in the MSB defines the number as negative.

Unfortunately, if two signed numbers are added and their sum exceeds 7-bits, the sign bit will be changed. For example, assume that a program adds $+73_{10}$ and $+96_{10}$. The addition looks like this:

$$\begin{array}{ll} \underline{0}100\ 1001_2 & +73_{10} \\ \underline{0}110\ 0000_2 & +96_{10} \\ \hline \underline{1}010\ 1001_2 & 169_{10} \end{array}$$

The answer is correct if all the binary numbers represent unsigned quantities. However, using two's complement, the underlined bits represent sign bits. Therefore, the answer does **not** represent 169_{10}. Instead, it represents -87_{10}. The reason for this error is that there was an overflow from bit 6 into the sign bit (bit 7). This is one of the situations that the V flag indicates.

When two's complement numbers having the same sign are added, the sum should have the same sign. That is, when two positive numbers are added, the sum should be positive. By the same token, when two negative numbers are added, the sum should be negative. However, an overflow can cause the sign to be reversed. The overflow logic detects this situation and sets the V flag whenever an overflow occurs.

The sign bit can also be upset during subtract operations. For example, when a negative number is subtracted from a positive number, the results should be positive. Remember that subtracting a negative number is tantamount to adding a positive number. However, in certain cases, an overflow can reverse the sign bit. This type of overflow occurs when the signs of the minuend and subtrahend are opposite and the difference has the sign of the subtrahend. This condition also sets the V flag.

Conditional Branch Instructions

The conditional branch instructions available in our hypothetical microprocessor are shown in Figure 4-11. While these are largely self-explanatory, a couple of points should be mentioned.

INSTRUCTION	MNEMONIC	OPCODE	BRANCH IF
Branch If Carry Clear	BCC	24	C=0
Branch If Carry Set	BCS	25	C=1
Branch If Not Equal Zero	BNE	26	Z=0
Branch If Equal Zero	BEQ	27	Z=1
Branch If Plus	BPL	2A	N=0
Branch If Minus	BMI	2B	N=1
Branch If Overflow Clear	BVC	28	V=0
Branch If Overflow Set	BVS	29	V=1

Figure 4-11
Conditional Branch Instructions.

The first instruction, Branch If Carry Clear (BCC), monitors the C register. If the carry register is reset to 0, the branch is implemented. Notice that the words "clear" and "reset" are used interchangeably in this regard. They both mean the register contains a 0.

The branch instructions that monitor the Z register can also be confusing. The Branch If Equal Zero (BEQ) instruction implements a branch when the Z register is set to 1. Recall that the Z register is set to 1 when the number in the accumulator is zero. Thus, you must remember that a 0 in the Z register means that the number in the accumulator is **not** zero.

These conditional branch instructions can be used with other instructions to make a wide range of decisions. They greatly increase the power of the microprocessor. More than any other type of instruction, the conditional branches are responsible for the MPU's "intelligence." In the next section, you will see how these instructions are used.

Self-Test Review

10. What is the difference between an unconditional branch instruction and a conditional branch instruction?

11. What condition is tested by the branch if minus (BMI) instruction?

12. When is the N flag set?

13. When is the Z flag set?

14. During an add operation, the C flag is set. What does this represent?

15. During a subtract operation, the C flag is set. What does this indicate?

16. Often, when two positive 2's complement numbers are added, the sign bit of the answer will indicate a negative sum. This "error" can be spotted by checking which flag?

17. Under what condition will the BEQ instruction cause a branch to occur?

18. Under what condition will the BPL instruction cause a branch to occur?

19. When subtracting unsigned binary numbers, which flag indicates that the difference is a negative number?

Answers

10. An unconditional branch instruction always causes a branch operation to occur. On the other hand, the conditional branch instruction implements a branch operation only if some specified condition is met.

11. The BMI instruction tests the Negative (N) register to see if it is set.

12. Generally speaking, the N flag is set if the previous instruction left a 1 in the MSB of the accumulator.

13. Generally, the Z flag is set if the previous instruction left all zeros in the accumulator.

14. During an add operation, the carry bit is set if there is a carry from bit 7 of the accumulator.

15. During a subtract operation, the carry bit is set if bit 7 had to "borrow" a bit to complete the subtraction.

16. This condition results from a two's complement overflow. Thus, the V flag will be set if this condition occurs.

17. The BEQ instruction causes a branch to occur only if the Z register is set.

18. The BPL instruction causes a branch to occur only if the N register is clear.

19. The carry flag.

MICROCOMPUTER PROGRAMMING

As the programs you write increase in complexity and length, the need for some type of organization for problem solving becomes quite evident.

The exact method of problem solving will vary from person to person. Some may have an intuitive "feel" for program development and may write programs "off the top of their head". If you can do this, you are fortunate indeed. Most people, however, need a formal "plan of attack" when solving problems and writing programs.

Essentially, there are three steps to writing a program. The first is to **define the problem**. This may seem like a relatively easy task but it sometimes proves to be the most difficult. Unfortunately, there is no set procedure for defining problems. Some problems will lend themselves to mathematical definitions while others may require a logical or graphical approach. We can only advise you to analyze each situation carefully before you attempt to define the problem.

The last step in creating a program is the **writing of that program** using the instruction set for your microprocessor. You already know a little bit about writing programs and you will be learning much more as you progress through the course. What we are primarily concerned with here is the second step in creating a program: mapping or **flowcharting** the solution.

The Flowchart

Given a well structured blueprint, a carpenter can construct even the most complex project with little or no difficulty. The same is true of a programmer with a good flowchart. As a matter of fact, some flowcharts are so detailed that little remains for the programmer to do other than fill in the appropriate instructions. For our purposes, we'll use a simple flowcharting technique using the five most common symbols. These are shown in Figure 4-12.

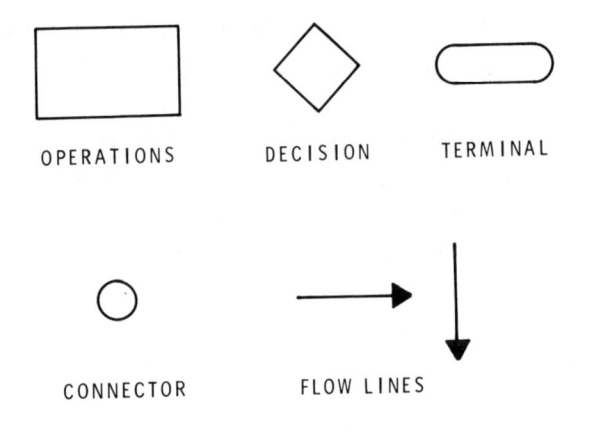

Figure 4-12
Flowchart Symbols.

THE SYMBOLS

All flowcharts have a beginning, and most flowcharts will have an end. These are referred to as the "terminal" points of the flowchart and they are represented by the **terminal** symbol. The terminal symbol seen in Figure 4-13 is simply labeled "start" or "stop", to denote its meaning.

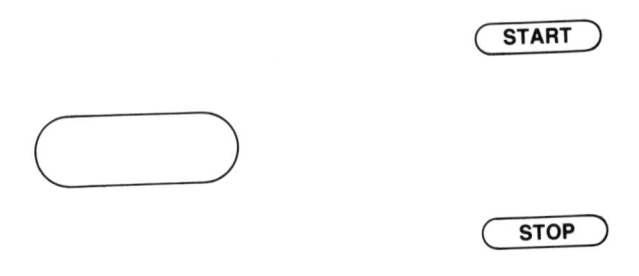

Figure 4-13
Terminal Symbol.

The **operations box** is probably the most frequently used flowchart symbol. It may represent a transfer process such as moving or loading data or an algebraic process like addition or multiplication. It can also be used for such statements as "print" or "set"; which we will get into later. If you have a process that is not specified by one of the other symbols, use the operations box. Later we will introduce some additional flowchart symbols. Some examples of the operations box use are shown in Figure 4-14.

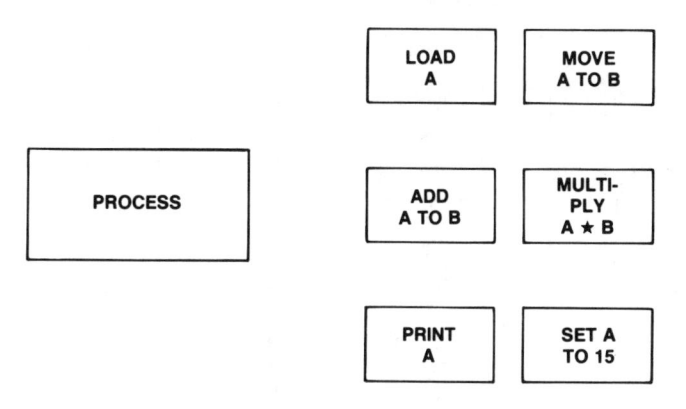

Figure 4-14
Operation Box.

The diamond-shaped **decision box** is really the "heart" of the flowchart. It indicates a logical choice between two conditions and, therefore, it controls the direction of program flow. If a condition is satisfied, the "yes" route is taken. If the condition is not satisfied, then the "no" route is selected. Typical examples for using the decision box are shown in Figure 4-15. The yes and no routes can originate in any corner of the diamond.

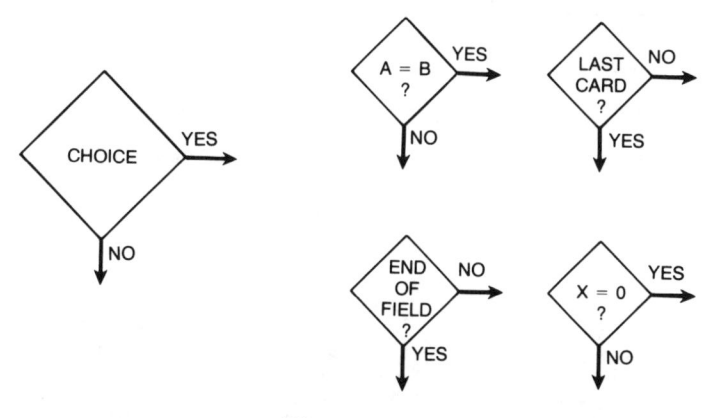

Figure 4-15
Decision Box.

Flow lines and **connectors** are used to tie the symbols and sections of the flowchart together. Normally, the chart will be arranged to flow from top to bottom and from left to right. However, there is no set rule in regard to this and the flowchart could just as well flow in the opposite direction. The use of flow lines as well as connectors is demonstrated in Figure 4-16. The connector symbols direct you from one section of the program to another. The connectors are labeled with values to indicate where the connection takes place; 1A connects with 1A, 2A connects with 2A, etc.

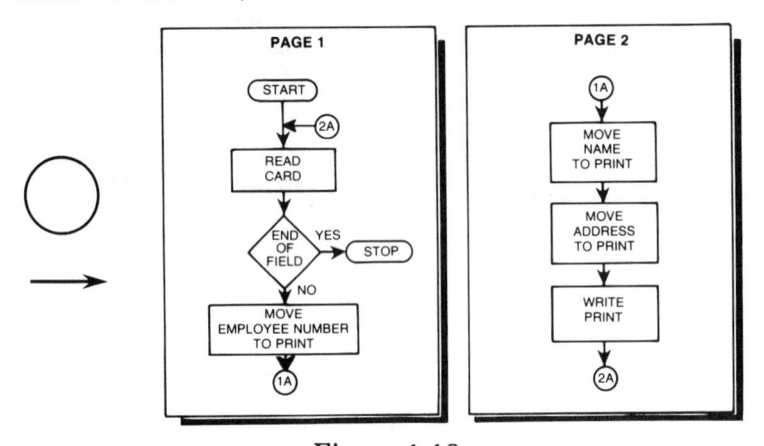

Figure 4-16
Connectors and Flowlines.

MATHEMATICAL SYMBOLS

Usually, sophisticated flowcharts use mathematical symbols to represent the decision making process. These symbols allow us to illustrate our decision quickly and concisely. In Figure 4-17A you see the five most frequently used symbols and their meanings. Figure 4-17B shows some examples of their use.

A

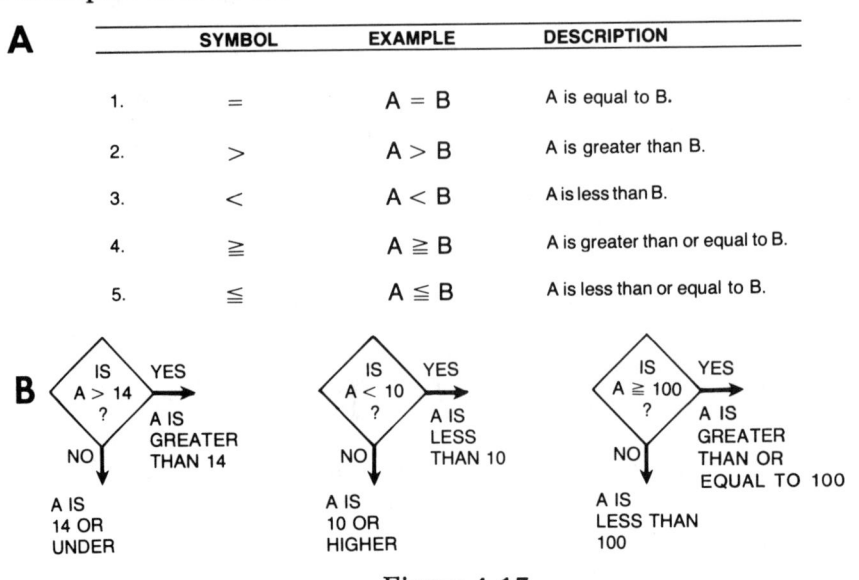

	SYMBOL	EXAMPLE	DESCRIPTION
1.	=	A = B	A is equal to B.
2.	>	A > B	A is greater than B.
3.	<	A < B	A is less than B.
4.	≧	A ≧ B	A is greater than or equal to B.
5.	≦	A ≦ B	A is less than or equal to B.

Figure 4-17
Mathematical Decision Making
Symbols and Their Use.

MICROPROCESSORS

Introduction to Programming | 4-31

CONSTRUCTING THE FLOWCHART

Now that you can identify flowchart symbols, it's time to solve a few problems using flowcharts. The first, to add three numbers and produce a sum, is shown in Figure 4-18. The problem and the mathematical expression of the problem are shown on the left. The mathematical expression serves as a definition of the problem. Our flowchart is on the right.

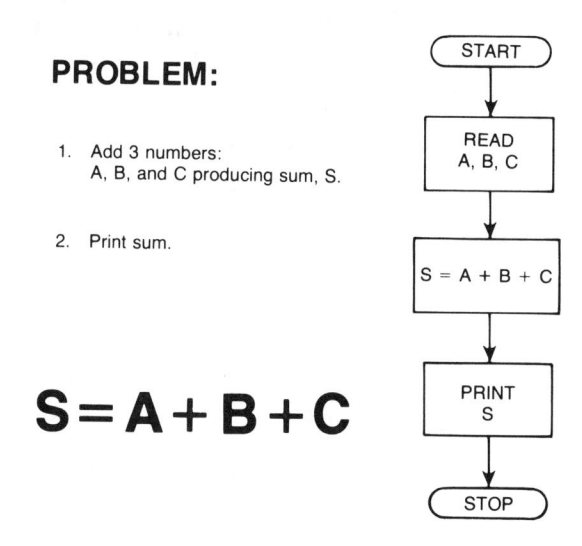

PROBLEM:

1. Add 3 numbers:
   A, B, and C producing sum, S.

2. Print sum.

$$S = A + B + C$$

Figure 4-18
Flowchart Construction.

It begins with the start terminal symbol. In a flowchart of this size you might think that this symbol is unnecessary. But, no matter how simple you think a flowchart is, always use the start terminal symbol. You will see later on in this course that flowcharts can get quite lengthy, and it is often necessary to return to the beginning of your flowchart. The start terminal symbol allows you to do this with ease. If you use it all the time, even when it seems unnecessary, then you'll never get into difficulty locating the beginning of the program.

Next we find an operation box that tells the computer to read, or identify, the variables A, B, and C. This process would actually move the numbers from memory into the microcomputer. Again, you might think that this box is unnecessary or that it could be combined with the next operations box. But, remember, the more detailed the flowchart, the easier it is to write your program from it.

In the second operations box, the computer is instructed to add A, B, and C, giving you the total S. The final operations box tells the computer to print the solution, S. Finally, the stop terminal symbol is used to end the process.

Now that you have seen how it is done, it's time to look at a more complex problem. In Figure 4-19 you see a drawing of a traffic intersection. Main Street is a busy thoroughfare while Side Street handles only a moderate amount of traffic. A traffic study shows that if traffic on Main Street is allowed to move for two minutes, while traffic on Side Street is allowed to move for one minute, the intersection controls traffic very efficiently. Light A has been assigned for control of traffic on Main Street and light B for control of traffic on Side Street.

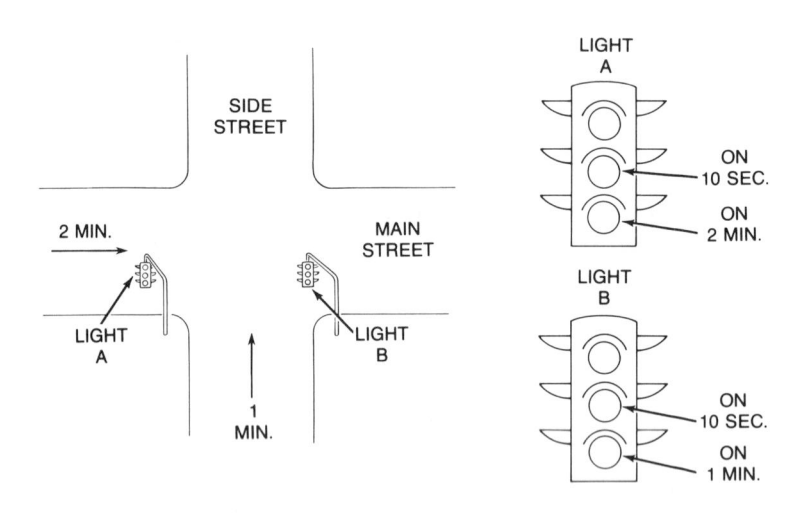

Figure 4-19
The Traffic Problem.

It is not necessary at this point, but you might like to try to draw this flowchart yourself. If not, just read along while we work our way through this problem. Before you can attempt to draw a flowchart, you must carefully examine the problem. That is, you must carefully determine exactly what each light must do.

Light A must remain green for two minutes. Naturally, you want a caution light between red and green. We suggest a yellow light duration of 10 seconds. The duration of the red light will be controlled by light B. Light B, on the other hand, will be green for one minute and yellow for ten seconds. When light B turns red, light A turns green and the cycle repeats.

MICROPROCESSORS

With this information, you should encounter little difficulty drawing the flowchart for this problem. Defining the problem in detail will always simplify problem solving. If you care to try your hand at this flowchart, grab a pencil and some paper and give it a try. If not, just continue reading. You'll find our solution in Figure 4-20.

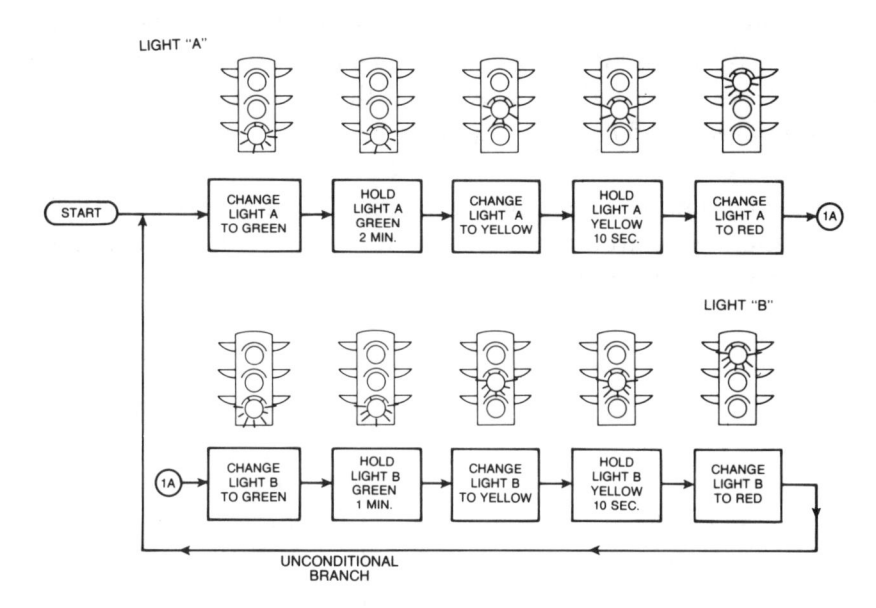

Figure 4-20
The Traffic Solution.

The flowchart begins in the top left-hand corner of Figure 4-20. The first five operation blocks control the operation of light A. You begin the program at the box that changes light A to green. The second process holds the light green for two minutes. After this, light A must change to yellow and hold there for ten seconds as the next two blocks indicate. Finally, light A is changed red by the fifth operation.

Connector 1A tells you that the flow of the program picks up at the corresponding 1A connector in the bottom left-hand corner of the illustration. Here, you enter the light B routine that controls the traffic on Side Street. Now that the traffic on Main Street has a red light, it is safe to change light B to green. Light B is held green for one minute, then it is changed to yellow and held for ten seconds. Finally, light B changes to red. Of course, you want this process to repeat so you draw a flow line from the end of the light B cycle back to the beginning of the light A cycle.

This type of a flow line is called an unconditional branch because it must always point to a particular point in the program. The unconditional branch in a flowchart would correspond to an unconditional branch in the actual program.

There are other flow lines that originate at a decision box rather than at an operation box. These are called conditional branches because the flow of the program along these lines is based on the conditions stated in the box. Conditional branches in a flowchart are related to conditional branches in an actual program.

Figure 4-21 demonstrates the use of the decision box and the conditional branch. The problem is stated on the left and the flowchart solution is shown on the right.

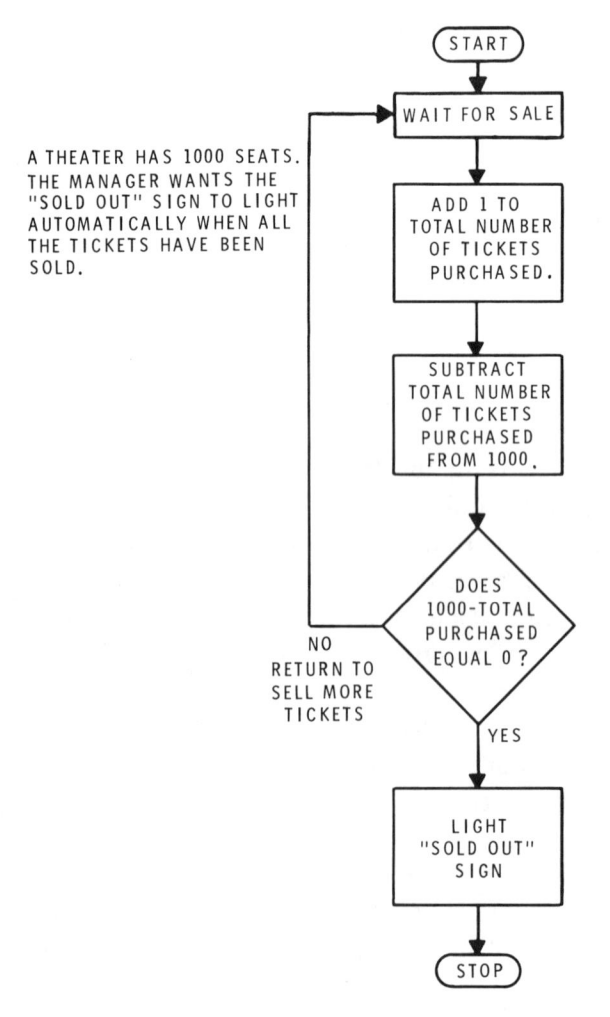

A THEATER HAS 1000 SEATS. THE MANAGER WANTS THE "SOLD OUT" SIGN TO LIGHT AUTOMATICALLY WHEN ALL THE TICKETS HAVE BEEN SOLD.

Figure 4-21
The Use of the Decision Box.

Again, the chart begins with the terminal start symbol. As each ticket is purchased, it is added to the total number of tickets purchased. Then the total number of tickets sold is subtracted from the number of seats available.

Now the decision must be made. If all tickets have not been sold, you must branch to the beginning of the flowchart and resume the count. If all tickets are sold, that is if the result of the subtraction is zero, then branch forward and light the "SOLD OUT" sign. Once the sign is lit, you complete the flowchart with the stop terminal symbol. Although the problem is very simple, there is no way to solve it without using a decision box and conditional branches in the flowchart.

Self Review Questions

20. The five most common flowcharting symbols are the:

    A. _____
    B. _____
    C. _____
    D. _____
    E. _____

21. You are permitted to use mathematical symbols in a flowchart.
    _____
    (True/False)

22. The flowchart should always begin with a start terminal symbol.
    _____
    (True/False)

23. The _____ _____ in a flowchart corresponds to the unconditional branch in the actual program.

24. The _____ _____ in a flowchart are related to the conditional branch in an actual program.

Self Review Answers

20. The five most common flowcharting symbols are the:

    A. **Terminal Symbol**
    B. **Operations Box**
    C. **Decision Box**
    D. **Flow Lines**
    E. **Connectors**

21. **True.** Flowcharts make use of mathematical symbols.

22. **True.** The flowchart should always begin with a start terminal symbol.

23. The **unconditional branch** in a flowchart corresponds to the unconditional branch in the actual program.

24. The **conditional branch** in a flowchart is related to the conditional branch in an actual program.

ALGORITHMS

An algorithm is a step-by-step procedure for doing a particular job. It generally involves doing a complex task by stringing together a series of simple steps. To illustrate the use of an algorithm, consider the following very simple example.

Multiplying by Repeated Addition

Most microprocessors do not have hardware multiply capabilities. That is, they do not have a multiplication circuit nor a multiply instruction. Nevertheless, the microprocessor can be made to multiply by use of an algorithm. One procedure for doing this was discussed earlier. It involved adding the multiplicand to itself the number of times indicated by the multiplier. In the previous example, this was done by using a separate ADD instruction for each addition. This procedure is unsatisfactory for two reasons. First, it results in excessively long programs. Second, you must know the value of the multiplier so that you know how many ADD instructions to include.

A better approach, although still far from ideal, is to use a program loop that will multiply two numbers by repeated addition. For the time being, assume that the two numbers are both positive and that the product does not exceed 255_{10}. Let's further assume that we use only the instructions which have been discussed up to this point. In fact, we will restrict ourselves to the instructions shown in Figure 4-22.

INSTRUCTION	MNEMONIC	IMMEDIATE	DIRECT	RELATIVE	INHERENT
Load Accumulator	LDA	86	96		
Clear Accumulator	CLRA				4F
Decrement Accumulator	DECA				4A
Increment Accumulator	INCA				4C
Store Accumulator	STA		97		
Add	ADD	8B	9B		
Subtract	SUB	80	90		
Branch Always	BRA			20	
Branch If Carry Set	BCS			25	
Branch if Equal Zero	BEQ			27	
Branch if Minus	BMI			2B	
Halt	HLT				3E

Figure 4-22
Instructions to be used.

The algorithm for multiplying by repeated addition is quite simple. To multiply A times B, you merely add A to a specific location B times. For example, to multiply 5 times 3, you clear a location and then add 5. You continue the addition until 5 has been added 3 times. The number in the affected location will then be 15_{10} which is the product of 5 times 3.

The success of this operation depends on the microprocessor knowing when to stop. It must add 5 three times, but only three times. One way to keep track of the number of additions is to decrement the multiplier (3) each time an addition is made. When the multiplier reaches 0, the proper number of multiplications has been carried out.

Figure 4-23 is a flow chart that illustrates the algorithm. In the first two steps, the MPU clears the accumulator and stores the resulting number (0) in the product. This ensures that the product is zero before the first number is added. Next, it loads the multiplier and checks to see if the multiplier is 0. If so, the process is stopped since a multiplier of 0 dictates a product of 0.

In our example, the multiplier is 3; therefore, we exit the decision block via the "no" line. The next step tells us to decrement the multiplier. The new value of the multiplier (2) is stored for future use. Next, the product whose present value is 0 is loaded. Then, the multiplicand (5) is added so that the new value of the product becomes 5. This completes our first pass through the program. Remember that the multiplicand has been added once and that the multiplier has been reduced by one.

Notice that the program loops back to the input of the second block. The product which now has a value of 5 is stored back in memory. The multiplier (which is now 2) is loaded and tested. Because its value is not yet 0, the multiplier is decremented to 1 and stored again. The product (whose value is now 5) is then loaded and the multiplicand is added so that a new value of 10_{10} is obtained.

The program loops again and the new product (10_{10}) is stored. The multiplier (whose value is now 1) is loaded and tested. Because its value is still not 0, it is decremented again. Notice that the value of the multiplier is now 0. This value is stored away, the product (10_{10}) is fetched, and the multiplicand is added once more. The new value of the product becomes 15_{10}.

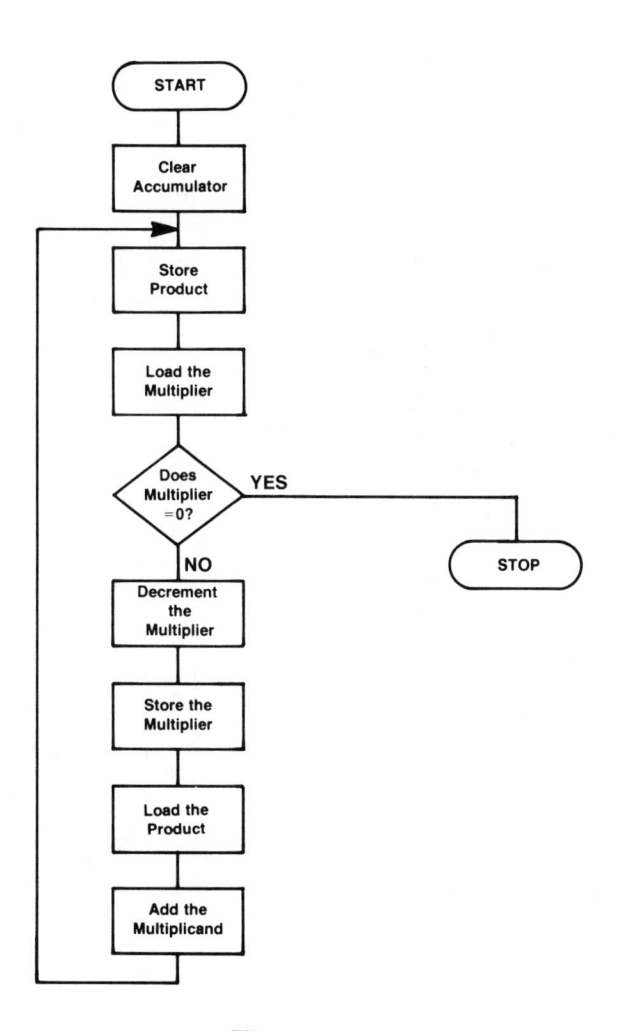

Figure 4-23
Flow chart for multiplying by repeated addition.

The program loops again and the product is stored. The multiplier is loaded and tested. Recall that the value of the multiplier is now 0. Consequently, we exit the decision block via the "yes" line. The program has accomplished its task and it now stops. Notice that the value of the product is 15_{10} which is the proper answer for 5 × 3.

The next task is to convert the flow chart to a program that the computer can execute. Figure 4-24 shows such a program. Carefully compare this program to the flow chart paying particular attention to the comments column. Work through the program on paper and verify that it will multiply the numbers at addresses 11_{16} and 12_{16}. Although 3 and 5 are used in this example, the program will work for any values of multiplier and multiplicand as long as the product does not exceed 255_{10}.

HEX ADDRESS	HEX CONTENTS	MNEMONIC/HEX CONTENTS	COMMENTS
00	4F	CLRA	Clear the accumulator.
01	97	STA	Store the product
02	13	13	in location 13_{16}.
03	96	LDA	Load the accumulator with the
04	12	12	multiplier from location 12_{16}
05	27	BEQ	If the multiplier is equal to zero,
06	09	09	branch down to the Halt instruction.
07	4A	DECA	Otherwise, decrement the multiplier.
08	97	STA	Store the new value of the
09	12	12	multiplier back in location 12_{16}.
0A	96	LDA	Load the accumulator with the
0B	13	13	product from location 13_{16}.
0C	9B	ADD	Add
0D	11	11	the multiplicand to the product.
0E	20	BRA	Branch back to instruction
0F	F1	F1	in location 01.
10	3E	HLT	Halt.
11	05	05	Multiplicand.
12	03	03	Multiplier.
13	–	–	Product.

Figure 4-24
This program multiplies the numbers at addresses 11_{16} and 12_{16}, and places their product at address 13_{16}.

Dividing by Repeated Subtraction

Another interesting algorithm is one that allows the microprocessor to divide by repeated subtraction. The technique is to keep track of the number of times that the divisor can be subtracted from the dividend. For example, suppose you wish to divide 47_{10} by 15_{10}. The divisor can be subtracted 3 times:

$$\begin{array}{ccc} \text{First subtraction} & \text{Second Subtraction} & \text{Third Subtraction} \\ \\ \begin{array}{r} 47_{10} \\ -15_{10} \\ \hline 32_{10} \end{array} \longrightarrow & \begin{array}{r} 32_{10} \\ -15_{10} \\ \hline 17_{10} \end{array} \longrightarrow & \begin{array}{r} 17_{10} \\ -15_{10} \\ \hline 2_{10} \end{array} \end{array}$$

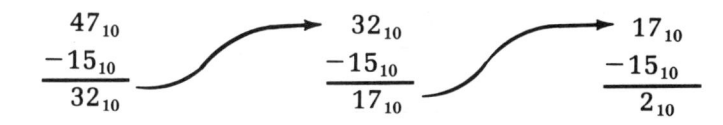

Because three subtractions occurred, the quotient is 3. Also, because 2 was left after the last subtraction, the remainder is 2. We can verify this by long division:

$$\text{divisor} \longrightarrow 15_{10} \overline{\smash{\big)}\, \begin{array}{r} 3_{10} \quad \leftarrow \text{Quotient} \\ 47_{10} \quad \leftarrow \text{Dividend} \\ 45_{10} \\ \hline 2_{10} \quad \leftarrow \text{Remainder} \end{array}}$$

The microprocessor keeps track of the number of subtractions by incrementing the quotient by one each time a subtraction occurs. Of course, the quotient must be initially set to zero.

The divisor is subtracted from the dividend until any further subtraction would result in a negative number. The MPU can use the BMI instruction to check for a negative result on each loop. The negative result is the indication that the process is finished.

A flow chart for this algorithm is shown in Figure 4-25. The actual program is shown in Figure 4-26. the program is arbitrarily placed in locations 00 through 10_{16}. The dividend (47_{10}) is at address 11_{16} while the divisor (15_{10}) is at address 12_{16}. When executed, the program will produce the quotient at location 13_{16} and the remainder at location 11_{16}.

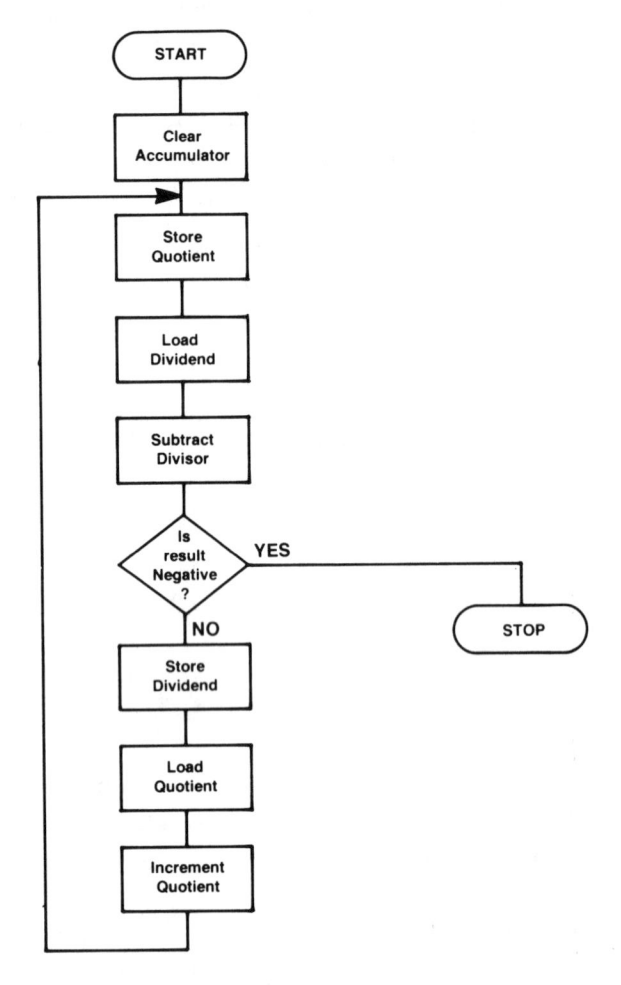

Figure 4-25
Flow chart for dividing by repeated subtraction.

MICROPROCESSORS

Introduction to Programming 4-43

HEX ADDRESS	HEX CONTENTS	MNEMONIC/HEX CONTENTS	COMMENTS
00	4F	CLRA	Clear the accumulator.
01	97	STA	Store in the quotient which
02	13	13	is at address location 13_{16}.
03	96	LDA	Load the accumulator with the
04	11	11	dividend from location 11_{16}.
05	90	SUB	Subtract the
06	12	12	divisor from the dividend.
07	2B	BMI	If the difference is negative, brach
08	07	07	down to the Halt instruction.
09	97	STA	Otherwise, store the difference
0A	11	11	back in location 11_{16}.
0B	96	LDA	Load the accumulator with the
0C	13	13	quotient.
0D	4C	INCA	Increment the quotient by one.
0E	20	BRA	Brach back to instruction
0F	F1	F1	in location 01.
10	3E	HLT	Halt.
11	2F	2F	Dividend (47_{10}).
12	0F	0F	Divisor (15_{10}).
13	—	—	Quotient.

Figure 4-26
This program divides by
repeatedly subtracting the divisor
from the dividend.

Refer to the flow chart and the comments column of the program. Before reading further, try running through the program on paper. This will give you a feel for how the computer solves the problem.

Now let's go through the program to see what it does. The first two instructions clear the quotient. Next, the dividend (47_{10}) is loaded into the accumulator and the divisor (15_{10}) is subtracted. The BMI instruction is used to examine the difference (32_{10}). Since the difference is not minus, the branch does not occur. Consequently, the next instruction stores the difference (32_{10}) back in the location from which the dividend came. In effect, the difference becomes the new dividend. Next the quotient (0) is loaded and is incremented to 1. The program then branches back to the instruction in location 01. This instruction stores the quotient (1) back in location 13_{16}.

On the next pass through the program, the new dividend (32_{10}) is loaded and the divisor (15_{10}) is subtracted again. This produces a difference of (17_{10}). Since the difference is not negative, the BMI instruction does not cause a branch. Thus, the difference is stored back in location 11_{16}. The quotient is loaded into the accumulator and is incremented to 2. The BRA instruction causes the program to loop once again. The STA instruction in location 01 stores the quotient (2) back in location 13_{16}.

On the third pass the dividend (17_{10}) is loaded and the divisor (15_{10}) is subtracted a third time. The difference (02) is still not negative so no branch occurs. The difference is stored away; the quotient is loaded and is incremented to 03. Notice that this is the proper final value for the quotient. Therefore, on the next pass, the MPU should be able to break out of the loop.

The quotient is stored back in location 13_{16}. The dividend, which now has a value of 2, is loaded. The divisor (15_{10}) is subtracted, leaving a negative number (-13_{10}) in the accumulator. The BMI instruction recognizes that this is a negative number and implements a branch operation. Notice that the MPU branches forward to the HLT instruction. Thus, the program ends with the quotient set to 3. The remainder is at address 11_{16}. That is, the remainder is what remains of the dividend after the third subtraction.

It may bother you that there were four subtractions and that a negative difference resulted from the last subtraction. However, you will recall that the quotient was incremented only on the first three of these subtractions. Thus, the final quotient is 3. Moreover, the negative difference that resulted during the last subtraction was never stored. Consequently, the remainder was 2 when the program ended.

This program does have some drawbacks. For one thing, neither the dividend nor the divisor can exceed 127_{10}. Also, only positive numbers can be used. Finally, the program gets hung up in an endless loop if the initial value of the divisor is zero. While division by zero is not allowed in mathematics, some provision would be made in a practical program to recognize this eventuality. Since the program is for demonstration purposes, we will live with these shortcomings for the time being.

Converting BCD to Binary

When a microprocessor is used with a terminal such as a teletypewriter, numerals are entered as ASCII characters. For example, the number 237_{10} is entered into memory as three ASCII characters:

Numeral	ASCII Character
2	0011 0010
3	0011 0011
7	0011 0111

Notice that the four least significant bits of the ASCII character represent the BCD value of the corresponding numeral. Thus, we can convert these ASCII characters to BCD numbers simply by eliminating the four most significant bits. This technique was demonstrated in an earlier experiment.

While the microprocessor does have some BCD capability, it is often desirable to convert BCD numbers to binary. The technique for doing this illustrates another useful algorithm.

The BCD representation for 237_{10} is:

 0010 ← hundreds BCD digit
 0011 ← tens BCD digit
 0111 ← units BCD digit

Notice that in this example 0010 represents two hundred, 0011 represents thirty, and 0111 represents seven. Because of this, there is a simple procedure for converting BCD to binary. Starting with an initial value of zero, the MPU adds 100_{10} as many times as indicated by the hundreds digit. It then adds 10_{10} as indicated by the tens digit. Finally, the value of the units digit is added on to the result. The steps involved look like this:

```
   1100100₂      100₁₀  ⎫  One hundred added
   1100100₂      100₁₀  ⎭  2 times
     1010₂        10₁₀  ⎫
     1010₂        10₁₀  ⎬  Ten added three times
     1010₂        10₁₀  ⎭
     0111₂         7₁₀     7 units added
  ─────────    ───────
  11101101₂  =   237₁₀
```

As you can see, this procedure ends with a binary result of 1110 1101, which is the binary representation for 237_{10}.

A flow chart for this procedure is shown in Figure 4-27. Here, the first step is to clear the binary result. We will be adding to this result, so it must start out at zero.

Next the program enters a loop in which it adds 100_{10} to the binary result the number of times indicated by the hundreds digit of the BCD number. The hundreds digit is loaded and tested for zero. If it is not zero, the hundreds digit is decremented and stored back in memory. Then the binary result is loaded and 100_{10} is added. The result is stored away and the loop is repeated. In our example, the hundreds digit was initially 2. Thus, this loop is repeated twice. The binary result will have the value 1100 1000_2 (200_{10}) when the hundreds digit is reduced to zero. At that time, the program exits the decision block via the "yes" line and immediately encounters a second loop.

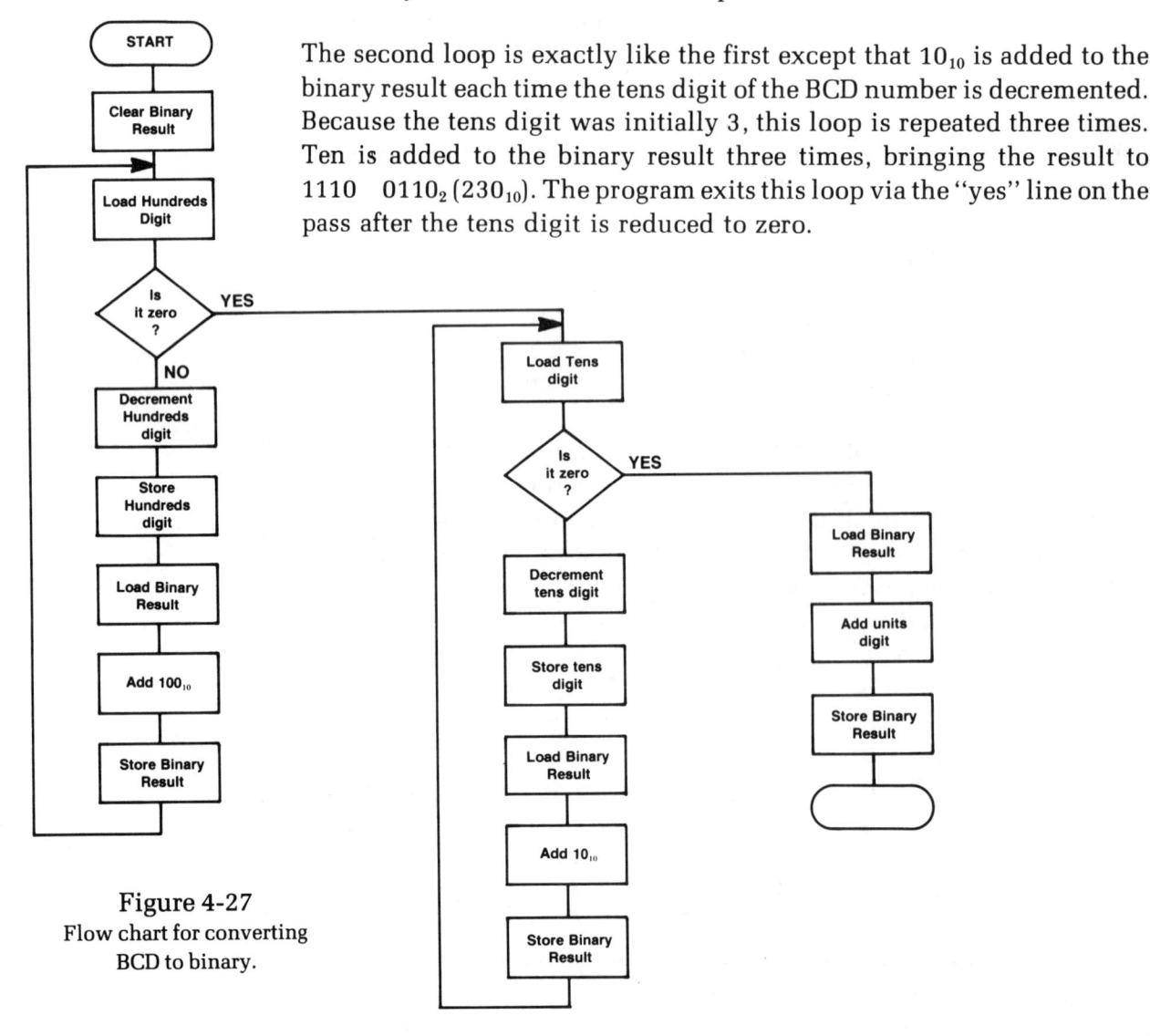

The second loop is exactly like the first except that 10_{10} is added to the binary result each time the tens digit of the BCD number is decremented. Because the tens digit was initially 3, this loop is repeated three times. Ten is added to the binary result three times, bringing the result to 1110 0110_2 (230_{10}). The program exits this loop via the "yes" line on the pass after the tens digit is reduced to zero.

Figure 4-27
Flow chart for converting BCD to binary.

The final three blocks add the units digit to the binary result. In our example, the units digit was 7_{10}. This brings the final binary result to $1110\ 1101_2$. Notice that this is the proper binary representation for the unsigned number 237_{10}.

A program that carries out this operation is shown in Figure 4-28. The three digit BCD number is stored in locations 28_{16}, 29_{16}, and $2A_{16}$. the binary equivalent will be computed and placed in location $2B_{16}$. Before reading further, try to work through the program. Refer to the flow chart and the comments column as you trace out the sequence that the MPU will follow.

HEX ADDRESS	HEX CONTENTS	MNEMONIC/HEX CONTENTS		COMMENTS
00	4F	CLRA		Clear the accumulator.
01	97	STA		Store 00
02	2B		2B	in location 2B. This clears the binary result.
03	96	LDA		Load direct
04	28		28	the hundreds BCD digit.
05	27	BEQ		If the hundreds digit is zero, branch
06	0B		0B	forward to the instruction in location 12_{16}.
07	4A	DECA		Otherwise, decrement the accumulator.
08	97	STA		Store the result as the new
09	28		28	hundreds BCD digit.
0A	96	LDA		Load direct
0B	2B		2B	the binary result.
0C	8B	ADD		Add immediate
0D	64		64	100_{10} to the binary result.
0E	97	STA		Store away the new
0F	2B		2B	binary result.
10	20	BRA		Branch
11	F1		F1	back to the instruction in location 03_{16}.
12	96	LDA		Load direct
13	29		29	the tens BCD digit.
14	27	BEQ		If the tens BCD digit is zero, branch
15	0B		0B	forward to the instruction in location 21_{16}.
16	4A	DECA		Otherwise, decrement the accumulator.
17	97	STA		Store the result as the new
18	29		29	tens BCD digit.
19	96	LDA		Load direct
1A	2B		2B	the binary result.
1B	8B	ADD		Add immediate
1C	0A		0A	10_{10} to the binary result.
1D	97	STA		Store away the new
1E	2B		2B	binary result.
1F	20	BRA		Branch
20	F1		F1	back to the instruction in location 12_{16}.
21	96	LDA		Load direct
22	2B		2B	the binary result.
23	9B	ADD		Add direct
24	2A		2A	the units BCD digit.
25	97	STA		Store away the new
26	2B		2B	binary result.
27	3E	HLT		Halt.
28	02		02	Hundreds BCD digit.
29	03		03	Tens BCD digit.
2A	07		07	Unit BCD digit.
2B	—		—	Reserved for the binary result.

Figure 4-28
Program for converting BCD to binary.

Now let's briefly go through the program. The first two instructions clear the location at which the binary number will be formed.

Next, the program enters the first loop, which is shown as the first shaded area. In this loop, the hundreds digit is loaded and tested for zero. If not zero, it is decremented and stored away. Then the binary result is loaded and 100_{10} is added. The result is stored away and the loop is repeated. Because the hundreds digit was 02 initially, 100_{10} will be added to the binary result twice. Thus, upon leaving this loop, the binary result will have the value 200_{10}. The MPU escapes this loop when the BEQ instruction at address 05 detects that the hundreds digit has been reduced to zero. The branch is to the second loop which is shown as an unshaded area.

In the second loop, the tens digit is loaded and tested for zero. If not zero, it is decremented and stored away. Then the binary number is loaded, 10_{10} is added, and the result is stored away. This loop is repeated until the tens digit is reduced to zero. Because the tens digit was initially three, the loop is repeated three times so that thirty is added to the binary number. The BEQ instruction at address 14_{16} allows the MPU to escape the loop and branch to the final program segment.

This final segment is the last shaded area. Here, the binary result is loaded and the units digit is added. This brings the binary result to 237_{10}. Then the result is stored and the program halts. While the number 237_{10} was used in this example, the program will convert any BCD number between 000 and 255_{10} to its binary equivalent.

Converting Binary to BCD

A microprocessor generally manipulates data in the form of straight binary numbers. However, before the results can be transmitted to the outside world, the data is often converted back to BCD. Frequently, this is an intermediate step in converting back to ASCII.

The binary-to-BCD conversion is the reverse of the process that occurred in the previous program. The MPU must determine how many times 100_{10} can be subtracted from the binary number. The answer becomes the hundreds BCD digit. After the 100_{10} has been subtracted as many times as possible, 10_{10} is subtracted repeatedly from the remaining number. The number of subtractions becomes the tens BCD digit. Finally, after 10_{10} has been subtracted as many times as possible, the remaining number becomes the units BCD digit.

For the number 1110 1101_2 (237_{10}), the process looks likes this:

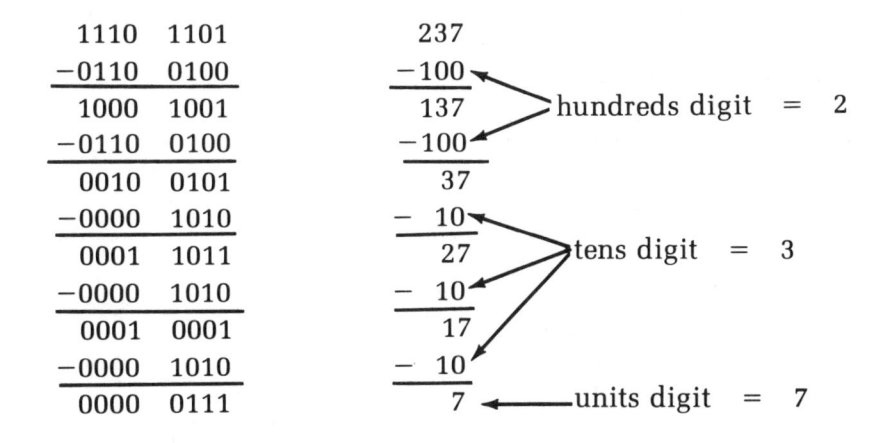

```
    1110  1101              237
   -0110  0100             -100 ⟵
    1000  1001              137    ⟩ hundreds digit  =  2
   -0110  0100             -100 ⟵
    0010  0101               37
   -0000  1010             - 10 ⟵
    0001  1011               27    ⟩ tens digit  =  3
   -0000  1010             - 10 ⟵
    0001  0001               17
   -0000  1010             - 10
    0000  0111                7 ⟵——— units digit  =  7
```

One hundred can be subtracted twice. Thus, the hundreds digit is 2_{10} or 0010_2. From the remainder, ten can be subtracted three times. Thus, the tens digit is 3_{10} or 0011_2. Finally, the remainder of 7_{10} or 0111_2 becomes the units digit. The BCD representation is 0010 0011 0111.

Figure 4-29 shows the flow chart for this procedure. The first three blocks clear the hundreds, tens, and units digits of the BCD result. Then the binary number that is to be converted to BCD is loaded and 100_{10} is subtracted. The outcome is tested to see if a negative number resulted. If not, the result is stored away. The hundreds digit is loaded, incremented, and stored away. The loop is repeated until 100_{10} can no longer be subtracted. In our example, 100_{10} can be subtracted twice. Therefore, the hundreds digit is incremented to 2. The third subtraction of 100_{10} gives a negative result. This allows the MPU to escape the first loop.

The second loop increments the tens digit to the proper value by subtracting 10_{10} repeatedly and keeping track of the number of subtractions. In our example, this loop is repeated three times. Consequently, the tens digit is incremented to 3. The binary number that is left over after 10_{10} is subtracted the proper number of times becomes the units digit. That is, upon escaping the second loop, the remaining binary number is stored in the units digit. In our example, the remaining number, and therefore the units digit, is 7.

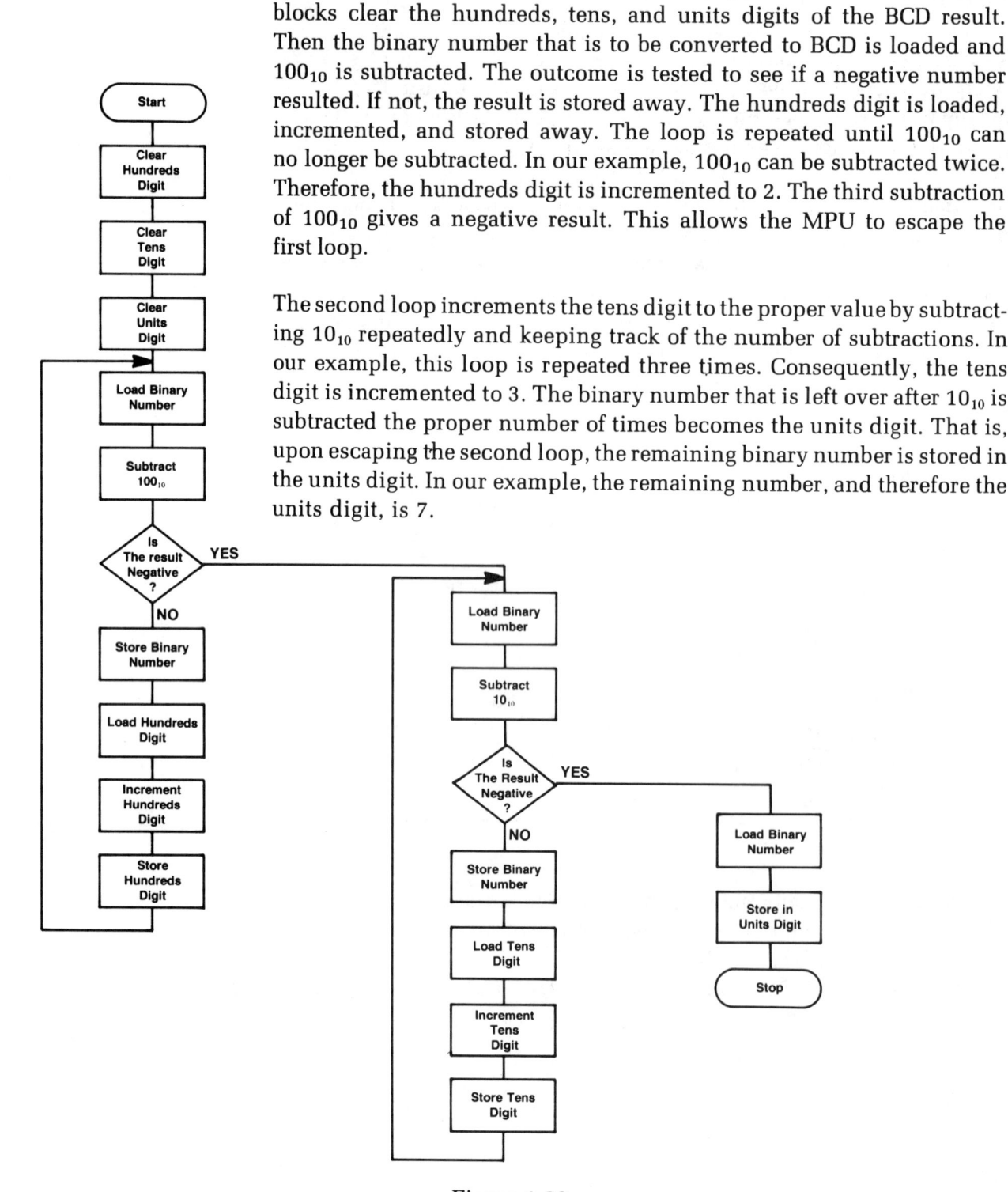

Figure 4-29
Flow chart for converting a binary number to a BCD number.

MICROPROCESSORS
Introduction to Programming | 4-51

The program that carries out this procedure is shown in Figure 4.30. At this point, you should be able to interpret the program from the comments given. However, a couple of points should be explained briefly. Any unsigned binary number from 0000 0000 to 1111 1111 can be placed at address $2A_{16}$. The computer will convert this number into its BCD equivalent. The hundreds digit will appear at address $2B_{16}$, the tens digit at $2C_{16}$, and the units digit at $2D_{16}$. The decision making instructions at addresses $0B_{16}$ and $1A_{16}$ are Branch if Carry Set (BCS) instructions. Because these instructions follow immediately after SUB instructions, the carry flag will indicate whether or not a borrow occurred. In effect, the BCS instructions decide: "Was the result of the subtraction a negative number?"

HEX ADDRESS	HEX CONTENTS	MNEMONIC/HEX CONTENTS	COMMENTS
00	4F	CLRA	Clear the accumulator.
01	97	STA	Store 00
02	2B	2B	in location $2B_{16}$. This clears the hundreds digit.
03	97	STA	Store 00
04	2C	2C	in location $2C_{16}$. This clears the tens digit.
05	97	STA	Store 00
06	2D	2D	in location $2D_{16}$. This clears the units digit.
07	96	LDA	Load direct
08	2A	2A	the binary number to be converted.
09	80	SUB	Subtract immediate
0A	64	64	100_{10}.
0B	25	BCS	If a borrow occurred, branch
0C	09	09	forward to the instruction in location 16_{16}.
0D	97	STA	Otherwise, store the result of the subtraction
0E	2A	2A	as the new binary number.
0F	96	LDA	Load direct
10	2B	2B	the hundreds digit of the BCD result.
11	4C	INCA	Increment the hundreds digit.
12	97	STA	Store the hundreds digit
13	2B	2B	back where it came from.
14	20	BRA	Branch
15	F1	F1	back to the instruction at address 07_{16}.
16	96	LDA	Load direct
17	2A	2A	the binary number.
18	80	SUB	Subtract immediate
19	0A	0A	10_{10}.
1A	25	BCS	If a borrow occurred, branch
1B	09	09	forward to the instruction in location 25_{16}.
1C	97	STA	Otherwise, store the result of the subtraction
1D	2A	2A	as the new binary number.
1E	96	LDA	Load direct
1F	2C	2C	the tens digit.
20	4C	INCA	Increment the tens digit.
21	97	STA	Store the tens digit
22	2C	2C	back where it came from.
23	20	BRA	Branch
24	F1	F1	back to the instruction at address 16_{16}.
25	96	LDA	Load direct
26	2A	2A	the binary number.
27	97	STA	Store it in
28	2D	2D	the units digit.
29	3E	HLT	Halt.
2A	—	—	Place binary number to be converted at this address.
2B	—	—	Hundreds digit ⎫
2C	—	—	Tens digit ⎬ Reserved for BCD result.
2D	—	—	Units digit ⎭

Figure 4-30
Program for converting a binary
number to a BCD number.

Self-Test Review

25. What is an algorithm?

26. What type of instruction is used to make a decision?

27. Refer to the program in Figure 4-24. If the multiplier is 8_{16} and the multiplicand is 15_{16}, how many times will the BEQ instruction be executed?

28. Refer to the program in Figure 4-26. What is the largest number that can be used as a dividend?

29. How could this program be modified so it could handle unsigned dividends up to 255_{10}?

30. When this program halts, where will the remainder be located?

31. Refer to the program in Figure 4-28. Assume that addresses 28_{16}, 29_{16}, and $2A_{16}$ contain 01, 09, and 08 respectively. How many times will 100_{10} be added to address $2B_{16}$?

32. How many times will 10_{10} be added?

33. Refer to the program in Figure 4-30. What is the purpose of the first four instructions?

34. What is the largest binary number that this program can convert to BCD?

Answers

25. An algorithm is a step-by-step procedure for doing a particular job.

26. Conditional branch instruction.

27. Nine times.

28. $+127_{10}$ or $0111\ 1111_2$.

29. Change the BMI instruction to BCS.

30. At address 11_{16}.

31. Once.

32. Nine times.

33. The first four instructions clear the locations where the BCD equivalent will be stored.

34. $1111\ 1111_2$ or 255_{10}.

ADDITIONAL INSTRUCTIONS

Before leaving this unit, you should also look at four additional instructions. The names, opcodes and mnemonics of these instructions are shown in Figure 4-31.

NAME	MNEMONIC	HEX OPCODE		
		IMMEDIATE	DIRECT	INHERENT
ADD WITH CARRY	ADC	89	99	
SUBTRACT WITH CARRY	SBC	82	92	
ARITHMETIC SHIFT ACCUMULATOR LEFT	ASLA			48
DECIMAL ADJUST ACCUMULATOR	DAA			19

Figure 4-31
Four new instructions.

Recall that the ALU always adds numbers as if they were unsigned binary numbers. When it adds 8-bit numbers, a carry often occurs from the MSB, setting the C flag. Thus, you can think of the carry flag as an extension of the accumulator. Let's look at some instructions that use the carry flag.

Add With Carry (ADC) Instruction

This instruction is similar to the ADD instruction discussed earlier with one important difference. If the carry bit is set to 1 before this instruction is executed, 1 is added to the LSB of the sum. However, if the carry bit is 0 prior to execution, then no carry is added. The effect is the same as having the carry bit from the previous operation added to the result of the present operation.

Like the ADD instruction, the ADC instruction has two addressing modes: immediate and direct. As shown in Figure 4-31, the opcode for "ADD With Carry Immediate" is 89_{16}, while the opcode for "Add With Carry Direct" is 99_{16}.

MICROPROCESSORS

Introduction to Programming 4-55

A primary use of the ADC instruction is to simplify **multiple-precision arithmetic**. Multiple-precision means that two or more bytes are used to represent a number. Recall that a single byte can represent unsigned binary numbers with values up to 255_{10}. However, much larger numbers can be represented by using two or more bytes. Two bytes (16 bits) can represent unsigned binary values up to $2^{16}-1$ or $65,535_{10}$. Three bytes can represent values to $16,777,215_{10}$; etc. Thus, the MPU can handle numbers of virtually any size simply by stringing the proper number of bytes together.

Suppose, for example, that two very large numbers are to be added. Figure 4-32 shows how the addition might look on paper. Notice that two 24-bit numbers are being added to form a 24-bit sum. The MPU is restricted to operating on data in 8-bit bytes. Thus, each quantity involved must be represented by three bytes.

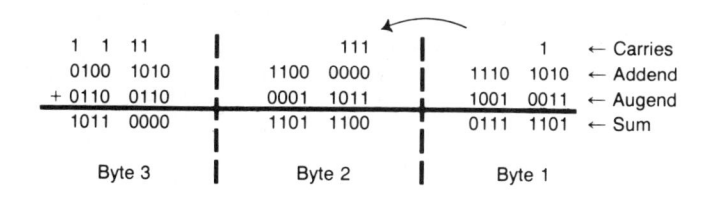

```
    1  1  11    |       111      |         1    ← Carries
    0100 1010   |   1100 0000    |   1110 1010  ← Addend
  + 0110 0110   |   0001 1011    |   1001 0011  ← Augend
    ─────────   |   ─────────    |   ─────────
    1011 0000   |   1101 1100    |   0111 1101  ← Sum

      Byte 3   |      Byte 2    |      Byte 1
```

Figure 4-32
Multiple-precision addition.

The MPU must be instructed to add the first byte of the addend to the first byte of the augend. This forms the first byte of the sum. Next the MPU must add the second bytes of the addend and augend. However, you will notice that there was a carry from the first byte to the second byte. If this carry is not added with the second bytes, the sum will be in error. The ADC instruction performs this operation automatically.

The program for adding the multiple-byte numbers could be written as shown in Figure 4-33. The three byte addend is stored in locations 13_{16} through 15_{16} while the augend is stored in locations 16_{16} through 18_{16}. Verify that the hexadecimal contents shown are the same as the binary values given in Figure 4-32.

HEX ADDRESS	HEX CONTENTS	MNEMONIC/HEX CONTENTS	COMMENTS
00	96	LDA	Load accumulator direct with
01	13	13	least significant byte of addend.
02	9B	ADD	Add direct
03	16	16	least significant byte of augend.
04	97	STA	Store result in
05	19	19	least significant byte of sum.
06	96	LDA	Load accumulator direct with
07	14	14	next byte of addend.
08	99	ADC	Add with carry direct
09	17	17	next byte of augend.
0A	97	STA	Store result in
0B	1A	1A	next byte of sum.
0C	96	LDA	Load accumulator direct with
0D	15	15	most significant byte of addend.
0E	99	ADC	Add with carry direct
0F	18	18	most significant byte of augend.
10	97	STA	Store result in
11	1B	1B	most significant byte of sum.
12	3E	HLT	Halt.
13	EA	EA	Least significant byte ⎫
14	C0	C0	⎬ Addend.
15	4A	4A	Most significant byte ⎭
16	93	93	Least significant byte ⎫
17	1B	1B	⎬ Augent
18	66	66	Most significant byte ⎭
19	—	—	Least significant byte ⎫
1A	—	—	⎬ Reserved for for sum.
1B	—	—	Most significant byte. ⎭

Figure 4-33
Program for multiple-precision addition.

The first two instructions add the least significant bytes of the addend and augend. The ADD instruction is used because the MPU need not consider earlier carries. The first byte of the resulting sum is stored in location 19_{16}.

The next two instructions add the next two bytes. This time the ADC instruction is used because the MPU must consider the carry from the previous addition. The second byte of the sum is placed in location $1A_{16}$.

Finally, the last two bytes are added using the ADC instruction. The final byte of the sum is stored in location $1B_{16}$. The program halts when the addition is completed.

Subtract With Carry (SBC) Instruction

This instruction simplifies multiple-precision subtraction. You will recall that during subtract operations the carry flag indicates whether or not a borrow operation occurred. For this reason, this instruction can be thought of as a subtract with borrow operation.

The SBC instruction subtracts the subtrahend from the minuend just as the SUB instruction did. However, the SBC instruction has an additional step in that the carry bit is also subtracted. As with the other add and subtract instructions, both immediate and direct addressing modes are possible. The opcodes for both modes are shown in Figure 4-31.

Figure 4-34 illustrates how multiple-precision numbers can be subtracted. Notice that, during the course of this subtraction, byte 1 must "borrow" a 1 from byte 2. The SBC instruction allows the MPU to do this.

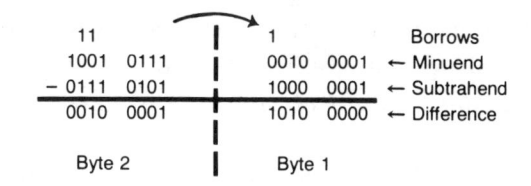

```
         11            |      1          Borrows
       1001  0111      |   0010  0001  ← Minuend
     − 0111  0101      |   1000  0001  ← Subtrahend
       0010  0001      |   1010  0000  ← Difference

        Byte 2         |    Byte 1
```

Figure 4-34
Multiple-precision subtraction.

HEX ADDRESS	HEX CONTENTS	MNEMONIC/HEX CONTENTS	COMMENTS
00	96	LDA	Load accumulator direct with
01	0D	0D	least significant byte of minuend.
02	90	SUB	Subtract direct
03	0F	0F	least significant byte of subtrahend.
04	97	STA	Store result in
05	11	11	least significant byte of difference.
06	96	LDA	Load accumulator direct with
07	0E	0E	most significant byte of minuend.
08	92	SBC	Subtract with carry
09	10	10	most significant byte of the subtrahend.
0A	97	STA	Store result in
0B	12	12	most significant byte of the difference.
0C	3E	HLT	Halt
0D	21	21	Least significant byte ⎱ Minuend.
0E	97	97	Most significant byte ⎰
0F	81	81	Least significant byte ⎱ Subtrahend.
10	75	75	Most significant byte ⎰
11	—	—	Least significant byte ⎱ Difference.
12	—	—	Most significant byte ⎰

Figure 4-35
Program for multiple-precision subtraction.

Figure 4-35 shows a simple program for performing the subtraction. The double-precision minuend is at addresses $0D_{16}$ and $0E_{16}$, while the subtrahend is at addresses $0F_{16}$ and 10_{16}. The program computes the difference and stores it in location 11_{16} and 12_{16}.

The first instruction loads the least significant byte of the minuend. Next, the corresponding byte of the subtrahend is subtracted. Since the subtrahend byte is larger, a borrow is indicated. Consequently, the carry flag is set to 1. Notice that the SUB rather than the SBC instruction is used. This is done because the first byte should not be affected by any previous borrow or carry. The result of the subtraction is stored away to become the least significant byte of the difference.

The most significant byte of the minuend is loaded next and the corresponding byte of the subtrahend is subtracted. However, this time the SBC instruction is used. And since the carry flag is set, an additional 1 is subtracted from the minuend to complete the borrow operation. The result of the subtraction becomes the most significant byte of the difference.

Arithmetic Shift Accumulator Left (ASLA) Instruction

The ASLA instruction shifts the contents of the accumulator to the left by one space. Figure 4-36 illustrates the repeated execution of this instruction. Figure 4-36A shows the condition of the accumulator and carry bit. In this example, the number in the accumulator is arbitrarily assumed to be 10_{10}. Also, the carry bit is arbitrarily assumed to be cleared.

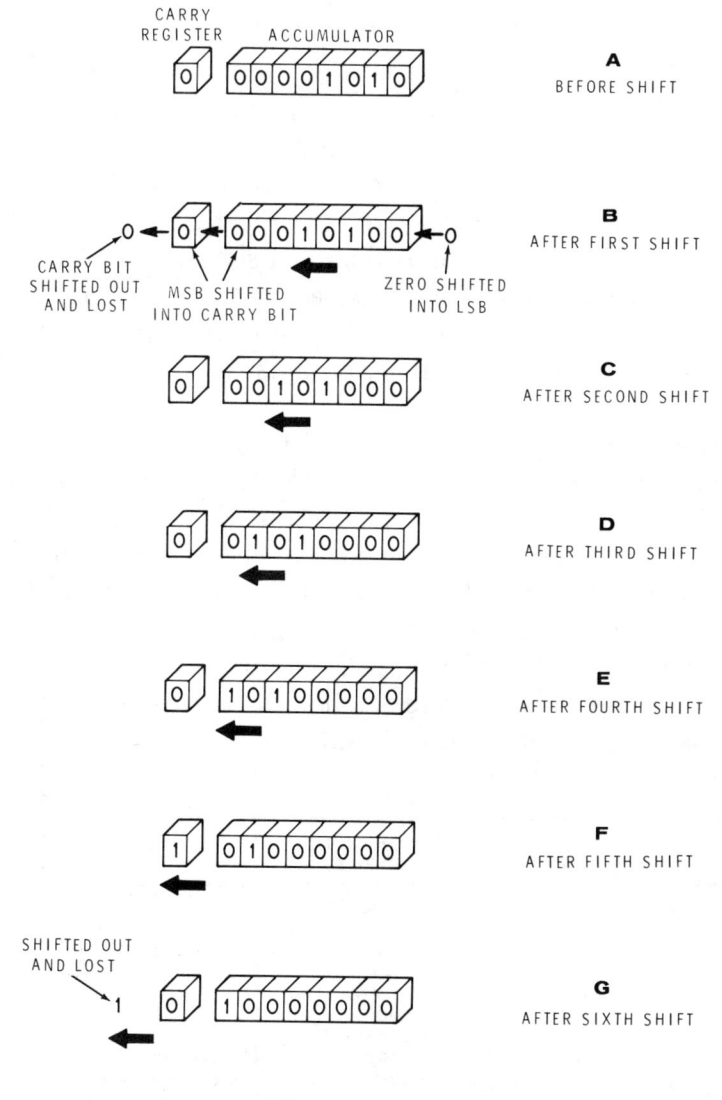

Figure 4-36
Repeatedly implementing the ASLA instruction.

Figure 4-36B shows the contents of the accumulator and carry bit after the ASLA instruction is executed. Notice that the number is shifted one bit to the left. Also, a 0 is shifted into the LSB. At the same time, the MSB is shifted into the carry bit. The old carry bit is shifted out and is lost.

You can understand one purpose of this instruction by examining the numbers in the accumulator before and after the instruction is executed. Before the shift, the number is 10_{10}; afterwards the number is 20_{10}. The number has been doubled. If you will try several different examples, you will see that any binary number can be multiplied by two simply by shifting the number one bit to the left. This holds true as long as the capacity of the accumulator is not exceeded.

Figures 4-36C through G show what happens if the MPU continues to execute ASLA instructions. The number continues to double. The number in the accumulator becomes 40_{10}, then 80_{10}, then 160_{10}. Each shift multiplies the number by two. On the fifth shift, the capacity of the accumulator is exceeded as the most significant 1 bit shifts into the carry bit. After the sixth shift, the leading 1 is lost altogether. When you use this technique to multiply by two or by a power of two, you must not exceed the capacity of the accumulator.

Another use of the ASLA instruction is to pack two BCD digits in a single byte. Earlier when we worked with BCD numbers, we assumed that each BCD digit resided in a separate memory byte. However, because a BCD digit has only 4 bits, memory space is wasted by assigning each digit a separate byte. Frequently, it is more desirable to "pack" two BCD digits into a single byte. A simple routine for doing this is shown in Figure 4-37. If dozens of BCD numbers are to be manipulated, a routine that uses a procedure similar to this can save substantial memory space. At the same time, it puts the BCD numbers into a more convenient and usable form.

HEX ADDRESS	HEX CONTENTS	MNEMONICS/HEX CONTENTS	COMMENTS
00	96	LDA	Load into the accumulator direct
01	0C	0C	the unpacked most significant BCD digit.
02	48	ASLA	
03	48	ASLA	Shift it four places to
04	48	ASLA	the left.
05	48	ASLA	
06	9B	ADD	Add
07	0D	0D	the unpacked least significant BCD digit.
08	97	STA	Store the result as
09	0B	0B	two packed BCD digits.
0A	3E	HLT	Halt
0B	—	—	Packed BCD digits.
0C	—	—	Most significant BCD digit (unpacked).
0D	—	—	Least significant BCD digit (unpacked).

Figure 4-37
Program for packing two
BCD digits into a single byte.

MICROPROCESSORS

The procedure carried out by the program is quite simple. The most significant BCD digit is loaded into the accumulator. It is then shifted four places to the left to make room for the least significant BCD digit. The least significant digit is then added to form a packed BCD number. The resulting single byte number is stored back in memory.

Decimal Adjust Accumulator (DAA) Instruction

Earlier in this unit, the problems of converting from BCD to binary and back again were considered. While this conversion is frequently necessary, many microprocessors have some limited BCD arithmetic capabilities. Our hypothetical MPU has an instruction that greatly simplifies BCD arithmetic. It is called the Decimal Adjust Accumulator (DAA) Instruction. When used in conjunction with the ADD or ADC instruction, it allows the MPU to add BCD numbers directly without an intermediate binary conversion.

Recall that the ALU adds input data bytes as if they were unsigned binary numbers. Therefore, if two BCD digits are added, the sum may be incorrect. For example, assume that the MPU adds the BCD digits 0111 and 0101. The ALU produces the result

```
      1
   0111
 + 0101
 ──────
   1100
```

This answer is the correct **binary** result, 12_{10}; but it is not the proper BCD result. Recall that in BCD, 12_{10} is represented as 0001 0010. Notice that you can obtain the proper BCD result by adding 0110_2 to the binary result. The addition of 0110_2 is necessary anytime that the binary result exceeds 1001_2.

To produce the proper BCD result when adding two BCD digits, the MPU must follow this procedure:

1. If the sum is 1001_2 or less, use the sum as the single digit BCD result.

2. If the sum is greater than 1001_2, add 0110_2 and use the result as a 2-digit BCD number.

The situation becomes more complex when packed BCD numbers are added. Consider adding 0111 1001$_{BCD}$ (79$_{10}$) to 0111 0011$_{BCD}$ (73$_{10}$). The ALU adds these packed BCD numbers as if they were unsigned binary numbers. The result is

```
  11    1
0111 1001
0111 0011
---------
1110 1100
```

Notice that the result is not a BCD number, since both 4-bit groups exceed 1001$_2$. Even so, the sum can be converted to BCD by adding 0110$_2$ to each 4-bit group. The result is

```
  1  1 1  1
    1110 1100
    0110 0110
    -----------
  1 0101 0010
```

There is a carry from bit 7 that sets the carry bit. This carry bit becomes the most significant BCD digit. Thus, the final BCD result is 0001 0101 0010$_{BCD}$ or 152$_{10}$.

If you consider all possible combinations of BCD numbers, you will find that four different situations exist:

1. When some BCD numbers are added, the binary result produced by the ALU is equal to the proper BCD representation. This occurs when both BCD digits of the result are 1001$_2$ or less.

2. The binary sum is adjusted by adding 06$_{16}$ if the least significant BCD digit exceeds 1001$_2$ but the most significant BCD digit does not.

3. The binary sum is adjusted by adding 60$_{16}$ if the most significant BCD digit exceeds 1001$_2$ but the least significant BCD digit does not.

4. The binary sum is adjusted by adding 66$_{16}$ if both BCD digits exceed 1001$_2$.

While this procedure could be programmed, it would be much better if the MPU performed these operations automatically. Fortunately, our hypothetical microprocessor does this. The programmer simply informs the MPU that the numbers being added are BCD numbers. The MPU automatically computes the proper BCD result. The way the programmer informs the MPU is via the DAA instruction. When the DAA instruction is placed immediately after an ADD or ADC instruction, the MPU automatically converts the sum to the proper BCD number.

Suppose, for example, that you wish to add two BCD numbers. Assume the numbers are 3792_{10} and 5482_{10}. Naturally, the sum should be 9274_{10}. A program for solving this problem is shown in Figure 4-38. The BCD addend (3792_{10}) is in addresses $0F_{16}$ and 10_{16}. The augend (5482_{10}) is in locations 11_{16} and 12_{16}. The BCD sum will be placed in locations 13_{16} and 14_{16}.

HEX ADDRESS	HEX CONTENTS	MNEMONICS/HEX CONTENTS	COMMENTS
00	96	LDA	Load into the accumulator direct
01	10	10	the least significant half of the addend.
02	9B	ADD	Add
03	12	12	the least significant half of the augend.
04	19	DAA	Decimal adjust the sum to BCD.
05	97	STA	Store the result as the
06	14	14	least significant half of the sum.
07	96	LDA	Load
08	0F	0F	the most significant half of the addend.
09	99	ADC	Add
0A	11	11	the most significant half of the augend.
0B	19	DAA	Decimal adjust the sum to BCD.
0C	97	STA	Store the result as the
0D	13	13	most significant half of the sum.
0E	3E	HLT	Halt
0F	37	37	} BCD Addend
10	92	92	
11	54	54	} BCD Augend.
12	82	82	
13	—	—	} Reserved for BCD sum.
14	—	—	

Figure 4-38
Program for adding multiple-precision BCD numbers.

The first two instructions add the least significant halves of the addend and augend. The ADD instruction is followed immediately by the DAA instruction. Therefore, the sum is adjusted to a packed BCD number. The result is stored in location 14_{16} as the lower half of the BCD sum.

Next, the upper halves of the addend and augend are added. This time, the ADC instruction is used because the carry from the previous addition must be added in. Again, the DAA instruction adjusts the sum to BCD. The result is stored as the upper half of the BCD sum.

The DAA instruction must be used properly. It can be used only with addition. Also, it must be used immediately after the addition instruction. It can not be used to convert just any binary number to BCD. It only converts the sum of BCD numbers to the BCD format.

Self-Test Review

35. How is the ADC instruction different from the ADD instruction?

36. How is the SBC instruction different from the SUB instruction?

37. A primary use of the ADC and SBC instructions is in _____-_____ arithmetic.

38. The accumulator contains the number 7_{10}. If two ASLA instructions are executed, what number will be in the accumulator?

39. What is the difference between packed and unpacked BCD numbers?

40. When adding unpacked BCD numbers, under what condition must 0110_2 be added to the sum in order to form a BCD sum?

41. What instruction is used to automatically adjust the sum to the proper BCD format when two BCD numbers are added?

42. Can the DAA instruction be used after a SUB instruction to produce the proper BCD difference when two BCD numbers are subtracted?

Answers

35. When the ADC instruction is executed, an additional 1 is added to the sum if the carry flag is set.

36. When the SBC instruction is executed, an additional 1 is subtracted from the difference if the carry flag is set.

37. Multiple-precision.

38. The first ASLA instruction multiplies the number by two, giving 14_{10}. The second ASLA doubles this number, giving 28_{10}.

39. With packed BCD numbers, each byte contains two BCD digits. With unpacked BCD numbers, each byte contains one BCD digit.

40. When two BCD digits are added, 0110_2 must be added to the sum if the sum exceeds 1001_2.

41. The decimal adjust accumulator (DAA) instruction.

42. No. The DAA instruction is used in conjunction with add instructions only.

UNIT 4 SUMMARY

1. The instructions in "straight line" programs are executed one after another in the order in which they are written.

2. The process called looping allows a section of a program to be repeated as often as it is needed.

3. Jump and branch instructions allow a programmer to create program loops.

4. Branch instructions use relative addressing to control the operation of the program loop.

5. The relative address is a value that is added to the MPU program counter to determine the address of the next instruction to be executed in the program.

6. The relative address is found in the second byte of a branch instruction.

7. Branching forward, the relative address is a positive value. Branching backward, the relative address is a negative value written in two's complement form.

8. The unconditional branch instruction forces the MPU to always branch when the instruction is executed.

9. The conditional branch instruction will only force the MPU to branch when a specified condition is met. If the condition is not met, the branch instruction will be ignored.

10. Conditional execution of a branch instruction is determined by the status of four condition code registers. These single bit registers are called carry, negative, zero, and overflow.

11. The carry condition code register acts as an extension of the accumulator. If a carry or borrow is generated during an arithmetic operation, the carry register bit is set. If no carry or borrow occurred, the bit is cleared.

12. The negative condition code register monitors the MSB of the accumulator. If that bit is one, the negative register is set. If the MSB of the accumulator is zero, the negative register bit is cleared. Not all accumulator operations affect the negative condition code register.

13. The zero condition code register monitors all bits of the accumulator. If they are all zero after an operation, the zero register bit is set. If any of the accumulator bits are one, the zero register bit is cleared. Most accumulator operations affect the status of the zero register.

14. The overflow condition code register monitors the status of the sign bits of the two numbers being added, subtracted, or compared, and the sign bit of the result. During addition, if the sign bits of the two numbers are different, there is no overflow, the register is cleared. If the sign bits of the two numbers, and the result are the same, there is, again, no overflow. If the sign bits of the two numbers are the same, but the sign bit of the result is different, there is an overflow, and the overflow register is set.

15. Writing complex and lengthy programs requires some form of organization for problem solving. Generally there are three steps to writing a program: define the problem, map or flowchart the solution, write the program.

16. A flowchart is a form of project blueprint.

17. Standard flowchart symbols should be used to allow any programmer to interpret the program solution.

18. The flowchart symbol terminal indicates the beginning and end of a flowchart.

19. The flowchart symbol operations box is used to represent a transfer process, an algebraic process, or any process that doesn't have a specific symbol.

20. The flowchart symbol decision box is used to indicate a logical choice between two conditions.

21. Flowchart flow lines and connectors are used to tie the symbols and sections in a flowchart together.

22. The five most common mathematical symbols used in a flowchart are: equal to, greater than, less than, greater than or equal to, and less than or equal to.

23. The unconditional branch in a flowchart corresponds to the unconditional branch in a program.

24. The conditional branch in a flowchart corresponds to the conditional branch in a program.

25. An algorithm is a step-by-step procedure for doing a particular job that cannot be handled directly by the microcomputer, such as multiplication.

26. Multiplication in a 6800-based microcomputer is best handled by a algorithm that uses a program loop to repeatedly add a number to itself the number of times specified by the multiplier.

27. Division in a 6800-based microcomputer is best handled by an algorithm that uses a program loop to repeatedly subtract the divisor from the dividend, and keep track of the count and any remainder.

28. Most data received by or transmitted from a microcomputer is in ASCII coded form.

29. The least significant four bits of an ASCII coded character represent the BCD value of the corresponding numeral.

30. To convert ASCII coded numerals to BCD code, subtract the binary value 00110000 from the ASCII code.

31. Multiple-digit BCD code is converted to binary by adding the positional weight of each code digit to itself, in binary, the number of times specified by the digit. Then all of the binary sums are added together.

32. Binary data is converted to BCD code by repeatedly subtracting the binary equivalent of the hundreds digit, the tens digit, and the ones digit from the binary value, beginning with the hundreds digit. The number of times each digit can be subtracted represents the BCD value for that decimal positional weight.

33. To convert BCD code to ASCII code, add the binary value 00110000 to the BCD code.

34. Multiple-precision numbers use two or more bytes to represent the number.

35. The add with carry and subtract with carry (borrow) instructions are used to simplify multiple-precision arithmetic.

36. The ASLA instruction shifts the MSB of the accumulator into the carry condition code register and a zero into the LSB.

37. The DAA instruction is used to adjust the result after a BCD arithmetic operation. A carry into the next digit position is recorded in the carry condition code register.

Perform Experiments 5 and 6 at the end of Book 2.

Unit 5

THE 6800 MICROPROCESSOR — PART 1

INTRODUCTION

Until now, we have confined our study to a simple hypothetical microprocessor. Obviously, though, this hypothetical model must be very close to the real thing, since we have been running its programs on the ET-3400 or ET-3400A Microprocessor Trainer. In this unit you will begin your study of the actual microprocessor upon which our hypothetical model is based. The microprocessor in the ET-3400 Trainer is called the 6800. It was first released by Motorola in the mid 1970's. Today, it is being second sourced by several other companies.

The microprocessor in the ET-3400A Trainer is called the 6808. The primary difference between the 6808 and 6800 microprocessors is the means by which clock signals are generated. The 6808 has an on-chip clock circuit, the 6800 does not. Because of this one difference, there will also be some chip pin assignments that are not identical. These differences will be discussed in more detail in Unit Seven of this course. However, in all other characteristics, such as the instruction set and internal registers, the 6800 and 6808 are identical. It is these identical characteristics which are the subject of this and the following unit. Therefore, throughout this unit reference is made to the 6800 microprocessor only. But, the data presented also applies to the 6808 in the ET-3400A Trainer.

There are other microprocessors that have similar instruction sets, architecture, and addressing modes. Thus, by becoming familiar with the 6800 (6808) you should be able to understand and use a wide range of microprocessors.

You already know a great deal about the 6800 and/or 6808 microprocessor. You have been programming this device for the past several units. The main difference between the 6800 (6808) microprocessor and our hypothetical model is complexity. As you will see, the 6800 (6808) is a vastly expanded version of our hypothetical model.

UNIT OBJECTIVES

When you have completed this unit you will be able to:

1. Draw a programming model of the 6800 MPU.

2. Explain the purpose of each block in a simplified block diagram of the 6800 MPU.

3. Using Appendix A and Figure 5-24 as references, explain the operation of all the instructions discussed in this unit.

4. Write simple programs that use indexed and extended addressing.

5. Using Figure 5-24 as a guide, find the opcode, number of MPU cycles, number of bytes, and effects on the condition code flags of every instruction discussed in this unit.

ARCHITECTURE OF THE 6800 MPU

In computer jargon, the word architecture is used to describe the computer's style of construction, its register size and arrangement, its bus configuration, etc. The architecture of our hypothetical microprocessor is shown for one last time in Figure 5-1. By now you should be quite familiar and comfortable with this architecture.

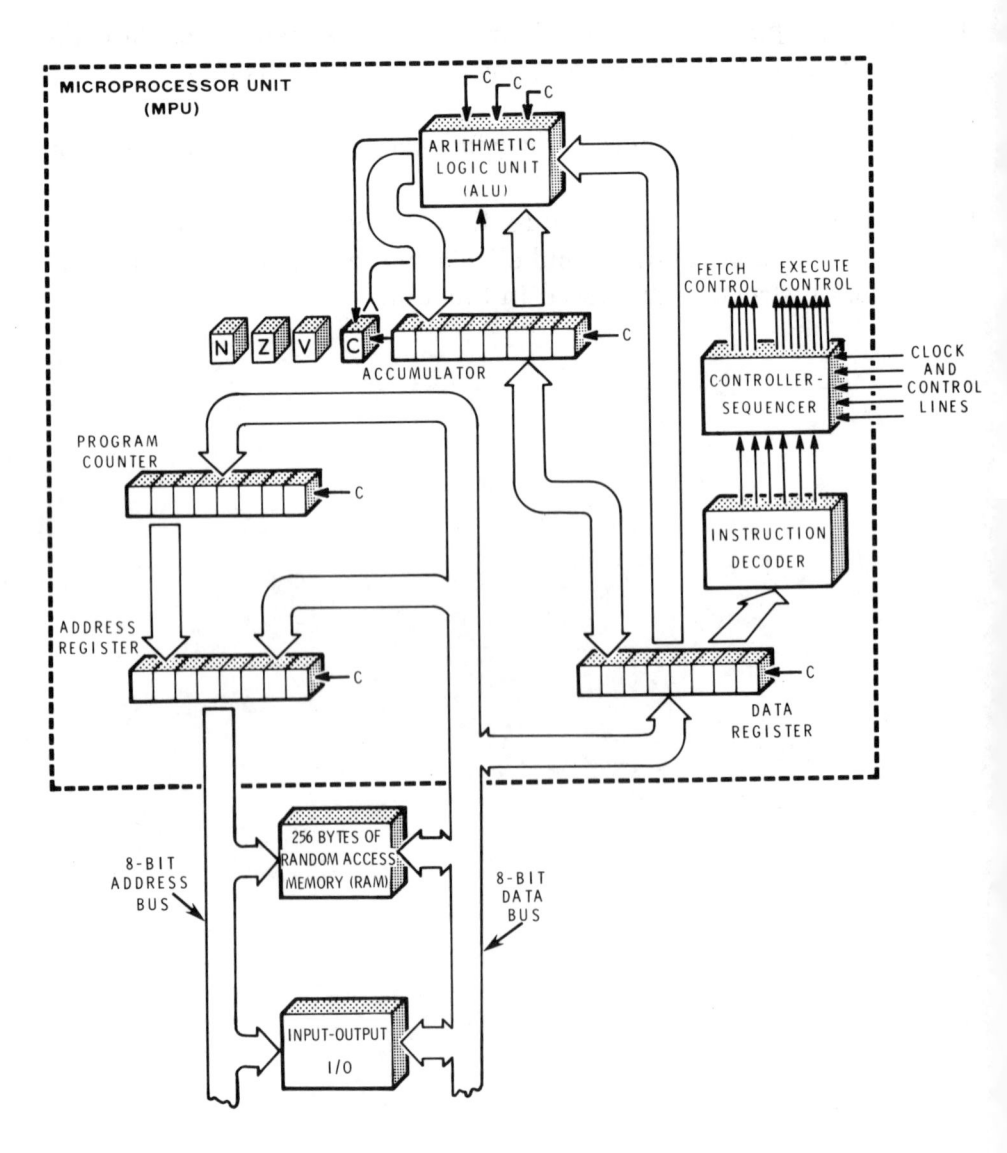

Figure 5-1
Architecture of the hypothetical microcomputer.

The only reason for showing the details of the model is to give you an idea of what goes on inside the integrated circuit. In an actual microprocessor the internal structure is often so complex that we become bogged down in details if we attempt to analyze it too closely. For this reason, a programming model is generally used when a microprocessor is being introduced for the first time. In the programming model, the emphasis is shifted upward by an order of magnitude. Any register or circuit that cannot be directly controlled by the programmer is simply ignored. Consider the data register for example. There are no instructions that give the programmer direct control over this register. That is, there are no instructions such as Load Data Register, Store Data Register, etc. All data register activity is controlled strictly by the MPU. Thus, the programmer can simply ignore the existence of this register. The same is true of the address register, the instruction decoder, the controller-sequencer, etc. Therefore, the programming model of our hypothetical MPU can be represented as shown in Figure 5-2. This simple diagram is sufficient for most programming applications since it shows all the registers that can be directly controlled by the program.

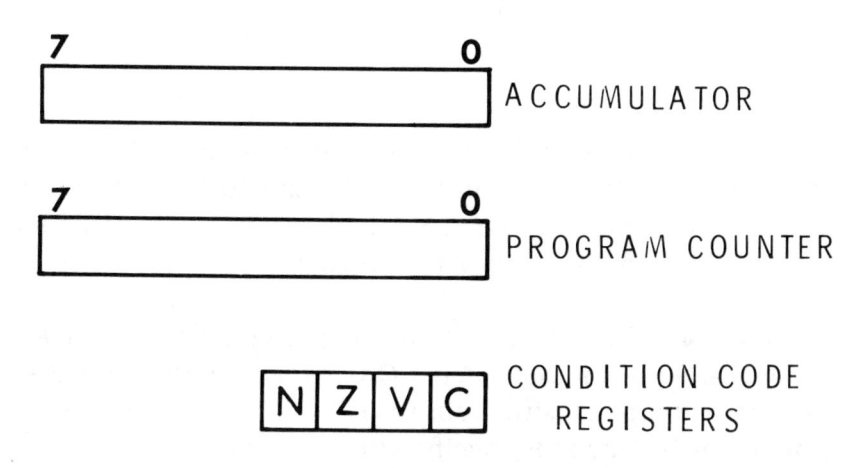

Figure 5-2
Programming model of the hypothetical MPU.

Programming Model of the 6800 MPU

The 6800 MPU is much more complex than our hypothetical MPU. Consequently, a programming model of the 6800 makes a good starting point. The programming model is shown in Figure 5-3.

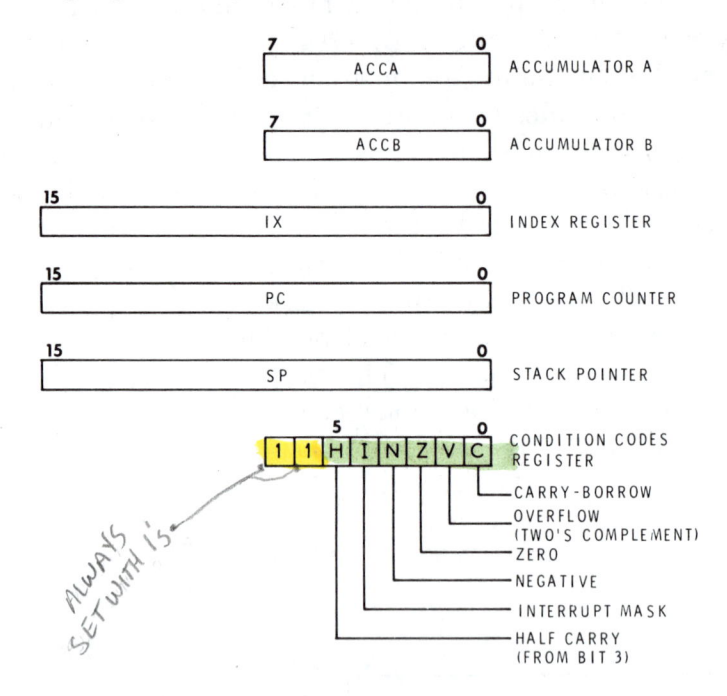

Figure 5-3
Programming model of the 6800 MPU.

You will notice immediately that the 6800 MPU has several additional registers. However, only two of these, the index register and the stack pointer, are actually new to you. Let's look at the major differences between this MPU and our hypothetical model.

Two Accumulators   The 6800 MPU has two accumulators instead of one. They are called accumulator A (ACCA) and accumulator B (ACCB). Each has its own group of instructions associated with it. The names and mnemonics of the instructions specify which accumulator is to be used. Thus, there are instructions such as:

>Load Accumulator A (LDAA)
>Load Accumulator B (LDAB)
>Store Accumulator A (STAA)
>Store Accumulator B (STAB)

Notice that a letter is added to both the name and the mnemonic to indicate which accumulator is being used.

From your previous programming experience, you can visualize the value of a second accumulator. For example consider a program in which the MPU counts the number of times that some operation occurs. In the past, we stored the number that the accumulator was presently working on, loaded the count into the accumulator; incremented the count; stored the count; and reloaded the original number. With a second accumuator, none of this is necessary. We can simply maintain the count in accumulator B while working with the number in accumulator A. In fact, we can perform any arithmetic or logic operation on two different numbers without having to shift the numbers back and forth between memory.

16-Bit Program Counter The program counter in the 6800 has 16_{10} bits rather than 8. Thus, it can specify $65,536_{10}$ different addresses. This means that a 6800 based microcomputer can have up to $65,536_{10}$ bytes of memory. Most applications require substantially less memory than this maximum number. Fortunately, we can use as little or as much memory as we need up to the 2^{16} byte limit.

Since the program counter has 16_{10} bits, the address bus must also be 16-bits wide. Contrast this with the 8-bit address bus of our hypothetical machine.

You may wonder how we specify a 16-bit address with an 8-bit byte. The obvious answer is that two 8-bit bytes are required. Recall that in the direct addressing mode, the address was specified by a single 8-bit byte. The 6800 microprocessor retains this addressing mode. However, since an 8-bit address can specify only 256_{10} addresses, the 6800 MPU can use this mode only if the operand is in the first 256_{10} bytes of memory. To reach higher addresses, a new addressing mode called **extended addressing** must be used. In the extended addressing mode, two bytes are used to represent each address. This addressing mode will be discussed in more detail later. For now, keep in mind that there are $65,536_{10}$ possible addresses. The lowest address is 0000_{16} and the highest is $FFFF_{16}$. Using extended addressing, we have access to any location in memory, but a 2-byte address is required.

Condition Code Registers The 6800 MPU has six condition codes. Four of these are almost identical to those discussed in an earlier unit. These include the negative (N), zero (Z), overflow (V) and carry (C) condition codes. The difference arises because there are two accumulators in the 6800 MPU. Thus, the carry flag is set whenever there is a carry from either accumulator. By the same token, an overflow in either accumulator will set the V flag. Later in this unit, you will see how the condition codes are affected by each instruction.

Two new condition codes are shown in Figure 5-3. The I flag is called an interrupt mask. We will discuss this flag later when you study interrupts. The other is called the half carry flag (H). The H flag is set when there is a carry from bit 3 of the accumulator. The MPU uses this flag to determine how to implement the decimal adjust instruction.

These six flags make up bits 0 through 5 of an 8-bit register. Bits 6 and 7 of the condition code register are not used and are always set to 1. Additional details of the condition codes will be brought out as the need arises.

Index Register The index register is a special-purpose, 16-bit register that greatly increases the power of the microprocessor. It allows a powerful address mode called indexed addressing. We will examine this addressing mode later in this unit. For now, consider the index register to be just another working register. The fact that it holds two bytes instead of one can be put to good use. The MPU has instructions that allow the index register to be loaded from two adjacent memory bytes. Another instruction allows us to store the contents of the index register in two adjacent memory locations. This allows us to move data in 2-byte groups. Also, the index register can be incremented and decremented. This lets us maintain 16-bit tallies.

Stack Pointer The stack pointer is another special-purpose 16-bit register. It allows the MPU and the programmer to use a section of RAM as a last in, first out (LIFO) memory. This capability is extremely valuable when using subroutines or when processing interrupts. These aspects of the stack pointer will be discussed in the next unit. For the time being let's consider the stack pointer to be another 16-bit working register. It too can be loaded from memory, stored in memory, incremented, and decremented.

Block Diagram of the 6800 MPU

Now that you have seen the programming model of the 6800 MPU, take a look at the block diagram. A simplified block diagram is shown in Figure 5-4. Several data paths, most control lines, and a temporary storage register have been omitted in favor of the major data paths and registers.

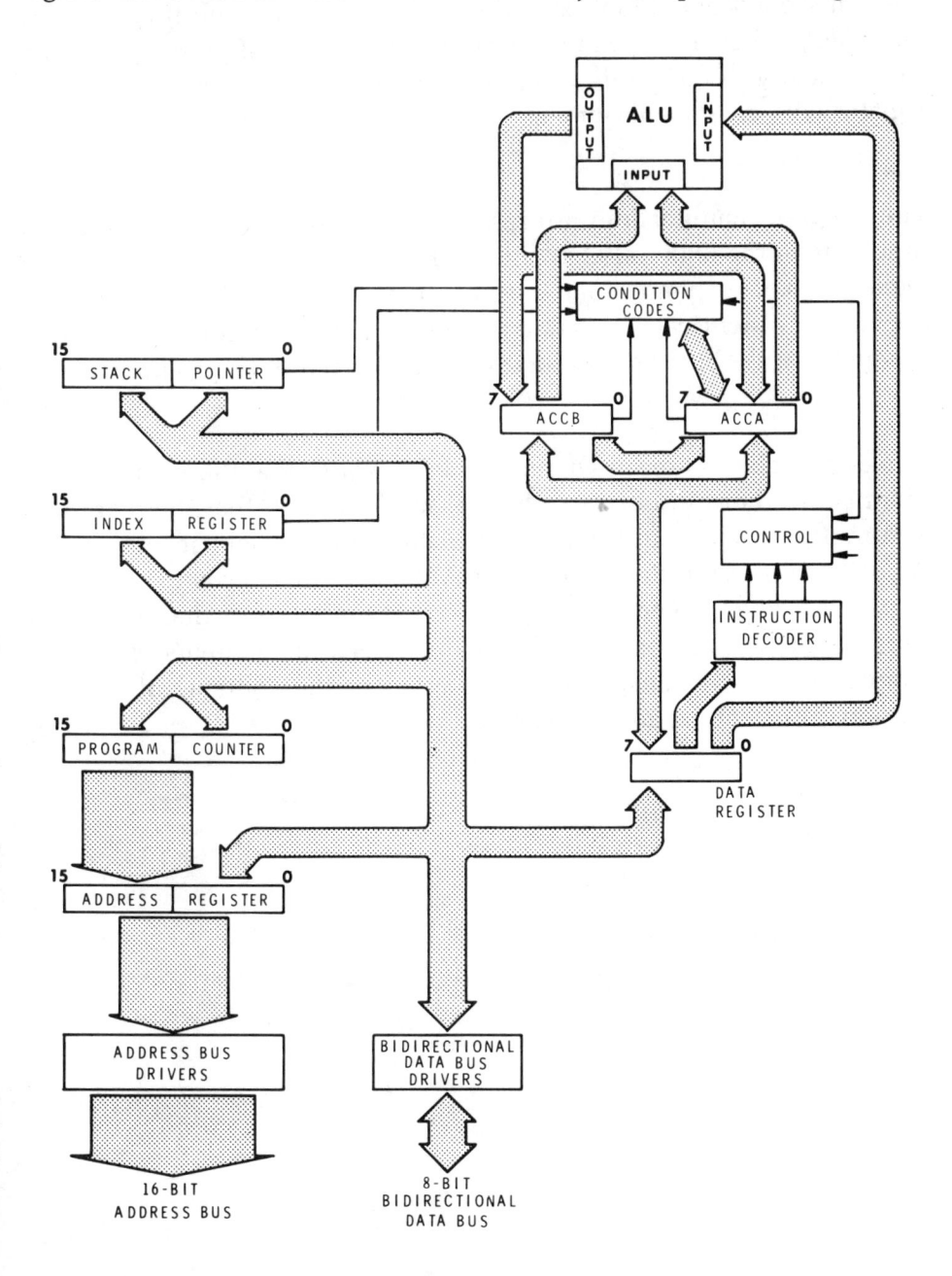

Figure 5-4
Simplified block diagram of the
6800 MPU.

The 16-bit registers are shown on the left. These registers are primarily concerned with addressing memory. Since the address bus has 16-bits, all registers associated with addressing must also have 16-bits. Any of the 16-bit registers can be loaded from the data bus. However, because the data bus has only 8-bits, two operations are required to load the 16-bit registers. The upper half of the affected register is always loaded first. Then, a second operation loads the lower half. Although this requires separate MPU cycles, the microprocessor takes care of these operations automatically. For example, a single instruction can load the 16-bit index register with two memory bytes.

The program counter and address register perform exactly the same functions in the 6800 MPU as they did in our hypothetical model. The fetch and execute phases for the immediate and direct addressing modes are virtually identical. The same is true of the relative addressing mode except that the 8-bit relative address is added to the 16-bit program count.

The 8-bit registers are shown on the right. Notice that these circuits are identical to those in our hypothetical model except that there are two accumulators. The condition code registers monitor both accumulators. Also, the two accumulators share the ALU. This allows you to keep track of two separate mathematical operations at more or less the same time. This arrangement is particularly flexible since the contents of one accumulator can be transferred to the other or the contents of the two accumulators can be added together.

Self-Test Review

1. The microprocessor on which our hypothetical model and the ET-3400 are based is the ___6800___ MPU.

2. A major difference between our hypothetical model and the 6800 MPU is that the latter has two ___ACCUMULATORS___.

3. The program counter in the 6800 MPU has ___16 BITS___ bits.

4. How wide is the address bus in a 6800-based microcomputer? ___16 BITS___

5. What is the range of addresses in the 6800 MPU? ___0000-FFFF___

6. List the six condition code flags. ___NZVCIH___

7. Besides the program counter, what other 16-bit registers are used in the 6800 MPU? ___INDEX STACK ADDRESS___

8. In the 6800 MPU, does each accumulator have its own carry flag? ___NO___

Answers

1. 6800.

2. Accumulators.

3. 16_{10}.

4. 16_{10} bits.

5. From 0000 to $65,535_{10}$ or 0000 to $FFFF_{16}$.

6. Carry — borrow (C)
   Overflow (V)
   Zero (Z)
   Negative (N)
   Interrupt Mask (I)
   Half Carry (H)

7. Index register and stack pointer.

8. No, the two accumulators share a common carry flag.

INSTRUCTION SET OF THE 6800 MPU

The 6800 MPU has about 100_{10} basic instructions. Moreover, when all the different addressing modes are considered, there are 197_{10} different opcodes to which the MPU will respond.

These instructions can be broken down into seven general categories. While some of the categories overlap, the general classifications of instructions are: arithmetic, data handling, logic, data test, index register and stack pointer, jump and branch, and condition code. In this unit we will discuss most of these instructions in detail. The handful of instructions that are not discussed in this unit will be described in the following unit.

In this section we will not be concerned with addressing modes. Therefore, no opcodes are given. Later, we will look at the various addressing modes and opcodes. For now, though, let's identify the instructions by their names, mnemonics, and operations. You will see what each instruction does and how it affects the various condition code registers.

Because of the large number of instructions covered in this section, the explanations will be general and brief. You are **not** expected to remember all the details of every instruction. Appendix A of this course contains a detailed listing of each instruction. It explains every detail of the various instructions. After reading this section, turn to Appendix A and look over the explanations given there. In the future, when you are in doubt as to exactly what a particular instruction does, look it up in Appendix A.

Arithmetic Instructions

Figure 5-5 shows the arithmetic instructions of the 6800 MPU. The name of each instruction is given on the left. The next column contains the mnemonics. The center column gives a shorthand description of what the instruction does. The right-hand columns show how the various condition code registers are affected.

ACCUMULATOR AND MEMORY OPERATIONS	MNEMONIC	BOOLEAN/ARITHMETIC OPERATION (All register labels refer to contents)	H (5)	I (4)	N (3)	Z (2)	V (1)	C (0)
Add	ADDA	A + M → A	↕	•	↕	↕	↕	↕
	ADDB	B + M → B	↕	•	↕	↕	↕	↕
Add Acmltrs	ABA	A + B → A	↕	•	↕	↕	↕	↕
Add with Carry	ADCA	A + M + C → A	↕	•	↕	↕	↕	↕
	ADCB	B + M + C → B	↕	•	↕	↕	↕	↕
Complement, 2's (Negate)	NEG	00 − M → M	•	•	↕	↕	①	②
	NEGA	00 − A → A	•	•	↕	↕	①	②
	NEGB	00 − B → B	•	•	↕	↕	①	②
Decimal Adjust, A	DAA	Converts Binary Add. of BCD Characters into BCD Format*	•	•	↕	↕	↕	③
Subtract	SUBA	A − M → A	•	•	↕	↕	↕	↕
	SUBB	B − M → B	•	•	↕	↕	↕	↕
Subract Acmltrs.	SBA	A − B → A	•	•	↕	↕	↕	↕
Subtr. with Carry	SBCA	A − M − C → A	•	•	↕	↕	↕	↕
	SBCB	B − M − C → B	•	•	↕	↕	↕	↕

*Used after ABA, ADC, and ADD in BCD arithmetic operation; each 8-bit byte regarded as containing two 4-bit BCD numbers. DAA adds 0110 to lower half-byte if least significant number >1001 or if preceding instruction caused a Half-carry. Adds 0110 to upper half-byte if most significant number >1001 or if preceding instruction caused a Carry. Also adds 0110 to upper half-byte if least significant number >1001 and most significant number = 9.

(Bit set if test is true and cleared otherwise)
① (Bit V) Test: Result = 10000000?
② (Bit C) Test: Result ≠ 00000000?
③ (Bit C) Test: Decimal value of most significant BCD Character greater than nine?
(Not cleared if previously set.)

Figure 5-5
Arithmetic instructions.

To be certain you have the idea, let's go through the first instruction in detail. The first instruction is the add instruction. Actually, since the 6800 has two accumulators, there are two add instructions. Their mnemonics are ADDA and ADDB. Notice that the final letter of the mnemonic indicates which accumulator (A or B) is involved. The shorthand representation of the operation is: A+M→A. The note at the top of this column tells you that the register labels refer to the contents of the register. Thus, A means the contents of accumulator A and M means the contents of the affected memory location. The symbol (→) means "Transfer into." Therefore, A+M→A means "Add the contents of accumulator A to the contents of the affected memory location and transfer the sum into accumulator A."

To see how the condition code flags are affected, you simply look over to the right under whatever condition code you are interested in. Generally, the condition code is either unaffected or is tested and set accordingly. When the condition code is unaffected, this is represented by the symbol (•). For example, none of the arithmetic instructions affect the I flag. Most of the arithmetic instructions test the condition codes and set them if the condition exists. For example, if the result of an arithmetic operation is zero, the Z flag is set to 1. If this condition does not exist, the Z flag is reset or cleared to 0. The symbol ($\updownarrow$) means "test and set if true; clear otherwise." Occasionally, a note is necessary to describe some unusual situation regarding the condition code. This is represented by a number within a circle. The notes are given at the bottom of the drawing.

The ADDA and ADDB instructions are self-explanatory. The ABA instruction adds the contents of accumulator A to the contents of accumulator B. The result is stored in accumulator A.

The add with carry instructions are identical to those discussed earlier for our hypothetical machine. Notice that the carry bit is added in with the sum.

Because two's complement arithmetic is used in the 6800 MPU, instructions are provided that allow us to take the two's complement of a number. The negate instruction subtracts the contents of the affected register from 00_{16}. This is the same as taking the two's complement of the number. The affected register can be any memory location (M) or either accumulator (A or B). Thus, there are three different negate instructions. Keep in mind that NEG means "take the two's complement of the affected memory location;" NEGA means "take the two's complement of accumulator A;" etc.

Notice that the NEG instruction allows us to operate on a byte in memory without first fetching the operand from memory. In the past, we have loaded the operand, performed the operation, and then stored the new operand. However, the 6800 allows us to perform certain operations on the operand without first fetching it from memory. Several examples of this will be pointed out as we progress through the instruction set.

The decimal adjust instruction performs exactly as it did in our hypothetical machine. The note immediately under the table summarizes its operation. It must also be pointed out that this instruction works only with accumulator A.

The subtract and the subtract with carry instructions are self-explanatory. They perform as described earlier for our hypothetical MPU. The 6800 MPU has an additional subtract instruction. The SBA instruction subtracts the contents of accumulator B from the contents of accumulator A. The resulting difference is placed in accumulator A.

Data Handling Instructions

Figure 5-6 shows the largest group of instructions used by the 6800 MPU. These can be loosely categorized as data handling instructions.

The clear instructions allow us to clear a memory location or either accumulator. In the past, we have cleared bytes of memory by first clearing the accumulator and then storing the resulting 00_{16} in the proper memory location. However, the CLR instruction allows us to clear a memory location with a single instruction. Notice that some new entries appear in the condition code registers column. R means that the condition code is always reset or cleared to 0. S means that the code is always set to 1.

The decrement instruction allows us to subtract 1 from a memory location or from either accumulator. The DEC instruction is especially valuable since it allows us to decrement a byte in memory with a single instruction. Previously we have loaded the byte, decremented it, and then stored it back in memory.

The increment instructions are similar except they allow us to add 1 to a memory location or one of the accumulators. Notice that the INC instruction allows us to maintain a tally in memory without having to load it, increment it, and then store it away.

MICROPROCESSORS

The 6800 Microprocessor — Part 1 | **5-17**

The load accumulator instructions are self-explanatory. Notice that either accumulator can be loaded from memory.

ACCUMULATOR AND MEMORY OPERATIONS	MNEMONIC	BOOLEAN/ARITHMETIC OPERATION (All register labels refer to contents)	H (5)	I (4)	N (3)	Z (2)	V (1)	C (0)
Clear	CLR	00 → M	•	•	R	S	R	R
	CLRA	00 → A	•	•	R	S	R	R
	CLRB	00 → B	•	•	R	S	R	R
Decrement	DEC	M − 1 → M	•	•	↕	↕	④	•
	DECA	A − 1 → A	•	•	↕	↕	④	•
	DECB	B − 1 → B	•	•	↕	↕	④	•
Increment	INC	M + 1 → M	•	•	↕	↕	⑤	•
	INCA	A + 1 → A	•	•	↕	↕	⑤	•
	INCB	B + 1 → B	•	•	↕	↕	⑤	•
Load Acmltr	LDAA	M → A	•	•	↕	↕	R	•
	LDAB	M → B	•	•	↕	↕	R	•
Rotate Left	ROL	M	•	•	↕	↕	⑥	↕
	ROLA	A	•	•	↕	↕	⑥	↕
	ROLB	B	•	•	↕	↕	⑥	↕
Rotate Right	ROR	M	•	•	↕	↕	⑥	↕
	RORA	A	•	•	↕	↕	⑥	↕
	RORB	B	•	•	↕	↕	⑥	↕
Shift Left, Arithmetic	ASL	M	•	•	↕	↕	⑥	↕
	ASLA	A	•	•	↕	↕	⑥	↕
	ASLB	B	•	•	↕	↕	⑥	↕
Shift Right, Arithmetic	ASR	M	•	•	↕	↕	⑥	↕
	ASRA	A	•	•	↕	↕	⑥	↕
	ASRB	B	•	•	↕	↕	⑥	↕
Shift Right, Logic	LSR	M	•	•	R	↕	⑥	↕
	LSRA	A	•	•	R	↕	⑥	↕
	LSRB	B	•	•	R	↕	⑥	↕
Store Acmltr	STAA	A → M	•	•	↕	↕	R	•
	STAB	B → M	•	•	↕	↕	R	•
Transfer Acmltrs	TAB	A → B	•	•	↕	↕	R	•
	TBA	B → A	•	•	↕	↕	R	•

④ (Bit V) Test: Operand = 10000000 prior to execution?
⑤ (Bit V) Test: Operand = 01111111 prior to execution?
⑥ (Bit V) Test: Set equal to result of N ⊕ C after shift has occurred.

Figure 5-6
Data handling instructions.

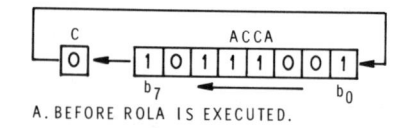

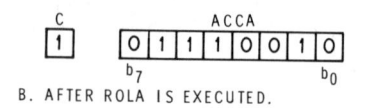

Figure 5-7
Executing the ROLA instruction.

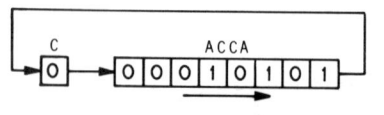

Figure 5-8
Executing the RORA instruction.

The rotate left instructions allow us to shift the contents of the accumulator or a memory location without losing bits of data. Consider the ROLA instruction as an example. When this instruction is executed, the A accumulator and the carry bit form a 9-bit circulating register. That is, they form a closed loop as shown in Figure 5-7A. When ROLA is executed, the data is rotated clockwise. The MSB of A shifts into the carry register. Simultaneously, the contents of A are shifted left. Notice that the carry bit is not lost. Instead it is shifted into the LSB of the accumulator.

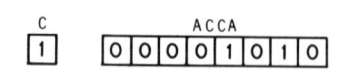

While the usefulness of this instruction may not be obvious, it is a valuable tool. For example, it could be used to determine parity. By repeatedly rotating left and testing the C flag, you could determine the number of 1's in the byte. Once you know this, you could easily generate the proper parity bit.

The ROL instruction allows you to rotate a memory byte to the left while it is still in memory. ROLB allows you to rotate the B accumulator to the left. In each case, the C register is used as a ninth bit.

The rotate right instructions are identical except that the direction of rotation is reversed. Figure 5-8 illustrates the execution of the RORA instruction. This instruction is also valuable. Suppose for example that we wish to know if the number in the accumulator is even or odd. This is determined by the LSB of the number. If LSB = 1, the number is odd; if LSB = 0, the number is even. One way to determine this is to rotate the number to the right so that the LSB is in the C register. We could then test the C register to see if it is set or cleared. Notice that the number could then be restored to its original value by the ROLA instruction.

The arithmetic shift left instruction was discussed earlier in our hypothetical MPU. The ASLA instruction performs exactly as described in the previous unit. However, notice that the 6800 MPU also has an ASLB instruction that performs the same operation with accumulator B. Also, it has an ASL instruction that allows us to perform this operation on a byte that is in memory. Figure 5-9 illustrates the execution of this instruction.

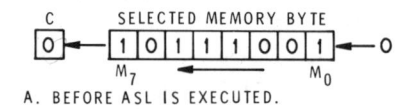

Figure 5-9
Executing the ASL instruction.

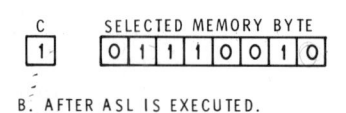

While there is only one type of shift left instruction, there are two types of shift right instructions. Let's discuss the arithmetic shift right instructions first.

When an **arithmetic** shift right instruction is executed, the number in the affected register is shifted right one position. The LSB goes into the C register. B_1 shifts to B_0, etc. B_7 shifts into B_6. However, B_7 itself remains unchanged. Figure 5-10 illustrates the execution of the ASRB instruction. Notice that there are also ASRA and ASR instructions listed in Figure 5-6. These perform the same type of shift operation but on accumulator A and the selected memory byte respectively.

The logic shift right instructions are different in that they do not retain the sign bit. When a logic shift right is executed, the contents of the affected register are shifted to the right. The LSB goes into the carry register. The MSB is filled with a 0. For example, the LSR instruction is illustrated in Figure 5-11. While this instruction shifts the selected memory locations, LSRA and LSRB can be used to perform similar operations on accumulators A and B respectively.

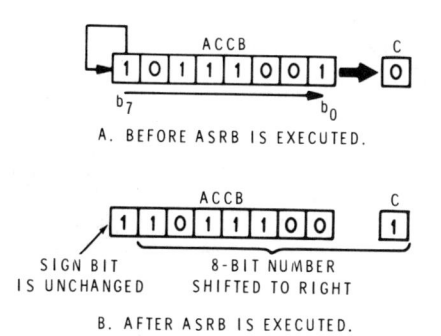

Figure 5-10
Executing the ASRB instruction.

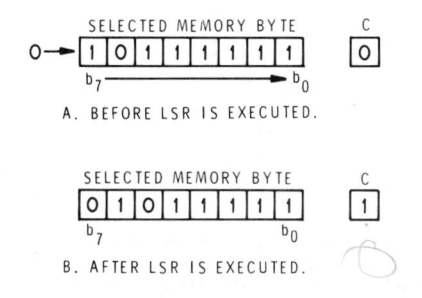

Figure 5-11
Executing the LSR instruction.

Referring back to Figure 5-6, the store accumulator instructions are self-explanatory.

The final data handling instructions are the transfer accumulator instructions. TAB copies the contents of accumulator A into accumulator B. After this instruction is executed, the number originally in accumulator A will be in both accumulators. TBA does just the opposite. It copies the contents of accumulator B into accumulator A. After TBA is executed, the number originally in accumulator B will be in both accumulators.

Logic Instructions

The logic instructions in the 6800 MPU are similar to those in our hypothetical MPU. Figure 5-12 shows the 6800's logic instructions.

ACCUMULATOR AND MEMORY OPERATIONS	MNEMONIC	BOOLEAN/ARITHMETIC OPERATION (All register labels refer to contents)	COND. CODE REG. 5 H	4 I	3 N	2 Z	1 V	0 C
And	ANDA	A • M → A	•	•	↕	↕	R	•
	ANDB	B • M → B	•	•	↕	↕	R	•
Complement, 1's	COM	$\overline{M}$ → M	•	•	↕	↕	R	S
	COMA	$\overline{A}$ → A	•	•	↕	↕	R	S
	COMB	$\overline{B}$ → B	•	•	↕	↕	R	S
Exclusive OR	EORA	A ⊕ M → A	•	•	↕	↕	R	•
	EORB	B ⊕ M → B	•	•	↕	↕	R	•
Or, Inclusive	ORA	A + M → A	•	•	↕	↕	R	•
	ORB	B + M → B	•	•	↕	↕	R	•

Figure 5-12
Logic instructions.

There is one AND instruction for each accumulator. The contents of the specified accumulator are ANDed bit-for-bit with the contents of the selected memory location. The result is placed back in the accumulator. This is identical to the AND instruction in our hypothetical machine.

The complement instructions allow you to take the 1's complement of the number in the affected register. COM allows you to complement a byte in memory.

COMA and COMB allow you to complement the contents of accumulators A and B respectively. In each case, all 1's are changed to 0's and all 0's are changed to 1's.

The exclusive OR instructions work like the one in our hypothetical MPU. The contents of the specified accumulator are exclusively ORed bit-for-bit with the contents of the selected memory location. The result is stored back in the specified accumulator.

The inclusive OR is similar except that the contents of the specified accumulator are inclusively ORed with the contents of the selected memory location.

Data Test Instructions

These are a powerful group of instructions that allow us to compare operands in several different ways. In previous units, you had experience comparing operands. The most frequently used method was to subtract one operand from another and test the result for zero or negative. In many cases, the numeric result of the subtraction was unimportant. We needed to know only if the result was zero or minus. The data test instructions allow us to make several different tests without actually producing an unwanted numeric result. These instructions are shown in Figure 5-13.

ACCUMULATOR AND MEMORY OPERATIONS	MNEMONIC	BOOLEAN/ARITHMETIC OPERATION (All register labels refer to contents)	H (5)	I (4)	N (3)	Z (2)	V (1)	C (0)
Bit Test	BITA	A • M	•	•	↕	↕	R	•
	BITB	B • M	•	•	↕	↕	R	•
Compare	CMPA	A − M	•	•	↕	↕	↕	↕
	CMPB	B − M	•	•	↕	↕	↕	↕
Compare Acmltrs	CBA	A − B	•	•	↕	↕	↕	↕
Test, Zero or Minus	TST	M − 00	•	•	↕	↕	R	R
	TSTA	A − 00	•	•	↕	↕	R	R
	TSTB	B − 00	•	•	↕	↕	R	R

Figure 5-13
Data test instructions.

The bit test instructions are very similar to the AND instructions. In both cases, the contents of the specified accumulator are ANDed with the contents of the selected memory location. The difference is that with the bit test instruction no logical product is produced. Neither the contents of the accumulator nor memory are altered in any way. However, the condition code registers are affected just as if the AND operation had taken place. Consider the BITA instruction. When executed, A is ANDed with M. If the result is 00_{16}, the Z register is set. Otherwise, the Z register is cleared. If the MSB of the result is 1, the N flag is set. However, the contents of the accumulator and memory are unaffected.

In the same way, the compare instructions are similar to subtract instructions except that the resulting numeric difference is ignored. For example, when the CMPA instruction is executed, the contents of the selected memory location are subtracted from the contents of accumulator A. The condition codes are affected just as if a difference had been produced. However, the original contents of accumulator A and memory are unaffected.

The compare accumulators instruction (CBA) works the same way. The condition codes are set as if the contents of B were subtracted from the contents A. However, the contents of the accumulators are unaffected.

Finally, the test for zero or minus instruction allows you to test the number in one of the accumulators or the memory to see if it is negative or zero. When this instruction is executed, the MPU looks at the number in question and sets the N and Z flags accordingly. The number itself is not changed.

Index Register and Stack Pointer Instructions

The index register and stack pointer are 16-bit registers. Figure 5-14 shows eleven instructions that allow us to control the operation of these registers. Because of the 16-bit format, the load, store, and compare instructions are slightly different from those discussed earlier.

INDEX REGISTER AND STACK POINTER OPERATIONS	MNEMONIC	BOOLEAN/ARITHMETIC OPERATION	5 H	4 I	3 N	2 Z	1 V	0 C
Compare Index Reg	CPX	$(X_H/X_L) - (M/M+1)$	•	•	①	↕	②	•
Decrement Index Reg	DEX	$X - 1 \rightarrow X$	•	•	•	↕	•	•
Decrement Stack Pntr	DES	$SP - 1 \rightarrow SP$	•	•	•	•	•	•
Increment Index Reg	INX	$X + 1 \rightarrow X$	•	•	•	↕	•	•
Increment Stack Pntr	INS	$SP + 1 \rightarrow SP$	•	•	•	•	•	•
Load Index Reg	LDX	$M \rightarrow X_H, (M+1) \rightarrow X_L$	•	•	③	↕	R	•
Load Stack Pntr	LDS	$M \rightarrow SP_H, (M+1) \rightarrow SP_L$	•	•	③	↕	R	•
Store Index Reg	STX	$X_H \rightarrow M, X_L \rightarrow (M+1)$	•	•	③	↕	R	•
Store Stack Pntr	STS	$SP_H \rightarrow M, SP_L \rightarrow (M+1)$	•	•	③	↕	R	•
Indx Reg → Stack Pntr	TXS	$X - 1 \rightarrow SP$	•	•	•	•	•	•
Stack Pntr → Indx Reg	TSX	$SP + 1 \rightarrow X$	•	•	•	•	•	•

① (Bit N) Test: Sign bit of most significant (MS) byte of result = 1?
② (Bit V) Test: 2's complement overflow from subtraction of LS bytes?
③ (Bit N) Test: Result less than zero? (Bit 15 = 1)

Figure 5-14
Index register and stack pointer instructions.

The compare index register (CPX) instruction allows us to compare the 16-bit number in the index register with any two consecutive bytes in memory. Recall that the index register (X) will hold two bytes. The higher byte is identified as X_H while the lower byte is called X_L. When the CPX instruction is executed, X_H is compared with the 8-bit byte in the specified memory location (M). Also, X_L is compared with the byte immediately following the specified memory location (M+1). The comparison is the same as if M and M+1 were subtracted from X_H and X_L except that no numeric difference is produced. Neither X nor M is changed in any way. However, the N, Z, and V condition codes are affected as shown in Figure 5-14. Generally, the Z code is the one we are interested in since it tells us whether or not an exact match exists between the index register and the two bytes in memory.

The next four instructions are self-explanatory. They allow us to increment and decrement either the index register or the stack pointer. For one thing, these instructions allow us to maintain two separate 16-bit tallies simultaneously. However, the real value of these instructions and their associated registers will be discussed later.

The load and store instructions for the 16-bit registers are shown next in Figure 5-14. Since these are two byte registers, the LDX and LDS instructions must load two bytes from memory. In the case of the index register, the specified memory byte (M) is loaded into the upper half of the index register (X_H). An instant later, the next byte in memory (M+1) is automatically loaded into the lower half of the index register (X_L). Thus, the operation can be described as: M→X_H, (M+1) → X_L.

Because the stack pointer is also a 16-bit register, the load stack pointer instruction (LDS) works the same way. Its operation can be described as: M → SP_H, (M+1) → SP_L. Here, SP_H refers to the upper half of the stack pointer while SP_L refers to the lower half.

When the contents of the 16-bit registers are being stored, the operation is reversed. For example, the STX instruction stores X_H in M and X_L in M+1. A similar instruction, STS, allows us to store the contents of the stack pointer in the same way.

The final two instructions in this group allow us to transfer numbers between these two 16-bit registers. The TXS instruction loads the stack pointer with the contents of the index register minus one. The TSX instruction loads the index register with the contents of the stack pointer plus one. A more detailed discussion of these two important registers and their associated instructions will be given in the next unit.

Branch Instructions

The branch instructions are shown in Figure 5-15. Two additional instructions are also thrown in since they affect the program counter.

BRANCH OPERATIONS	MNEMONIC	BRANCH TEST	5 H	4 I	3 N	2 Z	1 V	0 C
Branch Always	BRA	None	•	•	•	•	•	•
Branch If Carry Clear	BCC	C = 0	•	•	•	•	•	•
Branch If Carry Set	BCS	C = 1	•	•	•	•	•	•
Branch If = Zero	BEQ	Z = 1	•	•	•	•	•	•
Branch If ≥ Zero	BGE	N ⊕ V = 0	•	•	•	•	•	•
Branch If > Zero	BGT	Z + (N ⊕ V) = 0	•	•	•	•	•	•
Branch If Higher	BHI	C + Z = 0	•	•	•	•	•	•
Branch If ≤ Zero	BLE	Z + (N ⊕ V) = 1	•	•	•	•	•	•
Branch If Lower Or Same	BLS	C + Z = 1	•	•	•	•	•	•
Branch If < Zero	BLT	N ⊕ V = 1	•	•	•	•	•	•
Branch If Minus	BMI	N = 1	•	•	•	•	•	•
Branch If Not Equal Zero	BNE	Z = 0	•	•	•	•	•	•
Branch If Overflow Clear	BVC	V = 0	•	•	•	•	•	•
Branch If Overflow Set	BVS	V = 1	•	•	•	•	•	•
Branch If Plus	BPL	N = 0	•	•	•	•	•	•
No Operation	NOP	Advances Prog. Cntr. Only	•	•	•	•	•	•
Wait for Interrupt	WAI		•	①	•	•	•	•

① (Bit I) Set when interrupt occurs. If previously set, a Non-Maskable Interrupt is required to exit the wait state.

Figure 5-15
Jump and branch instructions.

MICROPROCESSORS

The 6800 Microprocessor — Part 1 | **5-25**

Nine of these instructions were discussed in the previous unit. These are: Branch Always (BRA); Branch If Carry Clear (BCC); Branch If Carry Set (BCS); Branch If Equal Zero (BEQ); Branch If Not Equal Zero (BNE); Branch If Minus (BMI); Branch If Plus (BPL); Branch If Overflow Clear (BVC); and Branch If Overflow Set (BVS).

Before we discuss the new branch instructions, here are some of the symbols we will be using. The symbol ($\geq$) means "is greater than or is equal to"; ($>$) means "is greater than"; ($\leq$) means "is less than or is equal to"; ($<$) means "is less than"; and ($\neq$) means "is not equal to."

Now consider the Branch If Greater Than or Equal instruction (BGE). This instruction is normally used after a subtract or compare instruction. It will cause a branch operation if the two's complement value in the accumulator is greater than or equal to the two's complement operand in memory. This condition is indicated by the N and V flags having the same value. The MPU determines if this condition is met by exclusively ORing N and V and examining the result.

Three simple examples may help illustrate the operation of this instruction. Let's start with a number in the accumlator that is greater than the operand in memory:

Number in Accumulator = 00000010_2
Operand in Memory   = 00000001_2

When the operand is subtracted, the result is 00000001_2. With this result, both N and V are cleared to 0. Notice that N and V are equal and N $\oplus$ V = 0. If the BGE instruction followed the subtract operation, the branch would be implemented.

Now see what happens when the number in the accumulator is equal to the operand:

Number in Accumulator = 00000010_2
Operand in Memory   = 00000010_2

When the operand is subtracted, the result is 00000000_2. Again N and V are cleared to 0. Thus, N and V are still equal and N $\oplus$ V = 0. Again, the BGE instruction would cause a branch to occur.

Finally, note what happens when the number in the accumulator is smaller:

$$\text{Number in Accumulator} = 00000001_2$$
$$\text{Operand in Memory} = 00000010_2$$

When the operand is subtracted, the result is 11111111_2. This time N is set but V is cleared. Thus, N and V are not equal. Therefore, N $\oplus$ V = 1. In this case, the BGE conditions are not met and no branch will occur. The branch occurs if the two's complement value in the accumulator is greater than or equal to the two's complement operand in memory.

Next, consider the Branch If Greater Than (BGT) instruction. This instruction is normally used immediately after a subtract or compare operation. The branch will occur only if the two's complement minuend was greater than the two's complement subtrahend. By trying several examples as we did above, you will find that the branch conditions are met when Z = 0 and N = V.

The Branch If Higher (BHI) instruction is similar to the BGT instruction except that it is concerned with **unsigned** numbers. BHI is normally used after a subtract or compare operation. The branch will occur only if the unsigned minuend was greater than the unsigned subtrahend. By trying several different examples, you can prove that this occurs only when the C and Z flags are both 0.

The Branch If Less Than or Equal (BLE) instruction allows you to compare two's complement numbers in another way. If it is executed immediately after a subtract or compare operation, the branch will occur only if the two's complement minuend was less than or equal to the two's complement subtrahend.

The Branch If Lower Or Same (BLS) instruction is similar to the BLE instruction except that **unsigned** numbers are compared. When it is executed immediately after a subtract or compare operation, the branch will occur only if the unsigned minuend was lower than or equal to the unsigned subtrahend.

The Branch If Less Than Zero (BLT) instruction is also similar to the BLE instruction except that the equal qualification is removed. If BLT is executed immediately after a subtract or compare operation, the branch occurs only if the two's complement minuend was less than the two's complement subtrahend.

Two additional instructions are included in Figure 5-15. Although they are not branch instructions, they are included here since they do not seem to fit any of the other categories.

The No Operation (NOP) instruction is a "do-nothing" instruction that simply consumes a small increment of time. It does not change the contents of any register except the program counter. It does increment the program counter by one and consumes two MPU cycles. In spite of this, the NOP is a very useful instruction. When writing a program, we frequently use too many instructions. Once the program is loaded in memory, it is often inconvenient to simply remove an instruction. The hole left in memory can be filled by moving back all instructions that follow. However, a faster way is to simply fill the hole with one or more NOP instructions.

The Wait For Interrupt (WAI) instruction is the 6800's version of a HLT instruction. In earlier units we used this instruction at the end of all our programs. We will continue to use it in the same manner in the future. However, as you will see in the next unit, there is more involved in executing the WAI instruction than simply stopping the MPU. For now, though, continue to think of the WAI as a simple halt instruction.

Condition Code Register Instructions

The 6800 MPU has eight instructions that allow us direct access to the condition codes. These are listed in Figure 5-16.

CONDITION CODE REGISTER OPERATIONS	MNEMONIC	BOOLEAN OPERATION	5 H	4 I	3 N	2 Z	1 V	0 C
Clear Carry	CLC	$0 \to C$	•	•	•	•	•	R
Clear Interrupt Mask	CLI	$0 \to I$	•	R	•	•	•	•
Clear Overflow	CLV	$0 \to V$	•	•	•	•	R	•
Set Carry	SEC	$1 \to C$	•	•	•	•	•	S
Set Interrupt Mask	SEI	$1 \to I$	•	S	•	•	•	•
Set Overflow	SEV	$1 \to V$	•	•	•	•	S	•
Acmltr A → CCR	TAP	$A \to CCR$	——————— (1) ———————
CCR → Acmltr A	TPA	$CCR \to A$	•	•	•	•	•	•

R = Reset
S = Set
• = Not affected

(1) (ALL) Set according to the contents of Accumulator A.

Figure 5-16
Condition code register instructions.

Most of these instructions are self-explanatory. The Clear Carry (CLC) instruction resets the C flag to 0 while the Set Carry (SEC) sets it to 1. In the same way, the CLV and SEV instructions allow us to clear and set the overflow flag. Also, the CLI and SEI instructions can be used to clear or set the interrupt flag.

You will notice that there are no instructions for individually clearing the N, Z, or H flags. However, we can still set or clear these flags with the Transfer Accumulator A to the Processor Status Register (TAP) instruction. Figure 5-17 illustrates the execution of this instruction. The contents of bits 0 through 5 of accumulator A are transferred to the condition code registers. Thus, this instruction allows us to set or clear all the condition codes at once.

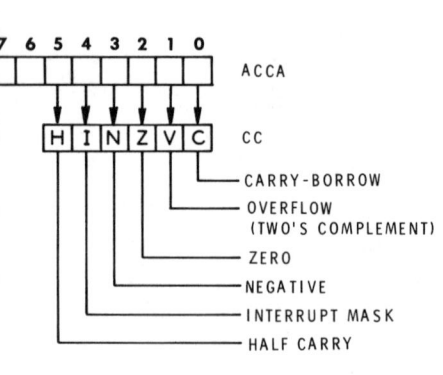

Figure 5-17
Executing the TAP instruction.

The final instruction is the Transfer Processor Status to Accumulator A (TPA) instruction. When this instruction is executed, the contents of the condition code registers are transferred to bits 0 through 5 of accumulator A. This operation is illustrated in Figure 5-18. Notice that bits 6 and 7 of the accumulator are set to 1.

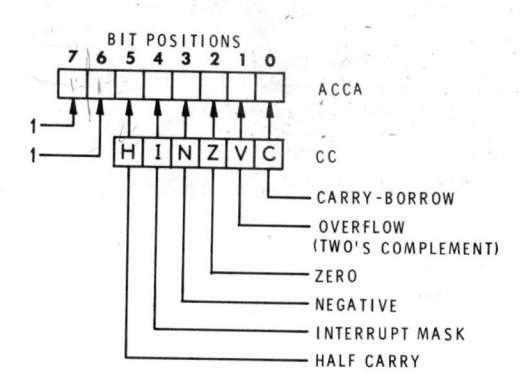

Figure 5-18
Executing the TPA instruction.

Summary of Instruction Set

As you can see, the 6800 MPU has a wide variety of instructions. In this section, most of the instructions have been mentioned briefly. However, a full explanation of some instructions must wait until additional new concepts have been covered.

In one short section, it is very difficult to cover every instruction in detail. And, it is virtually impossible for the reader to remember all the details of each instruction. Remember, all of the instructions available to the 6800 MPU are explained in detail in Appendix A of this program. Also, they are arranged alphabetically by their mnemonics for easy reference. Refer to Appendix A any time you are in doubt about what an instruction does. Be sure to look over the introductory material in the Appendix so that you understand all the conventions and symbols.

Self-Test Review

9. List the seven general categories of instructions.

10. What is meant by the shorthand notation: A+B → A?

11. How is the C flag affected by the "add" and "add with carry" instructions?

12. Is the C flag changed when the AND instruction is executed?

13. Explain the difference between the NEG instruction and the COM instruction.

14. Explain the difference between the ANDA instruction and the BITA instruction.

15. The decimal adjust instruction is associated with which accumulator?

16. When the RORA instruction is executed the LSB of accumulator A is shifted into the _____ register.

17. List eleven operations that can be performed directly to an operand in memory without first loading it into one of the MPU registers.

MICROPROCESSORS

The 6800 Microprocessor — Part 1 | 5-31

18. Explain the difference between the SUBB instruction and the CMPB instruction.

19. List the four types of logic operations that the 6800 MPU can perform.

20. When the LDX instruction is executed, from where is the index register loaded?

21. List four conditional branch instructions that are commonly used after a compare or subtract instruction to compare two's complement numbers.

22. Explain the difference between the BGT and BHI instructions.

23. Which instruction is often used to fill in a hole left in a program after an unwanted byte is removed?

24. Which instruction in the 6800 roughly corresponds to the halt instruction in our hypothetical machine?

25. Which of the condition codes can be individually set or cleared?

26. When you have some doubt as to exactly what operation is performed by a given instruction, where can you look to find the answer?

Answers

9. Arithmetic, data handling, logic, data test, index register and stack pointer, jump and branch, condition code.

10. Add the contents of accumulator A to the contents of accumulator B; transfer the result to accumulator A.

11. The C flag is set if a carry occurs; it is cleared otherwise.

12. No, the C flag is unaffected by the AND instruction.

13. The COM instruction replaces the operand with its 1's complement. The NEG instruction replaces the operand with its 2's complement.

14. With the ANDA instruction, the result of the AND operation is placed in accumulator A. With the BITA instruction, the condition code registers are set according to the result but the result is not retained.

15. The decimal adjust instruction works only with the A accumulator.

16. Carry (C).

17. A byte in memory can be: cleared, incremented, decremented, complemented, negated, rotated left, rotated right, shifted left arithmetically, shifted right arithmetically, shifted right logically, and tested.

18. With the SUBB instruction, a difference is produced and placed in accumulator B. With CMPB, the flags are set as if a difference were produced, but the difference is not retained.

19. Complement, AND, inclusive OR, and exclusive OR.

20. The upper half of the index register is loaded from the specified memory location; the lower half from the byte following the specified memory location.

21. BGE, BGT, BLE, BLT.

22. BGT is used to test the result of subtracting two's complement numbers. BHI is used to test the result of subtracting unsigned numbers.

23. NOP.

24. WAI.

25. C, I, and V.

26. Appendix A of this course.

NEW ADDRESSING MODES

In previous units, we have discussed four addressing modes. Let's briefly review these.

In the immediate addressing mode, the operand is the memory byte immediately following the opcode. These are generally two byte instructions. The first byte is the opcode, the second is the operand. However, there are exceptions to the two-byte rule. Some operations involve the 16-bit index register and stack pointer. In these cases, the operand is the **two** bytes immediately following the opcode. These are three byte instructions. The first byte is the opcode, the second and third are the operand.

In the direct addressing mode, the byte following the opcode is the address of the operand. These are always two byte instructions. The first byte is the opcode; the second is the address of the operand. An eight-bit byte can specify addresses from 00 to FF_{16}. Thus, when the direct addressing mode is being used, the operand must be in the first 256_{10} bytes of memory. Since the 6800 MPU can have up to $65,536_{10}$ bytes of memory, another means must be used to address the upper portion of memory.

The relative addressing mode is used for branching. These are two byte instructions. The first byte is the opcode, the second is the relative address. Recall that the relative address is added to the program count to form the absolute address. Since the 8-bit relative address is a two's complement number, the branch limits are $+127_{10}$ and -128_{10}.

In the inherent addressing mode either there is no operand or the operand is implied by the instruction. These are one byte instructions.

In this section, we will discuss two new addressing modes. These are called **extended addressing** and **indexed addressing**. We will discuss extended addressing first.

Extended Addressing

Extended addressing is similar to direct addressing but with one significant difference. Recall that with direct addressing the operand must be in the first 256_{10} bytes of memory. Since this represents less than one percent of the addresses available to the 6800 MPU, a more powerful addressing mode is needed. The extended addressing mode fills this need.

The format of an instruction that uses extended addressing is shown in Figure 5-19. The instruction will always have three bytes. The first byte is the opcode. The second and third bytes form a 16-bit address. Notice that the most significant part of the address is the byte immediately following the opcode. Since this instruction has a 16-bit address, the operand can be at any one of the $65,536_{10}$ possible addresses.

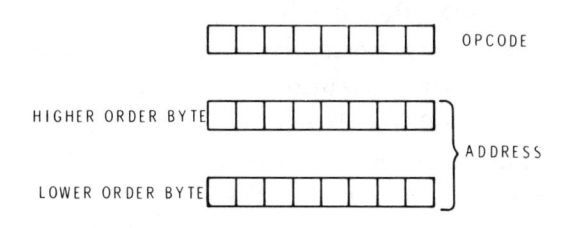

Figure 5-19
Format of an instruction that uses the
extended addressing mode.

Suppose, for example, that you wish to load the operand at memory location 2134_{16} into accumulator B. The instruction would look like this:

F6	Opcode for LDAB extended
21	Higher order address
34	Lower order address

By the same token, if you wish to increment the number in memory location $AA00_{16}$, the instruction would be:

7C	Opcode for INC extended
AA	Higher order address
00	Lower order address

The extended addressing mode allows us to address an operand at any address including the first 256_{10} bytes of memory. Thus, if you wish to load the operand at address 0013_{16} into accumulator A, you can use extended addressing:

        B6   Opcode for LDAA extended
        00   Higher order address
        13   Lower order address

Or, you can use direct addressing:

        96   Opcode for LDAA direct
        13   Address

Notice that, with direct addressing, the higher order address can be ignored since it is always 00. Because it saves one memory byte and one MPU cycle, direct addressing is normally used when the operand is in the first 256_{10} bytes of memory. Extended addressing is used when the operand is above address $00FF_{16}$. However, as you will see later, some instructions do not have a direct addressing mode. In these cases, extended addressing must be used even if the operand is in the first 256_{10} memory locations.

Indexed Addressing

The most powerful mode available to the 6800 MPU is indexed addressing. Recall that the 6800 MPU has a 16-bit index register. There are several instructions associated with this register. They allow us to load the register from memory and to store its contents in memory. Also, we can increment and decrement the index register. We can even compare its contents with two consecutive bytes in memory. These capabilities alone make the index register a very handy 16-bit counter. However, the real power of the index register comes from the fact that we can use this counter as an address pointer. Since this is a 16-bit register, it can point to any address in memory.

Purpose Before going into the details of how indexed addressing works, let's see why it is needed. Let's assume that we wish to add a list of 20_{16} numbers, and that the numbers are in 20_{16} consecutive memory locations starting at address 0050. Using the addressing modes discussed earlier, our program might look like this:

```
CLRA    Clear Accumulator A.
ADDA    Add the first number
50      To accumulator A.
ADDA    Add the second
51      number to accumulator A.
ADDA    Add the third number
52      to accumulator A.
  .        .
  .        .
  .        .
ADDA    Add the last number
6F      to accumulator A.
WAI     Wait.
```

While this accomplishes the desired result, it requires a long repetitive program. The above program would require 66_{10} bytes of memory. Notice that all the ADDA instructions are identical except that each successive address is one larger than the previous address. Indexed addressing can greatly simplify programs of this type.

Instruction Format The format of an instruction that uses indexed addressing is shown in Figure 5-20. Notice that this is a two-byte instruction. The first byte is the opcode, and the second is called an offset address. The offset address is an **unsigned** 8-bit binary number. It is added to the contents of the index register to determine the address at which the operand is located.

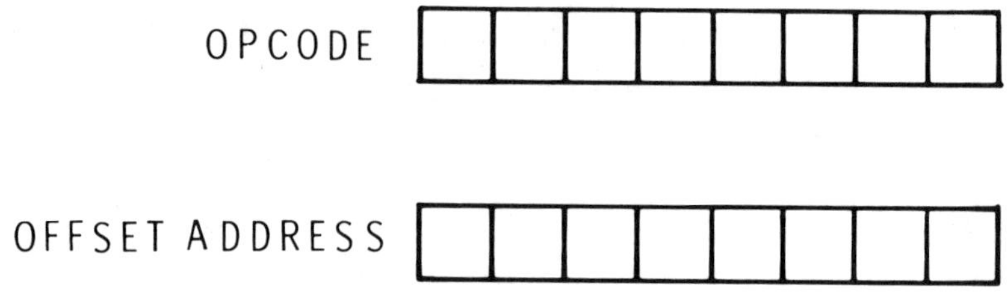

OPCODE ☐☐☐☐☐☐☐☐

OFFSET ADDRESS ☐☐☐☐☐☐☐☐

Figure 5-20
Format of an instruction that uses
the indexed addressing mode.

Every instruction that involves an operand in memory can use the indexed addressing mode. In this unit, we will use the following convention to indicate indexed addressing:

LDAA, X
STAA, X
ADDB, X
etc.

In each case, the X tells us that indexed addressing is used. For example, the first instruction means: "using indexed addressing, load the contents of the specified memory location into accumulator A." Now let's see how the address of the operand is determined.

Determining the Operand Address When indexed addressing is being used, the address of the operand is determined by the offset address and the number in the index register. Specifically, the 8-bit offset address is added to the 16-bit address in the index register. The 16-bit sum becomes the address of the operand. Figure 5-21 illustrates this.

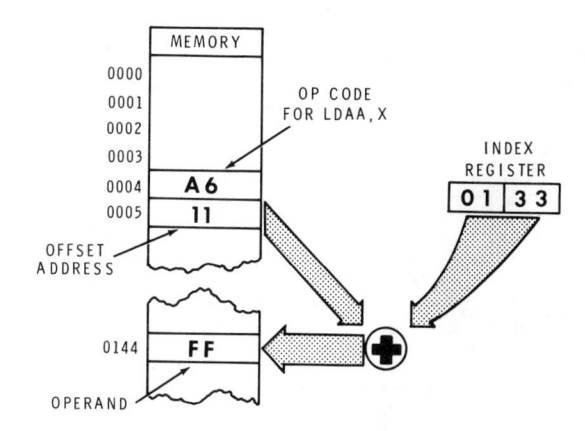

Figure 5-21
The operand address is formed by adding the offset address to the contents of the index register.

Here, the instruction in memory location 0004_{16} is LDAA, X. The offset address is 11_{16}. The contents of the index register are 0133_{16}. When the LDAA, X instruction is executed, the address of the operand is formed by adding the offset address to the number in the index register. In this case, the operand address will be:

$$\begin{array}{r} 0133_{16} \\ +11_{16} \\ \hline 0144_{16} \end{array}$$

The operand at this address is loaded into accumulator A. In this example, the operand FF is loaded into accumulator A when the instruction at location 0004 is executed. It is important to remember that this does not change the contents of the index register in any way. That is, the index register will still contain 0133_{16} after the instruction is executed.

Adding a List of Numbers To see how this addressing mode saves instructions, consider the problem given earlier. Recall that we were to add 20_{16} numbers stored in consecutive memory locations starting at address 0050. Using indexed addressing for the add instruction, our program looks like the one shown in Figure 5-22.

HEX ADDRESS	HEX CONTENTS	MNEMONICS/ HEX CONTENTS	COMMENTS
0010	CE	LDX #	Load index register immediate with the
0011	00	00	address of the
0012	50	50	first number in list.
0013	4F	CLRA	Clear accumulator A
0014	AB	ADDA, X	Add to accumulator A using indexed addressing
0015	00	00	with an offset address of 00.
0016	08	INX	Increment index register.
0017	8C	CPX #	Compare the contents of the index register
0018	00	00	with an address that is one greater than the
0019	70	70	address of the last number in the list.
001A	26	BNE	If not equal, branch back
001B	F8	F8	to the ADDA, X instruction.
001C	3E	WAI	Otherwise, halt.

Figure 5-22
Program for adding a list of
20_{16} numbers.

The first instruction is load index register immediate. Notice that a new symbol is used in this program. The symbol # is used to indicate the immediate addressing mode. Thus, the LDX# instruction causes the operand immediately following the opcode to be loaded into the index register. Recall that the index register can hold two 8-bit bytes. The operand is the two-byte number 0050_{16}. You may recognize that this is the address of the first number in the list of numbers that is to be added.

The next instruction clears accumulator A. The sum will be accumulated in this register, so it is important that it be cleared initially.

The third instruction (ADDA, X) is the only instruction in the program that uses indexed addressing. Notice that the symbol X indicates the indexed addressing mode. The offset address is 00. Recall that the operand address is determined by adding the offset to the contents of the index register. The index register contains 0050_{16} from a previous instruction. Since the offset is 00, the operand address is 0050_{16}. That is, the contents of memory location 0050 are added to the contents of accumulator A. Recall that 0050_{16} is the address of the first number in the list.

The fourth instruction increments the index register to 0051_{16}. Notice that the index register now points to the address of the second number in the list.

The fifth instruction compares the number in the index register with a number that is one greater than the address of the last number in the list.

If a match occurs, the Z flag will be set. Of course in this case, no match occurs yet. Notice once again that the symbol # indicates the immediate addressing mode. Thus, the contents of the index register are compared with the next two bytes in the program or 0070.

The BNE instruction tests the Z flag to see if the two numbers matched. If no match is indicated, the relative address (F8) directs the program back to the ADDA, X instruction. The first pass through the loop ends with the first number in accumulator A.

The second pass through the loop begins with the ADDA, X instruction being executed again. This time the index register points to address 0051. Therefore, the second number in the list is added to accumulator A. Accumulator A now contains the sum of the first two numbers. The index register is then incremented to 0052. Its contents are again compared with 0070. No match exists so the BNE instruction causes the loop to be repeated again.

The loop is repeated over and over again. Each time, the next number in the list is added to accumulator A. This process continues until the last number in the list is added. At that time, the index register will be incremented to 0070. Thus, when the CPX# instruction is executed, the Z flag will be set because the two numbers match. The BNE instruction recognizes that a match has occurred. Consequently, it does not allow the branch to occur and the next instruction in sequence is executed. Because this is the WAI instruction, the program halts. At this time, the sum of the 20_{16} numbers in the list will be in accumulator A.

Adding a list of numbers is a classic example of how indexing can be used to shorten a program. However, this example does not illustrate the full power of indexed addressing. For example, it does not illustrate the advantage of the offset address. Because indexed addressing is so important, let's look at another example.

Copying a List Let's assume we have a list of 10_{16} numbers that we wish to copy from one location to another. For simplicity, assume that the list is presently in addresses 0030 through 003F and that we wish to copy the list in location 0040 through 004F. Without using indexed addressing, our program might look like this:

>LDAA
>30
>STAA
>40
>LDAA
>31
>STAA
>41
>•
>•
>•
>LDAA
>3F
>STAA
>4F
>WAI

As you have seen; long, repetitive programs such as this are excellent candidates for indexed addressing.

Using indexed addressing, our program might look like that shown in Figure 5-23. The first step is to load the index register with the first address in the original list. The LDAA, X instruction has an offset address of 00. Therefore, accumulator A is loaded from the address specified by the index register (0030). That is, the first number in the original list is loaded into accumulator A when the LDAA, X instruction is executed.

HEX ADDRESS	HEX CONTENTS	MNEMONICS/ HEX CONTENTS	COMMENTS
0010	CE	LDX #	Load index register immediate with
0011	00	00	the first address of the original
0012	30	30	list.
0013	A6	LDAA, X	Load accumulator A indexed with
0014	00	00	an offset of 00.
0015	A7	STAA, X	Store accumulator A indexed with
0016	10	10	an offset of 10_{16}.
0017	08	INX	Increment index register.
0018	8C	CPX #	Compare index with one greater
0019	00	00	than last
001A	40	40	address in original list.
001B	26	BNE	If not equal, branch back to the
001C	F6	F6	LDAA, X instruction.
001D	3E	WAI	Otherwise, halt.

Figure 5-23
Program for copying a list from
addresses 0030 — 003F into
addresses 0040 — 004F.

The STAA, X instruction illustrates the use of the offset address. Notice that the offset is 10. This number is added to the address in the index register to form the effective address at which the contents of accumulator A are stored. Thus, the contents of accumulator A are stored at address 0040. Remember, this does not change the number in the index register in any way. By using the offset, we can load the accumulator indexed from one address and store the accumulator indexed at another.

Next, the index register is incremented to 0031. It is then compared with 0040. Since no match exists, the BNE instruction directs the program back to the LDAA, X instruction. The loop is repeated until the entire list is rewritten in locations 0040 through 004F. After the last entry in the list is copied, the index register is incremented to 0040. Thus, the CPX# instruction sets the Z flag allowing the BNE instruction to divert the program from the loop. The program halts after the last entry in the list is written in its new position in memory.

Instruction Set Summary

You have now been introduced to most of the instructions available to the 6800 MPU. You have also been introduced to all of the addressing modes. Now let's look at the complete instruction set.

Figure 5-24 summarizes the 6800's instructions and addressing modes. This 2-page Figure contains a wealth of information. For your convenience, this information is repeated on the Instruction Set Summary card provided with the course. You should keep this card handy. After a while, you will be able to write long, complex programs using only the card for reference.

The left-hand column of Figure 5-24 lists the names and mnemonics for each of the instructions. In many cases, a single name such as "add" is associated with more than one mnemonic. For example, ADDA is an add operation that involves accumulator A while ADDB is an add operation that involves accumulator B.

The center column gives important information about the addressing modes. Notice that the ADDA instruction can have any one of four addressing modes: immediate, direct, indexed, or extended. Three facts are given for each addressing mode. The hexadecimal opcode is given in the OP column. For example, the opcode for ADDA immediate is 8B while the opcode for ADDA direct is 9B.

The column labeled (~) tells the number of MPU cycles required to execute the instruction. This information is important because it allows us to determine exactly how long it will take to run a given program. As you will see later, an MPU cycle is equal to one cycle of the MPU clock. For example, if the clock frequency is 1 MHz, one MPU cycle will be one microsecond. With this clock rate, 2 microseconds are required to execute the ADDA immediate instruction while 5 microseconds are required for the ADDA indexed instruction.

The column labeled (#) indicates the number of bytes required by the instruction. ADDA immediate, ADDA direct, and ADDA indexed are two-byte instructions while ADDA extended is a three-byte instruction.

The next column to the right gives the shorthand notation for the Boolean or arithmetic operations performed. Finally, the right-hand column indicates how the condition code registers are affected by each instruction.

If you study the instruction set carefully, you will find that there are a few instructions that we have not yet discussed. These will be described in the next unit.

MICROPROCESSORS

The 6800 Microprocessor — Part 1 | **5-45**

ACCUMULATOR AND MEMORY OPERATIONS	MNEMONIC	IMMED OP	~	#	DIRECT OP	~	#	INDEX OP	~	#	EXTND OP	~	#	INHER OP	~	#	BOOLEAN/ARITHMETIC OPERATION (All register labels refer to contents)	5 H	4 I	3 N	2 Z	1 V	0 C
Add	ADDA	8B	2	2	9B	3	2	AB	5	2	BB	4	3				A + M → A	↕	•	↕	↕	↕	↕
	ADDB	CB	2	2	DB	3	2	EB	5	2	FB	4	3				B + M → B	↕	•	↕	↕	↕	↕
Add Acmltrs	ABA													1B	2	1	A + B → A	↕	•	↕	↕	↕	↕
Add with Carry	ADCA	89	2	2	99	3	2	A9	5	2	B9	4	3				A + M + C → A	↕	•	↕	↕	↕	↕
	ADCB	C9	2	2	D9	3	2	E9	5	2	F9	4	3				B + M + C → B	↕	•	↕	↕	↕	↕
And	ANDA	84	2	2	94	3	2	A4	5	2	B4	4	3				A • M → A	•	•	↕	↕	R	•
	ANDB	C4	2	2	D4	3	2	E4	5	2	F4	4	3				B • M → B	•	•	↕	↕	R	•
Bit Test	BITA	85	2	2	95	3	2	A5	5	2	B5	4	3				A • M	•	•	↕	↕	R	•
	BITB	C5	2	2	D5	3	2	E5	5	2	F5	4	3				B • M	•	•	↕	↕	R	•
Clear	CLR							6F	7	2	7F	6	3				00 → M	•	•	R	S	R	R
	CLRA													4F	2	1	00 → A	•	•	R	S	R	R
	CLRB													5F	2	1	00 → B	•	•	R	S	R	R
Compare	CMPA	81	2	2	91	3	2	A1	5	2	B1	4	3				A − M	•	•	↕	↕	↕	↕
	CMPB	C1	2	2	D1	3	2	E1	5	2	F1	4	3				B − M	•	•	↕	↕	↕	↕
Compare Acmltrs	CBA													11	2	1	A − B	•	•	↕	↕	↕	↕
Complement, 1's	COM							63	7	2	73	6	3				$\overline{M}$ → M	•	•	↕	↕	R	S
	COMA													43	2	1	$\overline{A}$ → A	•	•	↕	↕	R	S
	COMB													53	2	1	$\overline{B}$ → B	•	•	↕	↕	R	S
Complement, 2's (Negate)	NEG							60	7	2	70	6	3				00 − M → M	•	•	↕	↕	①	②
	NEGA													40	2	1	00 − A → A	•	•	↕	↕	①	②
	NEGB													50	2	1	00 − B → B	•	•	↕	↕	①	②
Decimal Adjust, A	DAA													19	2	1	Converts Binary Add. of BCD Characters into BCD Format	•	•	↕	↕	↕	③
Decrement	DEC							6A	7	2	7A	6	3				M − 1 → M	•	•	↕	↕	④	•
	DECA													4A	2	1	A − 1 → A	•	•	↕	↕	④	•
	DECB													5A	2	1	B − 1 → B	•	•	↕	↕	④	•
Exclusive OR	EORA	88	2	2	98	3	2	A8	5	2	B8	4	3				A ⊕ M → A	•	•	↕	↕	R	•
	EORB	C8	2	2	D8	3	2	E8	5	2	F8	4	3				B ⊕ M → B	•	•	↕	↕	R	•
Increment	INC							6C	7	2	7C	6	3				M + 1 → M	•	•	↕	↕	⑤	•
	INCA													4C	2	1	A + 1 → A	•	•	↕	↕	⑤	•
	INCB													5C	2	1	B + 1 → B	•	•	↕	↕	⑤	•
Load Acmltr	LDAA	86	2	2	96	3	2	A6	5	2	B6	4	3				M → A	•	•	↕	↕	R	•
	LDAB	C6	2	2	D6	3	2	E6	5	2	F6	4	3				M → B	•	•	↕	↕	R	•
Or, Inclusive	ORAA	8A	2	2	9A	3	2	AA	5	2	BA	4	3				A + M → A	•	•	↕	↕	R	•
	ORAB	CA	2	2	DA	3	2	EA	5	2	FA	4	3				B + M → B	•	•	↕	↕	R	•
Push Data	PSHA													36	4	1	A → M_{SP}, SP − 1 → SP	•	•	•	•	•	•
	PSHB													37	4	1	B → M_{SP}, SP − 1 → SP	•	•	•	•	•	•
Pull Data	PULA													32	4	1	SP + 1 → SP, M_{SP} → A	•	•	•	•	•	•
	PULB													33	4	1	SP + 1 → SP, M_{SP} → B	•	•	•	•	•	•
Rotate Left	ROL							69	7	2	79	6	3				M ⎫	•	•	↕	↕	⑥	↕
	ROLA													49	2	1	A ⎬ C ← b7...b0	•	•	↕	↕	⑥	↕
	ROLB													59	2	1	B ⎭	•	•	↕	↕	⑥	↕
Rotate Right	ROR							66	7	2	76	6	3				M ⎫	•	•	↕	↕	⑥	↕
	RORA													46	2	1	A ⎬ C → b7...b0	•	•	↕	↕	⑥	↕
	RORB													56	2	1	B ⎭	•	•	↕	↕	⑥	↕
Shift Left, Arithmetic	ASL							68	7	2	78	6	3				M ⎫	•	•	↕	↕	⑥	↕
	ASLA													48	2	1	A ⎬ C ← b7...b0 ← 0	•	•	↕	↕	⑥	↕
	ASLB													58	2	1	B ⎭	•	•	↕	↕	⑥	↕
Shift Right, Arithmetic	ASR							67	7	2	77	6	3				M ⎫	•	•	↕	↕	⑥	↕
	ASRA													47	2	1	A ⎬ b7...b0 → C	•	•	↕	↕	⑥	↕
	ASRB													57	2	1	B ⎭	•	•	↕	↕	⑥	↕
Shift Right, Logic.	LSR							64	7	2	74	6	3				M ⎫	•	•	R	↕	⑥	↕
	LSRA													44	2	1	A ⎬ 0 → b7...b0 → C	•	•	R	↕	⑥	↕
	LSRB													54	2	1	B ⎭	•	•	R	↕	⑥	↕
Store Acmltr.	STAA				97	4	2	A7	6	2	B7	5	3				A → M	•	•	↕	↕	R	•
	STAB				D7	4	2	E7	6	2	F7	5	3				B → M	•	•	↕	↕	R	•
Subtract	SUBA	80	2	2	90	3	2	A0	5	2	B0	4	3				A − M → A	•	•	↕	↕	↕	↕
	SUBB	C0	2	2	D0	3	2	E0	5	2	F0	4	3				B − M → B	•	•	↕	↕	↕	↕
Subract Acmltrs.	SBA													10	2	1	A − B → A	•	•	↕	↕	↕	↕
Subtr. with Carry	SBCA	82	2	2	92	3	2	A2	5	2	B2	4	3				A − M − C → A	•	•	↕	↕	↕	↕
	SBCB	C2	2	2	D2	3	2	E2	5	2	F2	4	3				B − M − C → B	•	•	↕	↕	↕	↕
Transfer Acmltrs	TAB													16	2	1	A → B	•	•	↕	↕	R	•
	TBA													17	2	1	B → A	•	•	↕	↕	R	•
Test, Zero or Minus	TST							6D	7	2	7D	6	3				M − 00	•	•	↕	↕	R	R
	TSTA													4D	2	1	A − 00	•	•	↕	↕	R	R
	TSTB													5D	2	1	B − 00	•	•	↕	↕	R	R

Figure 5-24
The 6800 instruction set.

5-46 UNIT FIVE

MICROPROCESSORS

INDEX REGISTER AND STACK POINTER OPERATIONS	MNEMONIC	IMMED OP	~	#	DIRECT OP	~	#	INDEX OP	~	#	EXTND OP	~	#	INHER OP	~	#	BOOLEAN/ARITHMETIC OPERATION	5 H	4 I	3 N	2 Z	1 V	0 C
Compare Index Reg	CPX	8C	3	3	9C	4	2	AC	6	2	BC	5	3				$(X_H/X_L) - (M/M+1)$	•	•	⑦	‡	⑧	•
Decrement Index Reg	DEX													09	4	1	$X - 1 \rightarrow X$	•	•	•	‡	•	•
Decrement Stack Pntr	DES													34	4	1	$SP - 1 \rightarrow SP$	•	•	•	•	•	•
Increment Index Reg	INX													08	4	1	$X + 1 \rightarrow X$	•	•	•	‡	•	•
Increment Stack Pntr	INS													31	4	1	$SP + 1 \rightarrow SP$	•	•	•	•	•	•
Load Index Reg	LDX	CE	3	3	DE	4	2	EE	6	2	FE	5	3				$M \rightarrow X_H, (M+1) \rightarrow X_L$	•	•	⑨	‡	R	•
Load Stack Pntr	LDS	8E	3	3	9E	4	2	AE	6	2	BE	5	3				$M \rightarrow SP_H, (M+1) \rightarrow SP_L$	•	•	⑨	‡	R	•
Store Index Reg	STX				DF	5	2	EF	7	2	FF	6	3				$X_H \rightarrow M, X_L \rightarrow (M+1)$	•	•	⑨	‡	R	•
Store Stack Pntr	STS				9F	5	2	AF	7	2	BF	6	3				$SP_H \rightarrow M, SP_L \rightarrow (M+1)$	•	•	⑨	‡	R	•
Indx Reg → Stack Pntr	TXS													35	4	1	$X - 1 \rightarrow SP$	•	•	•	•	•	•
Stack Pntr → Indx Reg	TSX													30	4	1	$SP + 1 \rightarrow X$	•	•	•	•	•	•

JUMP AND BRANCH OPERATIONS	MNEMONIC	RELATIVE OP	~	#	INDEX OP	~	#	EXTND OP	~	#	INHER OP	~	#	BRANCH TEST	5 H	4 I	3 N	2 Z	1 V	0 C
Branch Always	BRA	20	4	2										None	•	•	•	•	•	•
Branch If Carry Clear	BCC	24	4	2										$C = 0$	•	•	•	•	•	•
Branch If Carry Set	BCS	25	4	2										$C = 1$	•	•	•	•	•	•
Branch If = Zero	BEQ	27	4	2										$Z = 1$	•	•	•	•	•	•
Branch If ≥ Zero	BGE	2C	4	2										$N \oplus V = 0$	•	•	•	•	•	•
Branch If > Zero	BGT	2E	4	2										$Z + (N \oplus V) = 0$	•	•	•	•	•	•
Branch If Higher	BHI	22	4	2										$C + Z = 0$	•	•	•	•	•	•
Branch If ≤ Zero	BLE	2F	4	2										$Z + (N \oplus V) = 1$	•	•	•	•	•	•
Branch If Lower Or Same	BLS	23	4	2										$C + Z = 1$	•	•	•	•	•	•
Branch If < Zero	BLT	2D	4	2										$N \oplus V = 1$	•	•	•	•	•	•
Branch If Minus	BMI	2B	4	2										$N = 1$	•	•	•	•	•	•
Branch If Not Equal Zero	BNE	26	4	2										$Z = 0$	•	•	•	•	•	•
Branch If Overflow Clear	BVC	28	4	2										$V = 0$	•	•	•	•	•	•
Branch If Overflow Set	BVS	29	4	2										$V = 1$	•	•	•	•	•	•
Branch If Plus	BPL	2A	4	2										$N = 0$	•	•	•	•	•	•
Branch To Subroutine	BSR	8D	8	2											•	•	•	•	•	•
Jump	JMP				6E	4	2	7E	3	3				See Special Operations	•	•	•	•	•	•
Jump To Subroutine	JSR				AD	8	2	BD	9	3					•	•	•	•	•	•
No Operation	NOP										01	2	1	Advances Prog. Cntr. Only	•	•	•	•	•	•
Return From Interrupt	RTI										3B	10	1		⟵ ⑩ ⟶
Return From Subroutine	RTS										39	5	1	See special Operations	•	•	•	•	•	•
Software Interrupt	SWI										3F	12	1		•	S	•	•	•	•
Wait for Interrupt	WAI										3E	9	1		•	⑪	•	•	•	•

CONDITIONS CODE REGISTER OPERATIONS	MNEMONIC	INHER OP	~	=	BOOLEAN OPERATION	5 H	4 I	3 N	2 Z	1 V	0 C
Clear Carry	CLC	0C	2	1	$0 \rightarrow C$	•	•	•	•	•	R
Clear Interrupt Mask	CLI	0E	2	1	$0 \rightarrow I$	•	R	•	•	•	•
Clear Overflow	CLV	0A	2	1	$0 \rightarrow V$	•	•	•	•	R	•
Set Carry	SEC	0D	2	1	$1 \rightarrow C$	•	•	•	•	•	S
Set Interrupt Mask	SEI	0F	2	1	$1 \rightarrow I$	•	S	•	•	•	•
Set Overflow	SEV	0B	2	1	$1 \rightarrow V$	•	•	•	•	S	•
Acmltr A → CCR	TAP	06	2	1	$A \rightarrow CCR$	⟵ ⑫ ⟶
CCR → Acmltr A	TPA	07	2	1	$CCR \rightarrow A$	•	•	•	•	•	•

CONDITION CODE REGISTER NOTES:
(Bit set if test is true and cleared otherwise)

① (Bit V) Test: Result = 10000000?
② (Bit C) Test: Result = 00000000?
③ (Bit C) Test: Decimal value of most significant BCD Character greater than nine? (Not cleared if previously set.)
④ (Bit V) Test: Operand = 10000000 prior to execution?
⑤ (Bit V) Test: Operand = 01111111 prior to execution?
⑥ (Bit V) Test: Set equal to result of $N \oplus C$ after shift has occurred.
⑦ (Bit N) Test: Sign bit of most significant (MS) byte of result = 1?
⑧ (Bit V) Test: 2's complement overflow from subtraction of LS bytes?
⑨ (Bit N) Test: Result less than zero? (Bit 15 = 1)
⑩ (All) Load Condition Code Register from Stack. (See Special Operations)
⑪ (Bit I) Set when interrupt occurs. If previously set, a Non-Maskable Interrupt is required to exit the wait state.
⑫ (ALL) Set according to the contents of Accumulator A.

LEGEND:
- OP   Operation Code (Hexadecimal);
- ~   Number of MPU Cycles;
- #   Number of Program Bytes;
- +   Arithmetic Plus;
- —   Arithmetic Minus;
- •   Boolean AND;
- M_{SP} Contents of memory location pointed to be Stack Pointer;
- +   Boolean Inclusive OR;
- ⊕   Boolean Exclusive OR;
- $\overline{M}$ Complement of M;
- →   Transfer Into;
- 0   Bit = Zero;
- 00   Byte = Zero;
- H   Half-carry from bit 3;
- I   Interrupt mask
- N   Negative (sign bit)
- Z   Zero (byte)
- V   Overflow, 2's complement
- C   Carry from bit 7
- R   Reset Always
- S   Set Always
- ‡   Test and set if true, cleared otherwise
- •   Not Affected
- CCR Condition Code Register
- LS   Least Significant
- MS   Most Significant

Figure 5-24
(continued)

MICROPROCESSORS

The 6800 Microprocessor — Part 1 **5-4**

Self-Test Review

27. A disadvantage of direct addressing is that the operand must be in the first _____ bytes of memory.

28. The advantage of direct addressing is that only _____ bytes are required for each instruction.

29. Extended addressing can address _____ bytes of memory.

30. A disadvantage of extended addressing is that each instruction requires _____ bytes.

31. Can extended addressing be used to address an operand in the first 256_{10} bytes of memory?

32. The most powerful addressing mode available to the 6800 is called _____ addressing.

33. Indexed addressing requires _____ bytes for each instruction.

34. The second byte of an indexed addressing instruction is called the _____ address.

35. How is the address of the operand determined when indexed addressing is used?

36. Carefully examine the program shown in Figure 5-25. Determine what the program does and fill in the comments column. What number is loaded into the index register by the first instruction?

HEX ADDRESS	HEX CONTENTS	MNEMONICS/ HEX CONTENTS	COMMENTS
0010	CE	LDX #	
0011	00	00	
0012	50	50	
0013	6F	CLR, X	
0014	00	00	
0015	08	INX	
0016	8C	CPX #	
0017	00	00	
0018	60	60	
0019	26	BNE	
001A	F8	F8	
001B	3E	WAI	

Figure 5-25
Program for Self-Test Review

37. What location is cleared by the CLR, X instruction?

38. What is the number in the index register after the INX instruction is executed for the first time?

39. The loop will be repeated until the number in the index register is _____.

40. What does this program do?

41. Refer to Figure 5-24. What is the hexadecimal opcode for the LDAB extended instruction?

42. How many MPU cycles are required by the INC, X instruction?

43. How many bytes in the LDS # instruction?

Answers

27. 256_{10}.

28. Two.

29. $65,536_{10}$.

30. Three.

31. Yes. Although direct addressing is normally used when the operand is in the first 256_{10} bytes of memory, extended addressing can be used also.

32. Indexed.

33. Two.

34. Offset.

35. The offset address is added to the contents of the index register.

36. 0050_{16}.

37. 0050_{16}.

38. 0051_{16}.

39. 0060_{16}.

40. The program clears memory locations 0050_{16} through $005F_{16}$.

41. $F6_{16}$.

42. Seven.

43. Three.

UNIT 5 SUMMARY

1. In computer jargon, the word architecture is used to describe a microprocessor's style of construction.

2. From a programmer's point of view, the only parts of a microprocessor that are important are the registers that are accessible — the registers that can be directly modified by program code.

3. The programming model of the 6800 MPU contains the A and B Accumulators, the Index register, the Program Counter, the Stack Pointer, and Condition Codes register.

4. The A and B Accumulators in the 6800 MPU are 8-bit registers that operate as independent accumulators.

5. The 16-bit Program Counter can address up to 65,536 different addresses in memory.

6. The 6800 MPU has a 16-bit wide address bus.

7. Direct addressing is limited to the first 256 address locations in memory, because it uses an 8-bit address value.

8. Extended addressing uses a 16-bit (2-byte) address value, therefore it can access any address location in memory.

9. The Condition Code register in the 6800 MPU contains six 1-bit code registers. They are the:

    A. Carry code register that indicates if there was a carry from or borrow into the MSB of either accumulator.
    B. Overflow code register that indicates if there was an overflow from either accumulator.
    C. Zero code register that indicates if either accumulator is clear of 1-bits.
    D. Negative code register that indicates the state of the sign bit of either accumulator.
    E. Interrupt Mask code register that is used to determine how the 6800 MPU is effected by external interrupt requests.
    F. Half Carry code register that indicates if there was a carry from or borrow into the fourth bit of either 8-bit accumulator.

10. The Index register is a 16-bit register that can be used to hold 16-bit values and increment or decrement those values. It is also used to hold the 16-bit address values used in indexed addressing.

11. The Stack Pointer is another 16-bit working register that can be used to hold 16-bit values and increment or decrement those values. It is also used as an address pointer for "stack" operations.

12. When a 16-bit register is loaded with data, two 8-bit memory operations are used to supply that data. The first operation loads the upper half, or high-byte, of the register. The second memory operation loads the lower half, or low-byte, of the register.

13. The 6800 MPU has about 100_{10} basic instructions. Adding the different addressing modes brings the count to 197_{10} different opcodes.

14. There are seven general classifications of instructions: arithmetic, data handling, logic, data test, index register and stack pointer, jump and branch, and condition code.

15. Two's complement arithmetic is used within the 6800 MPU.

16. The add instructions add data in memory to an accumulator, or add the two accumulators together and store the sum in an accumulator.

17. The negate instructions perform a two's complement operation on data in memory or in either of the accumulators.

18. The decimal adjust instruction is used to convert the contents of the A accumulator into a valid BCD number after a BCD add operation.

19. The subtract instructions subtract data in memory or an accumulator from another accumulator and store the difference in an accumulator.

20. The clear instructions are used to clear (zero) a memory location or an accumulator.

21. The decrement instructions are used to subtract one from a value in a memory location, an accumulator, the Index register, or the Stack Pointer, and store the new value in the original location.

22. The increment instructions are used to add one to a value in a memory location, an accumulator, the Index register, or the Stack Pointer, and store the new value in the original location.

23. The rotate instructions are used to shift the eight bits in a memory location or accumulator and the carry condition code register bit one bit position left or right. On a rotate left, the MSB is shifted into carry, and the carry bit is shifted into the LSB. On a rotate right, the carry bit is shifted into the MSB, and the LSB is shifted into carry.

24. The shift instructions are used to shift the eight bits in a memory location or accumulator one bit position left or right. In each instance the carry condition code register bit is replaced by the bit shifted out of the accumulator or memory location. On a shift arithmetic left, the MSB is shifted into carry, and a zero is shifted into the LSB. On a shift arithmetic right, the LSB is shifted into carry, and the MSB is shifted back into the MSB as well as into the next bit position right. On a shift logical right, the LSB is shifted into carry, and a zero is shifted into the MSB.

25. The load instructions are used to move the contents of memory into either accumulator, the Index register, or the Stack Pointer.

26. The store instructions are used to save the contents of either accumulator, the Index register, or the Stack Pointer in memory.

27. The transfer instructions are used to load the contents of one accumulator into the other, load the contents of the Index register into the Stack Pointer, or load the contents of the Stack Pointer into the Index register.

28. The AND instructions are used to logically AND, bit-for-bit, the contents of an accumulator with a memory location, and store the result in the accumulator.

29. The OR instructions are used to logically OR, bit-for-bit, the contents of an accumulator with a memory location, and store the result in the accumulator.

30. The Exclusive OR instructions are used to logically XOR (EOR), bit-for-bit, the contents of an accumulator with a memory location, and store the result in the accumulator.

31. The complement instructions are used to perform a one's complement operation on a memory location or an accumulator.

32. The bit test instructions are used to logically AND, bit-for-bit, the contents of an accumulator with a memory location, and set the appropriate condition code register bits. The contents of the accumulator and memory location are not affected.

33. The compare instructions are used to subtract the contents of a memory location from an accumulator, an accumulator from an accumulator, or two memory locations from the Index register, and set the appropriate condition code register bits. The contents of the accumulators, Index register, and memory are not affected.

34. The test instructions are used to subtract zero from a memory location or an accumulator and set the appropriate condition code register bits. The contents of the accumulators or memory are not affected.

35. The unconditional branch instruction forces the MPU to execute the instruction pointed to by the relative address immediately following the branch instruction opcode. The relative address value is limited to $+127_{10}$ and -128_{10} bytes.

36. The conditional branch instruction causes the MPU to test the contents of the condition code register. If the proper conditions are met, the MPU is forced to execute the instruction pointed to by the relative address immediately following the branch instruction opcode. If the conditions are not met, the branch is ignored and the next sequential instruction is executed. The relative address is limited to $+127_{10}$ and -128_{10} bytes.

37. The no operation instruction is used to advance the Program Counter by one. You would use it to waste time in a program or reserve space in a program for future instructions.

38. The wait for interrupt instruction causes the MPU to go into a halt condition where it will only respond to an external interrupt.

39. The clear condition code instructions are used to clear to a zero state the carry, interrupt mask, or overflow register bits.

40. The set condition code instructions are used to set to a one state the carry, interrupt mask, or overflow register bits.

41. The transfer condition code register instructions are used to move the contents of the condition code register into the A accumulator, or the contents of the A accumulator into the condition code register.

42. In extended addressing, the second and third bytes of the instruction contain the high-order and low-order bytes, respectively, of the memory location being addressed.

43. In indexed addressing, the contents of the Index register are used as a pointer to the memory location being addressed. The second byte of the instruction contains an 8-bit, unsigned, offset value that is added to the Index register value to indicate the actual memory location being addressed.

Perform Experiments 7 and 8 at the end of Book 2.

PROGRAMMING CARD
6800/6808 INSTRUCTION SET

ACCUMULATOR AND MEMORY OPERATIONS	MNEMONIC	IMMED OP	~	#	DIRECT OP	~	#	INDEX OP	~	#	EXTND OP	~	#	INHER OP	~	#	BOOLEAN/ARITHMETIC OPERATION (All register labels refer to contents)	H (5)	I (4)	N (3)	Z (2)	V (1)	C (0)
Add	ADDA	8B	2	2	9B	3	2	AB	5	2	BB	4	3				A + M → A	‡	•	‡	‡	‡	‡
	ADDB	CB	2	2	DB	3	2	EB	5	2	FB	4	3				B + M → B	‡	•	‡	‡	‡	‡
Add Acmltrs	ABA													1B	2	1	A + B → A	‡	•	‡	‡	‡	‡
Add with Carry	ADCA	89	2	2	99	3	2	A9	5	2	B9	4	3				A + M + C → A	‡	•	‡	‡	‡	‡
	ADCB	C9	2	2	D9	3	2	E9	5	2	F9	4	3				B + M + C → B	‡	•	‡	‡	‡	‡
And	ANDA	84	2	2	94	3	2	A4	5	2	B4	4	3				A • M → A	•	•	‡	‡	R	•
	ANDB	C4	2	2	D4	3	2	E4	5	2	F4	4	3				B • M → B	•	•	‡	‡	R	•
Bit Test	BITA	85	2	2	95	3	2	A5	5	2	B5	4	3				A • M	•	•	‡	‡	R	•
	BITB	C5	2	2	D5	3	2	E5	5	2	F5	4	3				B • M	•	•	‡	‡	R	•
Clear	CLR							6F	7	2	7F	6	3				00 → M	•	•	R	S	R	R
	CLRA													4F	2	1	00 → A	•	•	R	S	R	R
	CLRB													5F	2	1	00 → B	•	•	R	S	R	R
Compare	CMPA	81	2	2	91	3	2	A1	5	2	B1	4	3				A − M	•	•	‡	‡	‡	‡
	CMPB	C1	2	2	D1	3	2	E1	5	2	F1	4	3				B − M	•	•	‡	‡	‡	‡
Compare Acmltrs	CBA													11	2	1	A − B	•	•	‡	‡	‡	‡
Complement, 1's	COM							63	7	2	73	6	3				$\overline{M}$ → M	•	•	‡	‡	R	S
	COMA													43	2	1	$\overline{A}$ → A	•	•	‡	‡	R	S
	COMB													53	2	1	$\overline{B}$ → B	•	•	‡	‡	R	S
Complement, 2's (Negate)	NEG							60	7	2	70	6	3				00 − M → M	•	•	‡	‡	①	②
	NEGA													40	2	1	00 − A → A	•	•	‡	‡	①	②
	NEGB													50	2	1	00 − B → B	•	•	‡	‡	①	②
Decimal Adjust, A	DAA													19	2	1	Converts Binary Add. of BCD Characters into BCD Format	•	•	‡	‡	‡	③
Decrement	DEC							6A	7	2	7A	6	3				M − 1 → M	•	•	‡	‡	④	•
	DECA													4A	2	1	A − 1 → A	•	•	‡	‡	④	•
	DECB													5A	2	1	B − 1 → B	•	•	‡	‡	④	•
Exclusive OR	EORA	88	2	2	98	3	2	A8	5	2	B8	4	3				A ⊕ M → A	•	•	‡	‡	R	•
	EORB	C8	2	2	D8	3	2	E8	5	2	F8	4	3				B ⊕ M → B	•	•	‡	‡	R	•
Increment	INC							6C	7	2	7C	6	3				M + 1 → M	•	•	‡	‡	⑤	•
	INCA													4C	2	1	A + 1 → A	•	•	‡	‡	⑤	•
	INCB													5C	2	1	B + 1 → B	•	•	‡	‡	⑤	•
Load Acmltr	LDAA	86	2	2	96	3	2	A6	5	2	B6	4	3				M → A	•	•	‡	‡	R	•
	LDAB	C6	2	2	D6	3	2	E6	5	2	F6	4	3				M → B	•	•	‡	‡	R	•
Or, Inclusive	ORAA	8A	2	2	9A	3	2	AA	5	2	BA	4	3				A + M → A	•	•	‡	‡	R	•
	ORAB	CA	2	2	DA	3	2	EA	5	2	FA	4	3				B + M → B	•	•	‡	‡	R	•
Push Data	PSHA													36	4	1	A → M$_{SP}$, SP − 1 → SP	•	•	•	•	•	•
	PSHB													37	4	1	B → M$_{SP}$, SP − 1 → SP	•	•	•	•	•	•
Pull Data	PULA													32	4	1	SP + 1 → SP, M$_{SP}$ → A	•	•	•	•	•	•
	PULB													33	4	1	SP + 1 → SP, M$_{SP}$ → B	•	•	•	•	•	•
Rotate Left	ROL							69	7	2	79	6	3				M ⎫	•	•	‡	‡	⑥	‡
	ROLA													49	2	1	A ⎬	•	•	‡	‡	⑥	‡
	ROLB													59	2	1	B ⎭	•	•	‡	‡	⑥	‡
Rotate Right	ROR							66	7	2	76	6	3				M ⎫	•	•	‡	‡	⑥	‡
	RORA													46	2	1	A ⎬	•	•	‡	‡	⑥	‡
	RORB													56	2	1	B ⎭	•	•	‡	‡	⑥	‡
Shift Left, Arithmetic	ASL							68	7	2	78	6	3				M ⎫	•	•	‡	‡	⑥	‡
	ASLA													48	2	1	A ⎬	•	•	‡	‡	⑥	‡
	ASLB													58	2	1	B ⎭	•	•	‡	‡	⑥	‡
Shift Right, Arithmetic	ASR							67	7	2	77	6	3				M ⎫	•	•	‡	‡	⑥	‡
	ASRA													47	2	1	A ⎬	•	•	‡	‡	⑥	‡
	ASRB													57	2	1	B ⎭	•	•	‡	‡	⑥	‡
Shift Right, Logic.	LSR							64	7	2	74	6	3				M ⎫	•	•	R	‡	⑥	‡
	LSRA													44	2	1	A ⎬	•	•	R	‡	⑥	‡
	LSRB													54	2	1	B ⎭	•	•	R	‡	⑥	‡
Store Acmltr.	STAA				97	4	2	A7	6	2	B7	5	3				A → M	•	•	‡	‡	R	•
	STAB				D7	4	2	E7	6	2	F7	5	3				B → M	•	•	‡	‡	R	•
Subtract	SUBA	80	2	2	90	3	2	A0	5	2	B0	4	3				A − M → A	•	•	‡	‡	‡	‡
	SUBB	C0	2	2	D0	3	2	E0	5	2	F0	4	3				B − M → B	•	•	‡	‡	‡	‡
Subract Acmltrs.	SBA													10	2	1	A − B → A	•	•	‡	‡	‡	‡
Subtr. with Carry	SBCA	82	2	2	92	3	2	A2	5	2	B2	4	3				A − M − C → A	•	•	‡	‡	‡	‡
	SBCB	C2	2	2	D2	3	2	E2	5	2	F2	4	3				B − M − C → B	•	•	‡	‡	‡	‡
Transfer Acmltrs	TAB													16	2	1	A → B	•	•	‡	‡	R	•
	TBA													17	2	1	B → A	•	•	‡	‡	R	•
Test, Zero or Minus	TST							6D	7	2	7D	6	3				M − 00	•	•	‡	‡	R	R
	TSTA													4D	2	1	A − 00	•	•	‡	‡	R	R
	TSTB													5D	2	1	B − 00	•	•	‡	‡	R	R

INDEX REGISTER AND STACK POINTER OPERATIONS

INDEX REGISTER AND STACK POINTER OPERATIONS	MNEMONIC	IMMED OP	~	#	DIRECT OP	~	#	INDEX OP	~	#	EXTND OP	~	#	INHER OP	~	#	BOOLEAN/ARITHMETIC OPERATION	5 H	4 I	3 N	2 Z	1 V	0 C
Compare Index Reg	CPX	8C	3	3	9C	4	2	AC	6	2	BC	5	3				$(X_H/X_L) - (M/M+1)$	•	•	⑦	‡	⑧	•
Decrement Index Reg	DEX													09	4	1	$X - 1 \to X$	•	•	•	‡	•	•
Decrement Stack Pntr	DES													34	4	1	$SP - 1 \to SP$	•	•	•	•	•	•
Increment Index Reg	INX													08	4	1	$X + 1 \to X$	•	•	•	‡	•	•
Increment Stack Pntr	INS													31	4	1	$SP + 1 \to SP$	•	•	•	•	•	•
Load Index Reg	LDX	CE	3	3	DE	4	2	EE	6	2	FE	5	3				$M \to X_H, (M+1) \to X_L$	•	•	⑨	‡	R	•
Load Stack Pntr	LDS	8E	3	3	9E	4	2	AE	6	2	BE	5	3				$M \to SP_H, (M+1) \to SP_L$	•	•	⑨	‡	R	•
Store Index Reg	STX				DF	5	2	EF	7	2	FF	6	3				$X_H \to M, X_L \to (M+1)$	•	•	⑨	‡	R	•
Store Stack Pntr	STS				9F	5	2	AF	7	2	BF	6	3				$SP_H \to M, SP_L \to (M+1)$	•	•	⑨	‡	R	•
Indx Reg → Stack Pntr	TXS													35	4	1	$X - 1 \to SP$	•	•	•	•	•	•
Stack Pntr → Indx Reg	TSX													30	4	1	$SP + 1 \to X$	•	•	•	•	•	•

JUMP AND BRANCH OPERATIONS

JUMP AND BRANCH OPERATIONS	MNEMONIC	RELATIVE OP	~	#	INDEX OP	~	#	EXTND OP	~	#	INHER OP	~	#	BRANCH TEST	5 H	4 I	3 N	2 Z	1 V	0 C
Branch Always	BRA	20	4	2										None	•	•	•	•	•	•
Branch If Carry Clear	BCC	24	4	2										$C = 0$	•	•	•	•	•	•
Branch If Carry Set	BCS	25	4	2										$C = 1$	•	•	•	•	•	•
Branch If = Zero	BEQ	27	4	2										$Z = 1$	•	•	•	•	•	•
Branch If ≥ Zero	BGE	2C	4	2										$N \oplus V = 0$	•	•	•	•	•	•
Branch If > Zero	BGT	2E	4	2										$Z + (N \oplus V) = 0$	•	•	•	•	•	•
Branch If Higher	BHI	22	4	2										$C + Z = 0$	•	•	•	•	•	•
Branch If ≤ Zero	BLE	2F	4	2										$Z + (N \oplus V) = 1$	•	•	•	•	•	•
Branch If Lower Or Same	BLS	23	4	2										$C + Z = 1$	•	•	•	•	•	•
Branch If < Zero	BLT	2D	4	2										$N \oplus V = 1$	•	•	•	•	•	•
Branch If Minus	BMI	2B	4	2										$N = 1$	•	•	•	•	•	•
Branch If Not Equal Zero	BNE	26	4	2										$Z = 0$	•	•	•	•	•	•
Branch If Overflow Clear	BVC	28	4	2										$V = 0$	•	•	•	•	•	•
Branch If Overflow Set	BVS	29	4	2										$V = 1$	•	•	•	•	•	•
Branch If Plus	BPL	2A	4	2										$N = 0$	•	•	•	•	•	•
Branch To Subroutine	BSR	8D	8	2											•	•	•	•	•	•
Jump	JMP				6E	4	2	7E	3	3				} See Special Operations	•	•	•	•	•	•
Jump To Subroutine	JSR				AD	8	2	BD	9	3					•	•	•	•	•	•
No Operation	NOP										01	2	1	Advances Prog. Cntr. Only	•	•	•	•	•	•
Return From Interrupt	RTI										3B	10	1		—⑩—
Return From Subroutine	RTS										39	5	1	} See special Operations	•	•	•	•	•	•
Software Interrupt	SWI										3F	12	1		•	S	•	•	•	•
Wait for Interrupt	WAI										3E	9	1		•	⑪	•	•	•	•

CONDITIONS CODE REGISTER OPERATIONS

CONDITIONS CODE REGISTER OPERATIONS	MNEMONIC	INHER OP	~	=	BOOLEAN OPERATION	5 H	4 I	3 N	2 Z	1 V	0 C
Clear Carry	CLC	0C	2	1	$0 \to C$	•	•	•	•	•	R
Clear Interrupt Mask	CLI	0E	2	1	$0 \to I$	•	R	•	•	•	•
Clear Overflow	CLV	0A	2	1	$0 \to V$	•	•	•	•	R	•
Set Carry	SEC	0D	2	1	$1 \to C$	•	•	•	•	•	S
Set Interrupt Mask	SEI	0F	2	1	$1 \to I$	•	S	•	•	•	•
Set Overflow	SEV	0B	2	1	$1 \to V$	•	•	•	•	S	•
Acmltr A → CCR	TAP	06	2	1	$A \to CCR$	—⑫—
CCR → Acmltr A	TPA	07	2	1	$CCR \to A$	•	•	•	•	•	•

CONDITION CODE REGISTER NOTES:
(Bit set if test is true and cleared otherwise)

① (Bit V) Test: Result = 10000000?
② (Bit C) Test: Result = 00000000?
③ (Bit C) Test: Decimal value of most significant BCD Character greater than nine? (Not cleared if previously set.)
④ (Bit V) Test: Operand = 10000000 prior to execution?
⑤ (Bit V) Test: Operand = 01111111 prior to execution?
⑥ (Bit V) Test: Set equal to result of N ⊕ C after shift has occurred.
⑦ (Bit N) Test: Sign bit of most significant (MS) byte of result = 1?
⑧ (Bit V) Test: 2's complement overflow from subtraction of LS bytes?
⑨ (Bit N) Test: Result less than zero? (Bit 15 = 1)
⑩ (All) Load Condition Code Register from Stack. (See Special Operations)
⑪ (Bit I) Set when interrupt occurs. If previously set, a Non-Maskable Interrupt is required to exit the wait state.
⑫ (ALL) Set according to the contents of Accumulator A.

LEGEND:
- OP — Operation Code (Hexadecimal);
- ~ — Number of MPU Cycles;
- # — Number of Program Bytes;
- + — Arithmetic Plus;
- − — Arithmetic Minus;
- · — Boolean AND;
- M_{SP} — Contents of memory location pointed to be Stack Pointer;
- + — Boolean Inclusive OR;
- ⊕ — Boolean Exclusive OR;
- $\overline{M}$ — Complement of M;
- → — Transfer Into;
- 0 — Bit = Zero;
- 00 — Byte = Zero;
- H — Half-carry from bit 3;
- I — Interrupt mask
- N — Negative (sign bit)
- Z — Zero (byte)
- V — Overflow, 2's complement
- C — Carry from bit 7
- R — Reset Always
- S — Set Always
- ‡ — Test and set if true, cleared otherwise
- • — Not Affected
- CCR — Condition Code Register
- LS — Least Significant
- MS — Most Significant